the Mantle of the Mountain Man

Rod Bell Sr.

Library of Congress Cataloging-in-Publication Data

Bell, Rod 1934-

   The mantle of the mountain man / Rod Bell, Sr.

      p. cm.

   ISBN 1-57924-272-3

   1. Bell, Rod. 1934-   . 2. Fundamentalist churches—United
States.   3. Christian biography—United States.   I. Title.

BX7800.F868B44   1999

289.9'5'092—dc21

[B]   99-28466

                                                        CIP

Cover photographs by PhotoDisc, Inc.

The Mantle of the Mountain Man

Edited by Becky J. Smith
Cover and design by Brad Sherman
Composition by David Harris

© 1999 by Bob Jones University Press
Greenville, South Carolina 29614

Printed in the United States of America

ISBN 1-57924-272-3

15   14   13   12   11   10   9   8   7   6   5   4   3   2   1

DEDICATION

To the wife of my youth. At the age of thirteen, I said to myself, "I am going to marry that girl. She is prettier than a speckled pup! She is built low to the ground and will make a jack rabbit hug a hound!" Five years later we were married. I owe her all my love and respect. She is my best friend, my dearest companion, my sweetheart, and a godly example to my wonderful children. She is my pearl of great price and my best critic.

Who can find a virtuous woman? for her price is far above rubies.
Proverbs 31:10

TABLE OF CONTENTS

FOREWORD

"Hill Bobby" Bell—he's the closest thing to a "Hill Billy" I've ever known. Bobby Lee Bell (Rod) was cut like a block of marble from the mountains of West Virginia and brought by God to Bob Jones University in 1958.

He was rough-hewn and unpromising, but eager to be shaped into the image of Christ by the hammer and chisel of God's Word in the hands of the faculty. The University probably never had a more willing and malleable piece of marble to work with. He knew what he wanted to be—a preacher. He knew it required some "learnin'." He knew his young bride, Lenore, would stand by him through the process. What he didn't know was the meaning of "quit." For a man who claimed not to know much, he knew a lot.

He possessed the character traits necessary for success: determination to finish the job, unapologetic confidence in the gifts and calling of God, tenderness of heart, a tireless work ethic, and love of Truth. Childlike faith and confidence in the faithfulness of God sustained him through the days of preparation and have remained part of the fabric of his character.

David the psalmist said that God's gentleness had made him great (II Sam. 22:36). God's omnipotence manifests itself in gentleness. Rod Bell resembles his God in that. He is one of the strongest and most unyielding men I know in matters of scriptural principle. Yet he is gentle and compassionate toward sinners, as Jesus is. He has never forgotten that he is a forgiven, redeemed sinner. His love for his Redeemer gives him the ability to weep over sinners, care for the dying, and snatch men in pity from sin and the grave. He draws a straight line between biblical truth and religious error, but he draws it with a feather rather than a baseball bat.

Men such as he who do the work of Christ with the spirit of Christ are going to be called upon for leadership. It is not surprising, therefore, that this amiable, transparent man traverses the globe preaching and calling preachers to be strong in the obedience of Christ.

The mountains of West Virginia have not yet been carried into the midst of the sea (Ps. 46:2), but a piece of stone from them has been cut out and carried to the sea of nations for the preaching of Him whose atonement is for the healing of the nations.

Rod Bell is my friend. He was my father's friend. He doesn't require his friends to pass a litmus test of total agreement with him on all theological matters. He makes some excessively narrow Baptists mad because of it. Dr. Ian Paisley, the Ulster Presbyterian, is Dr. Bell's treasured friend. They preach in each other's pulpits. They both understand that biblical separation doesn't center on denominational sectarianism but on violations of scriptural absolutes.

Dr. Bell is as narrow as the Bible. Where it is dogmatic, he is dogmatic. Where it isn't, he refuses to become like the Pharisees who measured the spiritual worth of others according to their adherence to the Pharisees' own preferences. I love him for that. He is my kind of Fundamentalist. He is biblically narrow, and he is healthily, biblically broad. That kind of balance has made many of us eager to follow his leadership as president of the Fundamental Baptist Fellowship. He is Spurgeon's kind of Fundamentalist as described in a sermon extract from C. H. Spurgeon preached in London in 1863:

> But all Christians can meet in the person of Christ; all true hearts can meet in the work of Christ. This is a banner that we all love, if we be Christians, and far hence be those who are not. Hither to thy cross, O Jesus, do we come! The Churchman, laden with his many forms and vestments; the Presbyterian, with his stern Covenant, and his love of those who stained the heather with their blood; the Independent, with his passion for liberty, and the separateness of the free churches; the Methodist, with his intricate forms of Church Government, sometimes forms of bondage, but still forms of power; the Baptist, remembering his ancient pedigree, and the days in which his fathers were

hounded even by Christians themselves, and counted not worthy of that name; they all come to Christ. Various opinions divide them; they see not eye to eye on many matters; here and there, they will have a skirmish for the old landmarks; and rightly so, for we ought to be jealous, as Josiah was, to do that which is right in the sight of the Lord, and neither decline to the right hand nor to the left. But we rally to the cross of Christ; and there, all weapons of internecine warfare being cast aside, we meet as brethren, fellow-comrades in a blessed Evangelical Alliance, who are prepared to suffer and to die for [H]is dear sake.

Rod Bell is a gentle, jovial, trustworthy friend and valued soldier in the good fight of Faith.

Do the mountains have any more like him to give the church?

Bob Jones III
Greenville, S.C.
May 1999

PREFACE

Who is Rod Bell? He is a twentieth-century demonstration of the eternal truth of God's impregnable Book. "For ye see your calling, brethren, how that not many wise men after the flesh, not many mighty, not many noble, are called. But God hath chosen the foolish things of the world to confound the wise; and God hath chosen the weak things of the world to confound the things which are mighty; And base things of the world, and things which are despised, hath God chosen, yea, and things which are not, to bring to nought things that are: That no flesh should glory in his presence" (I Cor. 1:26-29).

Who is Rod Bell?

A sinner saved by free grace!
A child of God!
A justified believer!
A man of God!
A preacher of the Word!
A pastor of God's flock!
A contender for the Faith!
A defender of the Truth!
A disturber of the satanic peace!
A follower of Christ!
An outside-the-camp pilgrim!
An unflinching soldier of the Cross!
A loving husband!
A tender-hearted father and grandfather!
A beloved brother!
A friend in deed and in truth!

And so I could go on and on . . .

In Revelation 4:7 the living creatures that surround the throne have four representations:

First, the Lion—

Rod Bell is a lion. He has lionlike courage and determination, and above all, a lion's heart. He is worth a whole battalion in the battle for the Truth. I have been with him in many controversies and conflicts, and he has never flinched under the force of the enemy's fire. He asks for no quarter and expects none. He fights to the finish, and his arrows are the first and last to do damage to the apostasy. For him there is no discharge in the wars of God.

Second, the Calf—

Rod Bell is a worker. Having put his hand to the plough, there is no looking back, let alone turning back, for him. He is the ox who sticks to the ploughing and then to the treading out of the corn. He is baptized with a continuing stickability, and that's why he gets the job in hand well done. You will be out of breath seeking to keep up to the pace he sets. He has learned to redeem the time because the days we live in are so evil. Like the calf, he is always ready for the sacrifice.

Third, the Man—

Rod Bell is every inch a man, a manly man, a giant of a man, but still a man for all that. He is a great man because he has a great heart. His tenderness is wondrous to behold. He has the simplicity of a child, the touch of a mother, yet the strong presence of a conqueror. He has these characteristics because he keeps company with the Lord of Glory, the Man Christ Jesus.

Fourth, the Flying Eagle—

Rod Bell has learned to pray and to mount up with wings as eagles. In all parts of the globe where we have travelled together, we have enjoyed blessed times of prayer.

> *Heaven has come down*
> *our souls to greet,*
> *and glory has crowned*
> *the mercy-seat.*

Rod Bell has learned how to preach. When he gets his preaching wings and the wind of God blows, his flight is glorious to behold! The passion, the power, and the inescapable captivity of the congregation result. Then the truth is mastering the preacher—not the preacher mastering the truth. That is the secret.

Go on, my brother, and may your bow abide in strength and your arms be continually empowered by the arms of the mighty God of Jacob.

Today for you the noise of battle, tomorrow the victor's song.

The reading of this, your life story, will be an inspiration indeed!

If you, reader, want to feel the heartthrob for revival and a divine intervention of God in the affairs of men, read this book and watch the sovereign hand of God at work in the life of one of His servants.

Ian R. K. Paisley, M.P.
Belfast, Northern Ireland
May 1999

ACKNOWLEDGMENT

If it had not been for Hap Barko's and his family's taking this on as a family project, *The Mantle of the Mountain Man* would not be in print. In the preparation, research, and late hours of volunteer time, this family show their love for their pastor and true servant hearts.

I would also like to thank all those who edited, typed, retyped, sent in old family photos, and many others too numerous to mention who had a part in preparing this book for publication.

Part 1:

An
Unsaved
Mountain Boy

CHAPTER 1:
Family Background

In the mountains of West Virginia, in the poor Appalachian Region, lay dying an old-fashioned, circuit-riding Methodist preacher by the name of Dr. Jake Ball. He was not a medical doctor, but he performed a variety of tasks. Sometimes a veterinarian, other times an obstetrician. He also prescribed "medicine," mostly homemade remedies. But foremost he was a mountain preacher. Dr. Ball was contemporary with Robert Sheffey, who also rode circuit through the mountains delivering babies, holding camp meetings, preaching to the Indians, preaching to the mountain people. He was trying to win for Christ those in the wilderness. West Virginia was called the "wilderness" in those days. It was the Indian's "happy hunting ground."

My ancestors, who were Scotch-Irish, came from the borders of Scotland by way of Ulster, Northern Ireland, into the Shenandoah Valley, Pennsylvania, and, later, into West Virginia. The earliest stories that I recollect are those my mother told me about her grandfather, Dr. Jake Ball, and the exploits he did for God. My heart would pound with excitement as I sat and listened to Mother telling about this mountain missionary traveling through blizzards, sometimes frozen into the horse's stirrups.

Though he was wrapped in a heavy coat with a mantle draped over his head and shoulders, his face would be cut from the ice and sleet and he would be almost frozen to death as he made his way back home. His family would run out and take him off the horse. Shaking the snow and ice from the heavy mantle, they would bring him inside and feed him warm soup and broth. The mantle would be hung to dry by the fireplace until he was ready for another circuit journey.

I was born on August 12, 1934. When I was just a few weeks old, my great-grandfather had a stroke. As he lay upon the bed with his Bible, my mother took me in to show to him. As Dr. Jake looked at his great-grandson, he began to weep while he pointed to the Bible, pointed to the baby, pointed to himself, and then pointed toward heaven. Several times he went through these motions—pointing to the Bible, to the baby, to himself, and then to heaven.

My mother later said, "Son, I don't know what Granddaddy was trying to say."

"Mom, I know. Granddaddy was saying that he was going to leave a mantle to this baby. 'He will take my mantle and preach the gospel.'"

I believe I have Dr. Jake's "mantle." I am the only preacher on my mother's side of the family. I have a great love for the mountain people and a burden to try to reach them for the Lord Jesus Christ.

Being brought up in the Appalachian Mountains of a Scotch-Irish descent is a story in itself. My grandfather on my daddy's side was from County Antrim in Northern Ireland. His great-grandfather, Levi Collins Bell, migrated from Scotland during the famine and worked in the potato plantation. He came from Ireland for "a piece of the American dream" and settled in the Shenandoah Valley and the Appalachian Mountains of West Virginia. On Mud River in Lincoln County, he staked out a settlement and cleared a homestead in a valley called "Big Ugly." Levi Collins Bell distinguished himself as a captain in the Confederate Army during the Civil War, fighting in the

Northern Regiment. He was renowned for raiding behind Union lines, burning Union trains, and blowing up their railroad lines.

In my childhood days, I remember living at the head of a hollow named "Ball Fork" at the headwaters of Turtle Creek. We moved from one shack to another.

My earliest memory of the Bell clan was that we were always "on the move." In fact, we moved ten or twelve times when I was a boy. One time in particular, when I was about five, we moved out of Ball Fork Hollow, down Low Gap, and up Sparrows Creek. Our mode of transportation was an old nag and a well-used wagon. We piled all the furniture on that wagon— pots, pans, all our worldly goods. My brothers and I rode in the back until we came to the top of Low Gap Mountain.

The air was filled with excitement because we were about to descend this long, steep mountain. I saw the look of concern on Mom's face as she held my baby brother, Dennis, in her arms. Our dog sensed the uneasiness as he ran alongside the wagon, barking. With the Coal Mountain air biting our cheeks, we made our way down the crooked dirt road. Pots, pans, and tubs rattled as the old wagon creaked and groaned. The descent was so steep I could smell the smoke from the heat as Dad "rode" the wooden brakes. Many times we feared the wagon would run over the horse; my heart was pounding so hard I thought it would leap from my chest!

Our dog, Luke, was "king of the holler." Every time we passed a homestead, he engaged the dogs there in a good scrap. Dad finally had enough and put him up in the wagon. "Hold this blasted dog, before we all get in a dogfight!"

We were challenged along the way by countless barks and yaps, and I was greatly tempted to let the dog loose. But Dad had spoken and I knew better! That move was the most exciting adventure a five-year-old boy could ask for.

We finally came to an old log house with three rooms. The kitchen had a dirt floor, and we all slept in one room. An old log fireplace kept the house warm. After we cleaned out the bats nested in the chimney, Dad started a nice wood fire to take off the chill.

I remember going out to explore and finding a toy wagon with three wheels. It was the most beautiful thing I had ever seen; it was "store bought." Someone had left it in the junk pile. We pulled it out and tried to make a wooden fourth wheel. I remember trying to figure out how we could make a round wheel—I thought I might be able to invent one. However, my round wheel ended up rather square. It was exciting, though, having a toy that was "store bought," even if it did have only three wheels!

DAD
~

My dad and mother were married at a young age. Dad was a poor mountain farmer, a hard worker, but he had a habit of drinking. He became a drunkard and a moonshine runner early in life. My three brothers and I were born at home with the help of the women on the hollow and the county doctor, if he arrived in time.

Dr. Pauley delivered us all, except me. I was born in a crude two-room mountain cabin on Low Gap in Boone County, West Virginia. The county was named after Daniel Boone and was near the Hatfield-McCoy feuding ground.

The doctor's fee for delivering a baby was always small. "Poor mountain folk have poor ways, but we always pay our way, and we always find a way to get the job done." This philosophy was drilled into us daily. So you paid the doctor whatever you could afford or in any commodity that could be turned into cash. The delivery of Woody (my oldest brother) had cost Dad a wagonload of corn.

But on that hot August 12 night in 1934, Dr. Pauley was late. I had already been born, "kicking and screaming." Mom would often say, "Son, you were born in a hurry, you have lived in a hurry, and you're going to die in a hurry!"

Dad asked the doctor how much he owed for my delivery. "I hain't got no money."

"Well, what do you have?"

"I have a wagonload of corn."

Dr. Pauley scratched his head. "Well, Raymond, the baby was already here and most of the hard work was already done. So I guess half a wagonload of corn should be sufficient."

My, how prices have changed in the last sixty-four years. Thank God for honest and fair mountain doctors who were not in the medical profession for money, just corn!

Dad was a no-nonsense type—hard work, hard living, and hard liquor. Hard times were a way of life to him. He was not a good disciplinarian; he was not authoritative but authoritarian. He loved us, but he felt that children "should be seen and not heard." His word was never to be questioned, only obeyed. He taught us to fight, never to run or quit. The way to settle an argument was to fight about it—the one left standing was right! Everybody knew Raymond Bell would fight you, and he was good at it. He would get even if it took a lifetime. "An eye for an eye and a tooth for a tooth" was his philosophy. We were taught that if we went down in a fight, never to be "stay downers" but to be "get uppers."

My life as a young lad was filled with fear, frustration, anxiety, and uncertainty from his knife fights, shootings, and arrests. Being a coal miner, Dad worked hard, but his money went fast on riotous living. I remember going to bed hungry or spending the night with my three brothers in one bed, humped up in the corner, afraid of the dark and of a drunken dad, knowing the authorities would come to arrest him. One night in particular after a drunken brawl, Dad came in covered with blood after being in a knife fight. With his shotgun in hand, he raised the window to look down the mountain trail, waiting for someone to come and arrest him. He bragged, "The only way they will take me off this mountain is feet first."

Needless to say, that was a long night for four little boys and their weary mother. We spent the night in fear. As a little lad I was praying, but I did not know to whom I was praying. I was scared and afraid of what might happen. Sometimes I had so much bitterness, anger, and hate in my heart toward my dad. I so badly wanted him just to do right.

MOM
~

My mother was a kind, loving, hard-working mountain woman; she told me she had been saved at the age of fourteen. Because of the influence of her grandfather Dr. Jake Ball, she went to church and felt the Lord had called her to be a missionary, but she married an unsaved man who kept her in bondage and poverty. She lived ten to twelve miles from the nearest church and just strayed from her commitment to Christ. (Late in life, at age fifty-two, she and Dad surrendered to be missionaries to Virginia Beach, Virginia. They served twenty years on the staff at Tabernacle Baptist Church.) Looking back on it now, I feel that my mother was truly saved in those early years. I have never seen a woman with so much character and determination, who would do whatever was necessary "to keep body and soul together" and to keep her boys, as she would say, "under the same roof."

Many evenings I would come home and my mother would be out in the woods collecting berries, polk salad, creasy greens, and mushrooms. "Mom, what are you doing?"

"Trying to get enough food to keep soul and body together, Honey. Run and do your chores, and we'll have something to eat after a while."

Little did I realize that she was doing her grocery shopping because we did not have any food in the house to eat. We would all come in to a meal of mountain herbs with a "pone" of cornbread. Thank God, she did help "keep soul and body together."

Some of my childhood memories are of my mother working like a man in the mountains. I have been cross-cut sawing with her, sawing down locust posts to build a chicken house or a shed.

I have been with her in the mountains picking blackberries and digging ginseng roots. She could get maple sap from a maple tree and boil it just right. It tasted mighty good on a "cat-head biscuit." She would make apple butter or lye soap in a big cast iron pot. Many times I would see her hands cracked open from scrubbing our "overall britches" on the scrub board. She never complained, but she did cry a lot.

I loved to hear my mother sing. I knew that when she was singing she was not hurting. As just a little lad, I would often go out behind the house at night and look up into the face of God and see that big, wonderful, starry sky and wonder if there was a God. If the God who made all of that bright, starry heaven really cared, did He know that there was a boy down in the midst of all those mountains, in the little three-room, tarpaper shack on the side of the hill?

Did that God really love me?

Did anybody love me?

Maybe it would be easier if I'd run off or die; there would be one less mouth to feed.

As I let those thoughts flood through my soul, off in the distance I would hear my mother singing. She would churn butter while sitting in a rocking chair and sing an old mountain song, "When all my labors and trials are o'er, and I am safe on that beautiful shore; just to be near the dear Lord I adore . . . that will be glory for me." I knew that the God who made the heavens was helping my mother not to be sad and not to weep and hurt that night. With those thoughts, I would drift off to sleep.

Many nights my mother would put us to bed early so that she could wash our clothes because we had only one pair of bibbed overalls. She did not want us running around "naked as a jaybird." She was a good mother, and I look forward to seeing her on that "beautiful shore" some day.

"Keeping body and soul together" was one of my mother's prime objectives. We dug holes in the ground in the winter and lined them with straw to store apples. We also dug potato and vegetable holes for the winter, covering them with straw and a piece of tin to keep our food fresh until the spring.

The fall of the year was always hog-killing time. All the neighbors would come in and help kill a couple of hogs. This was always a great time of feasting. We would have red-sop gravy, biscuits, and plenty of fresh ham. The hogs were always cured in the smokehouse and put up for the winter. There was no refrigeration or electricity, no phones, and no inside plumbing. It never dawned on us that we were missing any of these luxuries; we didn't know other people had them. Dad always said, "Poor folk have poor ways, but they get the job done."

Going through the depression was not easy in the mountains. My mother would go to the country store and shop for a dress. She would look at the feed sacks for different colors and prints. She made sure we bought "midlins" for the hog that had a nice pattern to be used to make a dress. She would get cloth and used clothes, as she would say, "almost new," to make shirts for her boys. We had only one pair of shoes. If the sole came off, a good piece of hay wire would always put it back together. Many times the homemade shoestand was not the best. When spring came, we would go barefoot from late May through the summer months. We were fortunate to get a pair of shoes in the middle of September.

BROTHERS

I have three brothers: Woody is the oldest, then me, then Dennis and Jim. We are all different, yet we are all the same. If you jumped on one Bell, you had to whip us all. We were loyal to one another. The backbone of the mountain man is his pride. No one could say anything about a member of our family and get away with it. This pride would plague me all my life—a pride not of what we possessed, but of what we were. We didn't need anyone or anybody. We took care of our own; we could handle any situation, no matter what!

Woody got in many fights to defend my honor. He would get the job done quickly and thoroughly. He was quite a scrapper when it came to using his fists. He always said, "You need to get in the first punch, and then you won't have to worry about the last."

Since he was the oldest, he always came to our rescue. I've seen him fight like cats and dogs because of something that was said about our family or because something had been done to one of us. Oh, the times he would defend me and keep me from being "beaten up" or seriously hurt. Woody feared neither man nor beast—his honor was at stake. He was a Bell and proud of it!

I got into a barroom fight once with four or five ruffians, and they threw me out into the street. I jumped up and went back because they had called my mother a bad name. With blood flying, I went back. Then I saw a strange look come over these ruffians—I saw *fear* on their faces. My brother Woody had just walked in behind me. Needless to say, he defended our mother's honor and kept his baby brother from being beaten up!

Woody was always there when I was mistreated or made fun of. One day at school, two bullies cut off my tie and humiliated me. The next thing I knew, Woody had "cleaned their plow," once again defending his little brother's honor. I will always be thankful to Woody for looking out for me.

I love my big brother—he was my idol, and I wanted to be just like him. I hope to see him one day in heaven with the rest of my family. He needs the Lord. In many ways, he is still my "idol": he has character, honesty, integrity, a strong will, and his word is his bond. But he is not saved (yet). I am praying that God will gently break the backbone of this mountain man—the proud, the self-sufficient, the "I-can-handle-the-situation" spirit. Pray that God will help him see his need of Christ, that success in material wealth is only temporal. His dear wife, Pat, is a sweetheart, but she also needs the Savior. Their salvation would make the family circle complete in eternity. I've had the privilege of seeing just about all my aunts and uncles come to Christ. Father, brothers, grandparents—what a terrible thought if just one were to be lost for eternity. Many times, my burden for them became so heavy I thought I'd burst. But our God is faithful.

My other brothers, Dennis and Jim, were made of the same stuff as Woody, if not more so. Jim was more like our mother as far as temperament—patient, longsuffering, yet willing to defend our honor and our integrity.

We were taught to fight and stand for principle—that is the way mountain men settled disagreements. The man that won was always right. If we ever ran from a fight, we paid for it with a beating from our dad when we got home. The day was wasted if we didn't have a good rock fight on the way to or from school; that was just planned on every day. Many times, the whole family got into it. There was a very "clique-ish" and clannish spirit in the mountains.

MY GRANDMAWS

The mountain people had their mountain ways; they made do with what they had. They didn't have much, so they learned how to live off the land. My grandmother always worked in the fields cutting timber, hoeing corn, gathering vegetables and fruit, or doing whatever else had to be done. She canned, helped butcher hogs, and milked the cows.

I remember my grandmother wearing long dresses, little pointed shoes, and a bibbed apron. I can almost see her sitting on the back porch churning. As she churned, I would watch her through the window and listen as she sang "How Tedious and How Tasteless the Hours" or some other kind of religious song. I can't remember what all the songs were, but I thought as a boy that they must be religious if Granny sang them.

Grandma Lori Baisden would often tell me that she needed some tobacco for her pipe. She smoked a clay pipe with a reed in it. I didn't go to the store; I went down to the barn to get "trash lugs" of tobacco. She didn't want anything but the trash lugs.

There are different grades of tobacco on the stalk—the higher it grows on the stalk, the more expensive it is. The middle leaves are more expensive; they are used to make cigarettes and cigars. Grandma wanted the bottom leaves—called the trash lugs.

She would sit in her rocking chair, crumbling up the trash lugs of tobacco and getting the stems out. She kept the lugs in her pocket. Then she would load up her old clay pipe. I thought maybe Granny would have some candy in those pockets, but there was never candy, just that old stinky, smelly tobacco. And you could smell Granny from almost thirty yards away when she would start smoking that pipe. When you came to visit her, you'd smell the pipe before you'd see Granny. She died at 104, and I believe that pipe finally killed her!

She was a very intelligent woman, I thought. She sure saved me some hard work. I would go dig potatoes for supper, and I remember her yelling across the creek, "Now, Son, before you carry those potatoes up the hill, you wash them off in the creek down there, and you won't have to carry water up the hill to wash them."

I thought, "My, that woman is smart."

So I'd go down to the creek and wash the potatoes off and take them up. Because we didn't have water on the mountain, we had to carry all of our water from the well or from a spring. Granny sure did save me some steps by telling me to wash the potatoes in the creek before I carried them back up the hill.

Being a mountain boy, I had only one pair of shoes, which had to last me all winter. Needless to say, when spring came, those shoes were just about completely gone. We went barefoot as much as we could, running and jumping on the rocks and logs. We would get stone bruises on our feet, and they would become like a carbuncle or a boil and have to be lanced.

My Grandmother Rosie had a great remedy for boils, carbuncles, and stone bruises. She knew how it do it. She made us go down to the barn and get a fresh pile of cow manure. Now this had to be fresh; it couldn't be old. She would put our foot right into that cow manure, wrap our foot up with a lot of blankets or feed sacks or whatever was available, and leave it on for twenty-four hours. Then we could take it off, and she would wash our foot good and make us sit with our foot in a bucket of hot salt water—as hot as we could stand it—and after it became just as white and wrinkly as it could be, all the corruption would be gone.

Granny would take a torn piece of bed sheet and wrap it around our foot. She'd say, "From Granny with love" and send us away. No hospital bills and no doctor bills whenever we lived in the mountains. I thought Granny was the smartest doctor who ever lived.

GRANDMA ON THE WARPATH

Being brought up in the Appalachian Mountains, we had many experiences that can't be re-created today. My Grandmother Bell was a Cherokee Indian, and I always have to chuckle when I remember the many times that she would "get on the warpath." She was a hard-working mountain woman who had her mountain ways, but she had a strong character and was determined to look after her own.

One day when all the men were gone, she saw some hoodlums coming up the holler, drinking, cursing, and carousing. She told us, "There's trouble brewing, and I'm going to handle it."

I can almost see her going out on the porch and yelling, "You fellows get out of the holler."

And those ruffians made a great, great mistake—they cursed Granny. Grandma Bell went back in the house, grabbed a shotgun, and shot right over the car. "I said get out of the holler, or I'll lower my aim."

Those fellows jumped in their vehicle and never came back.

CHAPTER 2:
Mountain Ways

A MULE NAMED JIM AND A SWARM OF YELLOW JACKETS

Being brought up in the ragged Appalachian Mountains produces some positive character strengths. You learn to work at a young age, or you may go hungry. The mountain people call it "digging a living out of the side of the hill." I learned early that we were all expected to work if we wanted to eat. Little did I realize that this was a biblical principle. All of my people believed in hard work, and they called it "live hard, die hard." In other words, live your life to the fullest, and live it on the edge.

When I was approaching my thirteenth birthday, my dad and my granddad gave me an old white mule named Jim and told me there was new ground back in the cove up the mountains with four or five acres of tobacco. They wanted me to take care of it. I took my mule and a four-pound lard bucket full of pinto beans, cornbread, and an onion. Jim and I spent all day at the new ground. Jim was not very cooperative. If he were a human being, I believe he would have been an independent Baptist! If I said, "Gee!" he would go "haw." He had a mind of his own and did generally what he wanted to do. I was all over the side of that mountain, trying to persuade him to plow straight.

I learned some valuable lessons that summer: I learned what it was to work hard and to be lonely. I learned what it was to be tired, and I also learned how to accept responsibility. Many times at the end of the row, at the end of the day, I would look up with a tired little body and say, "Dear God, if you're up there, answer one question for me: Why? There has to be more to life than this."

During the middle of the day, I would come under the shade and tie up old Jim, feed him a little, and give him some branch water as I ate my beans and drank water from the little stream that ran down by the side of the field.

One time I got Jim into a yellow jackets' nest. My, how that bunch of yellow jackets—just a little yellow and black instrument of the underworld—put Jim and me out of commission for a whole day. I went home crying. The mule went to the barn, harness, swingletree, and all, like a shot out of a gun.

My dad said to me, "Now, Son, listen. When I was a boy, I wouldn't let a little yellow jacket run me out of the field. If you'll ever be a man, you'll learn to whip yellow jackets. What you do is go back and take your brothers. Cut you a brush, and go in and whip those yellow jackets. If you're ever going to be a man and grow up, you've got to learn to stand your ground."

Like little fools that we were, we did not realize that he was jesting. We went up that mountain determined to be men and stand our ground. We each cut a brush and waded into those yellow jackets. First thing I knew, they were all over us—up our pant legs, down our shirt collars, working on us with their little sharp stingers. We were swinging the brush and crying, saying, "Don't run; stand your ground. Don't run; stand your ground." I learned a valuable principle that day: powerful things often come in small packages. Needless to say, those small yellow jackets put knots and burning welts on three boys in a hurry!

When we got home, Dad saw us red all over and crying from being stung. "What in the world have you boys done? I told you to stand and whip those yellow jackets. The reason you lost is because you ran. You'll never be a man; that is a job for men, Son."

I never will forget what I thought. I said in my heart, "Why, then, don't you go stand with us, if it's for a man?" But I was afraid to utter those words to my dad.

FRUIT ON THE LINE

Mountain people have a unique way of doing things; we call it "hillbilly ingenuity." Many times, "necessity is the mother of invention." We grew tobacco high on top of a mountain. There was no way to get the tobacco out of the back of the field on a sled or a wagon because there was no road, just a trail to the valley. So we took several hundred yards of heavy wire cable on a spool and anchored one end in the back of the field, then ran it down across the valley to the barn, cranking the spool up good and tight. We placed the tobacco on sticks with a wire hook, stretched the hooks over the cable, and turned them loose. At such a steep angle, the tobacco sailed like greased lightning out of the field and down to the tobacco barn. Someone then hung the tobacco to dry on the tiers of the tobacco barn. It was great fun to run the tobacco on the wire. Many times it went so fast sparks flew from the steel hook and the cable.

Sometimes, we would find a big watermelon, hook it in a sack, put it on the wire, and yell, "Fruit on the line!" Men would prepare to catch it at the bottom. If they failed to catch it, the watermelon smashed the backboard of the spool, flying into a million pieces. Many exciting things happen in the mountains. What a day it was to see the tobacco run!

LOST AND FOUND

Stories about this mountain boy and his dog could fill a book by itself. I had constant companions when I was a lad, and they were my dogs. Growing up in the mountains without a dog is almost like being in the sunshine without a shadow—it's impossible. I had coon dogs, rabbit dogs, squirrel dogs, fox-hounds, and the "Heinz 57" varieties. Some were "sooners": they'd sooner lie by the fire than run anything. Between the ages of eight and ten, I could be seen every day and every spare minute of my time groundhog hunting with Old Blue, my coon dog.

What a joy it was to take my mattock (a tool to dig with) and go groundhog hunting. Groundhogs could weigh thirty-five to forty pounds, almost as big as my dog. One time I had to tie the dog up in order to dig. Just as I was digging in closer, the dog started barking and growling. My heart was pounding! I heard the scratching and squealing of the groundhog as I closed in on him. How exciting it was to know that the fight was ready to begin! I turned the dog loose and let him in the hole. There was about a thirty-five-pound groundhog sitting on his legs, ready for battle. The battle raged, the groundhog struck, the dog lunged, the fight was on! I loved to see the fur fly, and if the groundhog got the best of my dog, which seldom happened, I used the mat-tock to whack the groundhog over the head. This experience was better than any fake wrestling matches we see today; it was the real McCoy, and I enjoyed every minute of it. With a big ground-hog hanging over my back, I'd proudly walk the mountain trail singing, "A-hunting we will go . . . Hi, Ho, Hi, Ho."

I loved to hunt rabbits—track them, trap them, any way that I could get them—to bring home fresh meat. Squirrel trap-ping and deer hunting were also exciting times in my life. My dog and I worked as a team to outsmart the furry creatures. It was always good for the family to have some meat on the table. My family called me "the bare-footed Indian" because I learned to glide through the woods without making a sound, learning to step over the twig, not on it.

The joy of my life was bringing home the kill and seeing my mom with a smile on her face. "We'll have meat to eat because the Indian is coming out in my little Irish boy."

My coon dogs and hunting dogs were constant companions and friends. We learned to trust each other and built a special relationship. I learned a valuable lesson when I was in the mountains hunting. I once found myself lost from my dogs and went the wrong way through the mountains. It was a cloudy day, and I could not see the sun. Darkness was creeping in, and shadows were getting long. The forest came alive with different sounds. The imagination of a young boy began to see and hear things that did not exist. Stories that we had heard about black panthers, wildcats, and bears began to run through my mind as I tried to find my way home.

Suddenly, the awesome truth dawned upon me: *I was lost.* It's one thing to be lost and not know it, but it's another thing to be lost and have the grim truth suddenly dawn upon you that you are indeed lost. Abruptly, the woods became silent. The only thing I heard was my heart; it was almost beating out of my chest. I thought, "I am lost."

Then the phantom sounds of the woods became a reality: I heard noises in the leaves. Someone or something was walking toward me. Through the darkness that crept upon the forest, I saw two eyes, and my heart began to leap as if it would come right out of my chest. I gripped my mattock, and then I realized it was Old Blue, my hound dog, who came up, licked me, and wagged his tail. I patted him on the head and said, "Let's go home, Blue." He knew the way, and I followed.

What a joy it was to have a friend who knew the way home! It was a joy to see the familiar places, familiar areas, and to know that I was on my way home. Off in the distance I saw a light on the side of the hill where a concerned Mom and Dad waited as their little hunter and his friend made their way through the darkness.

Years later, I saw the spiritual application in this experience. Thank God, I finally realized I was spiritually lost. The Savior found me and led me home! I can see the lights of home on Zion's Hill, and Mom and Dad and my loved ones waiting for me to arrive. Then there will be no more dark valleys, for the glory of God is the sweet light of that city!

THOUGHTS OF GOD

~

Many of my childhood memories are of being in the woods alone with my dog, hunting or tracking rabbits or trapping in the wild. It gave me time to think and contemplate the God of creation, who made all the hills and all the mountains and all the valleys, who caused the sun to shine and the moon and stars to glisten and whirl in their orbits through the darkness of the night.

Many nights I would camp out on top of the ridge and turn our foxhounds loose and let them run. Listening to them off in the distance as they chased a fox, I would look up into the starry heaven of God's universe and think, "Who made all this? Who made me? Where would I go if I were to die? Is there a God? If so, why does He not speak to me? Does He have something for me to do? Does He love me? Does He care about me?" There's nothing better than for a young boy to get alone and look into the starry heavens and think about his Creator and think about eternity.

We never went to church when I was a lad. The first time I ever went to church was for a funeral at Olive Branch Baptist Church on Turtle Creek (the church where I preached my first sermon about six months after I was saved). I was scared when I saw the dead person. I thought again, "I wonder where that person is? I wonder if he is still living?" I heard all kinds of remarks that he was a good man, or that he did this or he did that. I heard people say that he was with his Maker, and I wondered, "How do they know?"

We never had a Bible; we never read a Bible. I can remember my dad telling me, "Son, when you go to church, you sit and listen to that man called the preacher. Don't you dare open your mouth; you keep quiet and listen to what he has to say. He's a man of God."

I knew that's exactly what I'd better do, and I did it!

LESSONS TAUGHT BY A SINNER IN A CORNFIELD

In my family there were no "churchgoers," no Bible, no praying, no family altar, and not much talking about God. Yet we had a reverential respect for God.

One day as we were all hoeing corn, a black thundercloud came up. Granddad said, "It looks like we're going to get a downpour."

"Yep," said one of my uncles, "It sure looks like 'the Old Man upstairs' is moving His furniture around."

Immediately, my grandfather stopped his hoeing, cut him a stick, grabbed my uncle by the back of his overalls, and lashed him good. "Son, don't you ever let me hear you make jokes about the Almighty like that again."

That lesson made a deep impression upon me because I saw that my grandfather knew there was a God and that he respected Him. I never heard any one of those men call God "the Old Man upstairs" again!

I had another "religious" experience in that same cornfield on a hot summer day. My grandfather had me planting pole beans in each hill of corn: two kernels of corn, two beans. (This was "hillbilly ingenuity" again!) The cornstalk became the pole for the beans to climb, and they could then be easily picked.

My friend came down the hollow with an inner tube. "Come on! Let's go swimming!"

"I can't until I get all these beans in the ground."

"Oh, throw those ol' beans away and come on! He'll never know the difference!"

Foolish boy that I was! About that time, I saw a crawfish hole and I had a brilliant idea. Granddad had said, "Put all the beans in the ground." So I filled the hole with the beans, covered it over with a rock, and hurriedly put dirt over the rock. "Hey! Wait for me! I'm coming!"

I did what Grandpa had said, didn't I? I "put all the beans in the ground."

Later that month, Grandpa was plowing the corn and we were hoeing. I heard him stop the horses. "Rod, come over here, Son."

I thought, "Oh, no!" I could tell by the sound of his voice that I was in deep trouble. I made my way over to where he was, and it dawned on me that it was the spot where I had buried all those beans. Sure enough, in the middle of the corn row, there stood a bush with hundreds of bean sprouts.

"What is this, anyway? What happened here, Son?"

I sadly told Grandpa my story.

He said, "Let this be a lesson to you: *Be sure your sins will find you out!* And, by the way, there will be no more swimming for you for the rest of the summer."

I had to pay for my disobedience. I didn't understand it then, but here was a sinner, my grandpa, who still had woven into the fiber of his soul Bible truth. Even now, as I look back on it, many of the character traits that were drilled into us were biblical principles—respect for "the Almighty," respect for God's house, respect for God's man; the principle of sowing and reaping; a man's word is his bond, sealed with a handshake; paying for disobedience. These were all scriptural principles I learned living in an unsaved family.

We have lost so much in this country. These elementary elements of biblical truth are lost in our nation. We simply must pass on this mantle of God's truth to the next generation. My family almost lost them and, in my generation, they have almost been lost again. "Help, Lord; for the godly man ceaseth; for the faithful fail from among the children of men."(Ps. 12:1)

I can remember some of the ways our neighbors banded together to help in time of need, especially if there were strangers coming up the hollow. Dinner bells rang or three shots would be fired. Neighbors communicated by sending reflections from mirrors in the sun to let us know that strangers or "outsiders" were coming up the hollow. Our people did not trust outsiders, especially if they were the authorities, because the authorities had no business nosing around in our territory. I found out a little later that this was a carryover from the moonshine days when we were taught not to trust any strangers, just stand by our own.

We took care of ourselves; we didn't need anyone coming in and telling us what to do. The spirit of independence and self-reliance was drilled into me and would cause me trouble later in my life. I was self-confident, with the determination that I could achieve anything I wanted to do. There was no need of God or anyone else. I believe that's one of the reasons that, later in my life, God had to strip me of self-reliance.

BLEW UP THE WRONG DOG!

We often gathered on the end of the porch on a rainy day, and my dad and grandfather would tell stories. I remember one story they told about Old Blue and Old Sue, two foxhounds that were said to be the best in the mountains. They were twins and looked almost identical.

One day Old Blue got into the chicken house and sucked the eggs. Grandad told Dad to go out and shoot Old Blue that day and get rid of him because once a dog started sucking eggs, he was finished.

Dad told the story that when his dad (my grandpa) went to work that day, the last thing he said was, "Get rid of Old Blue." That day, he went by the smokehouse and got a stick of dynamite; he took the dog back in the woods and tied the dynamite around Old Blue's neck. With Blue's sad eyes looking up at him, Dad lit the fuse and ran behind a tree, fingers in his ears and shutting his eyes, waiting for Blue to make his final trip to the world beyond.

Suddenly, he felt something cold on his cheek. Opening his eyes, he realized it was Old Blue, licking him. The fuse on the dynamite was getting shorter and shorter! Dad jumped up and ran toward the house. As he ran, he looked over his shoulder and saw Old Blue following him, ears flapping and gaining ground. By the time Dad jumped over the fence, Old Blue was right behind him. Dad leapt to the porch and the dog went under the porch. Dad ran into the house, grabbed his mother, and they both went to the floor as he shielded her. The dynamite went off, blowing the porch off the cabin!

My granddad came in that evening and wanted to know, "What in the world happened?"

"Well, I got rid of Old Blue!"

"What happened to the porch?"

"I forgot to tie up Old Blue."

As he was telling Grandad what happened, they looked up and saw Old Blue coming around the smokehouse. Dad got the wrong dog! He had killed Old Sue instead of Old Blue.

Dad said, "The moral of the story is this: Make sure, boys, you always have the right dog before you light the fuse."

I sometimes wonder if that all happened just exactly the way my dad told it.

This is the way evenings were passed on the porch—stories told about the Hatfields and the McCoys, stories told about the wild adventures of the mountain people. That was all the world we knew. There was no radio, no telephone, no TV, no videos—just families telling stories on the porch. What fond memories!

A BOY TEN FEET TALL

I'll never forget the time I was helping Dad with a split-rail fence that kept the cow in. We had to split the logs and make rails. These were chestnut logs, and as we split them, I got a splinter beneath my thumbnail. It ran underneath my thumbnail and came out the top of my knuckle. Dad said, "Son, this is going to be bad."

I began to cry because it hurt so badly. But we didn't go to the emergency room; my dad knew what to do. He took his knife out, sharpened it up on a whetstone and the sole of his shoe, stuck it in the ground to sterilize it, put some kerosene on it, and set it on fire. Then he wiped it off real good and said, "Son, I've got to cut this out. Do you think you can stand it?"

"Yes, sir."

"Well, let me give you something. Maybe this will help you."

As tears rolled down my cheeks, he put a piece of wood in my mouth. "Bite on this. As it begins to hurt, you bite."

He began to cut. He split my nail open and dug out the chestnut splinter that was 1½ to 2 inches long. "Is it hurting, Son?"

"I don't know."

It was hurting so bad I could not feel it—I was gritting my teeth with everything I had. Dad cut it out, soaked my hand down in kerosene and some alcohol, wrapped it up, and rubbed me on the head. "You're going to be a great man. You're tough."

I felt ten feet tall and as big as a mountain.

A LIVE COWARD

After a hot summer's day of working in the fields and after all the chores were done, if I got a break, I would head to Low Gap swimming hole. The swimming hole was in Coal River, and it was approximately fifteen to twenty feet deep at the deepest part. There was a large tree leaning over the swimming hole, and we would get in the top of that tree and jump or dive out. That's where I learned to swim. An incident happened at the swimming hole that I will never forget.

There were huge rocks under the water, and there were caves underneath those rocks. We always played "dare devil" to see who could hold their breath and go through the underwater caves.

I took a dare and went in under there. I got stuck and couldn't get out. I couldn't hold my breath any longer, and I could see bubbles. I was fighting with every ounce of energy in me. I was kicking, frightened and scared. I believe that was one of the first times I ever thought I was going to die.

One of my uncles realized that I had been gone too long and must be in trouble. Diving down, he pulled me out feet first. He put me on the bank and worked with me; I was just about gone. I will never forget my uncle (it was Uncle "Junior" Bell) telling me, "It's better to be a live coward than a dead hero. Don't you ever take so foolish a dare again!"

HILLBILLY INGENUITY

Some of our greatest toys were created through what I call "hillbilly ingenuity." We played rolly-hole marbles. We would find a flat place and make eight holes in the ground about three feet apart. The surface had to be perfectly smooth; clay was best. The objective was to get your marble in the hole in one shot. After you sank your marble in a hole, you would place it on the ground again within a handsbreadth of that hole and shoot toward the next hole. If someone was trying to beat you to the other end and back, you could always knock his marble out and then go on. It was something similar to playing croquet. The one who went through all the holes first was the champion.

One of the Hager boys on the holler was the champion rolly-hole player, and we would all try to beat him. Sometimes we would bet a certain number of marbles, but marbles were so expensive that none of us had store-bought marbles. We learned to make our own marbles. We would shoot the insulators off the electric poles with a rifle and chip the insulators until they were pretty close to being round. Then we would put them between two pop bottles and twist them. The pop bottles would wear the marbles down until they were perfectly round. We could make them any size we wanted. We prohibited "steelies." "Steelies" were ball bearings. The marbles had to be made out of glass or a dish.

We were out to beat Hager, and we found that the insulator-made marble was the best to use. Often we played until dark, and even then we would put kerosene lights out so that we could finish the games. But I don't think any of us could beat old Hager because he spent most of his time practicing.

We also played horseshoes. I became pretty good with a horseshoe and thought I could beat just about anyone. But I discovered that some of my uncles were horseshoe champions. They had played for years, and it was hard to beat them. But playing horseshoes when we had some spare time kept us out of trouble.

We also had chicken fights. People would come from all over the holler for a good rooster fight. These were probably some of the greatest pastimes we had.

Another one of the toys we made used a wheel and wire. Every boy had a wheel (the best ones were made from steel), and he had a long piece of metal with a hook in it that fit around the wheel. All you had to do was start the wheel rolling, put the stick behind it, and keep it rolling. It was quite an art. Every boy rolled his wheel wherever he went. It was always interesting to see the boys rolling the wheels down the holler with their dogs running along behind them. I can see in my mind's eye now—boys going to their neighbors' or relatives' homes with their wheels and their dogs. That was the fad of the day—have a good wheel and a good dog!

DEFENDING MOM
~

My folks never had to worry about our getting into trouble when I was a little fellow because there was no trouble to get into. When we were too tired to play, we were in bed. We had to get up each morning between 4:30 and 5:00. Life was hard for all of us, and I often thought about running away or just ceasing to exist. I thought about ways I might make life easier for my mom. I never wanted to see or hear her cry again.

One time when I was thirteen, Dad was going to hurt Mom. He came in drunk, and she said something he didn't like. I got a stick of stove wood and jumped between them. With tears streaming down my cheeks, I screamed, "Don't you hurt my mom. You lay a hand on her, and I'm going to bust your head with this piece of stove wood."

Dad put his hands on his hips, chuckled, and said, "I like you, boy, you got some grit." Then he went off in a drunken laughter.

But I was trembling; I was so afraid I might hurt my dad whom I loved or that my dad might hurt the momma I loved.

As years went by, I became more like Dad, wanting to do the things he did to show him I could be just like him, not realizing what it was doing to me. If my mother had known how much it affected me, it would have torn her heart out. I became a very frustrated, hard, bitter, and determined young man. I was angry at the world because many nights we went to bed hungry and we didn't have clothes to wear. When we went to high school, we had a real culture shock. We couldn't be like other kids; we were embarrassed and humiliated. It's still difficult to talk about some of those things because the scars still remain.

CHAPTER 3:
School Days

GOING TO FIGHT
~

A very early remembrance of my school days begins on December 8, 1941. I remember walking out of the holler in West Virginia with my uncles and cousins, all going to the one-room schoolhouse at the mouth of the holler in Low Gap. There were eight grades in one room and one pot-bellied stove.

Some of my uncles, aged sixteen, seventeen, and eighteen, were in the eighth grade. They were old enough to join the army and go fight the Japanese. Coming out of the holler that morning, they were talking about joining up. I wished I were old enough to go with them. I thought, "If I could only find me a little Jap about my size, I'd knock some knots too." I wanted to go so badly, but I was only in the first grade. Many of my relatives were eager to go and did so. Some did not come back. But there was a patriotic spirit burning in the hearts of all the young people.

When we reached the one-room schoolhouse that morning, our teacher raised the American flag. As she stood on the porch before about twenty-five young people, praying the Lord's Prayer with tears rolling down her cheeks, she prayed for our country and for God's protecting hand to be upon us. I thought again, "Is there a God in heaven who really cares?"

We listened to an old battery-powered radio. All the neighbors and friends gathered around the only radio on the holler. As the radio cracked and popped, we heard a man whom they said was the president of the United States of America telling us that we were at war with Japan.

That night I did not sleep much. All I could think was that maybe the Japanese had come into the Appalachian Mountains and were ready to come down upon us at any moment. I remember the fear in my little heart, but I knew my daddy had his gun and would fight until the end. I finally drifted off to sleep.

THE FIRST TIME I SAW CHRIST

My first recollection of the Danville Grade School was as a lad of about ten or eleven. My teacher was a godly woman named Mrs. Robert Ferrell. Every day she would see me, pat me on the head, and pull me up to her side, saying to me with the sweetest voice, "Bobby Lee, Mrs. Ferrell loves you, and Jesus loves you too."

I needed to hear that because at times I didn't think anyone loved me. My dad never told me that he loved me. Mountain people do not show love by an outward expression. Only a sissy would say "I love you" to a person of the same sex.

The spirit with which Dad disciplined me left its impression and hurt more deeply than the whippings I received. But with Mrs. Ferrell it was different. Every time she saw me, she would put her arms around me, pull me up to her side, and tell me the same words again and again: "Bobby Lee, Mrs. Ferrell loves you, and Jesus loves you too."

One day she said to me, "Son, I teach Sunday school at the First Baptist Church in Danville. I teach the junior boys; that is my department. Why don't you come? I would love to have you in my Sunday school class."

I will never forget the first day in Sunday school. I got up, put on my blue shirt and bibbed overalls, and rubbed some grease on my hair. My mother and dad asked where I was going.

"I am going to Sunday school."

It was about a two-and-a-half-mile walk out of the holler to Sunday school. When I got there, Mrs. Ferrell met me at the door, took me in, and introduced me. She had me sit on the front row and then said something I'll never forget: "We are glad to have one of my best students with us today. He is our guest, and we are going to ask him if he will take up the offering this morning."

She gave me a little basket with a piece of red velvet in the bottom and asked me to take the offering. I felt like I was somebody because I passed the offering plate to those boys and saw them put their pennies, nickels, and dimes into my basket. I felt so bad because everybody put something in except me. I was ashamed. I thought, "Next Sunday I'll have something to give." I then took the basket and gave it to my teacher. I've enjoyed taking up offerings ever since!

"I DID NOT STEAL THAT DIME"

Time went on; so did life with Mrs. Ferrell. She was the first person in whom I really saw Jesus Christ. She showed me what it was to be a Christian. I remember getting into a fight because a boy accused me of stealing a dime out of his billfold. *I did not steal it*. The principal said he thought I did steal it and accused me wrongly. He interrogated me thoroughly. "Did you pick up Jackie Honiker's billfold?"

"Yes, I did."

"Did you see a dollar and a dime?"

"No."

"Yes, you did! You stole the dime!"

I remember thinking, "You foolish man. Do you think I would just take a dime when I could take a dollar?!"

I went down and found the boy who accused me of stealing his dime and we got into a fight. Another teacher took me to the principal's office and I got a spanking. In my heart I wanted to talk with somebody because I had been done wrong. I went down the hallway and I heard Mrs. Ferrell talking with someone (I thought it was the principal). I heard her call my name and say, "But he's a good boy; he just needs to be saved. He just needs to know the Lord."

I listened outside the room, but as I peeked around the corner, I realized no one was there. She had her head bowed and she was praying for this little mountain boy. I turned and ran down the hall because I was embarrassed. I didn't want her to know that I had heard her praying, but in my heart I felt, "That must be what God is like—loving, forgiving, caring, sharing, helping." I saw Christ in her life.

I would have done anything for Mrs. Ferrell because I knew she loved me. I went through her junior boys Sunday school being as faithful as I could be but still struggling inside about that great God who made the heavens and that great God who made the mountains, the great God who was so far away. I still wondered if He cared.

Mrs. Ferrell did not lead me to Christ. After college, I intended to go back and tell Mrs. Ferrell that I had received Christ, that she had planted the seed in my life. But I never got around to it; I just kept putting it off. I wanted to tell her just how much she meant to me and that I first saw the love of Christ in her life.

One time when I was home from college, Dad said, "Son, you know Mrs. Ferrell passed away; they're having her wake down at the Hunter and Hunter Funeral Home."

"Oh, no! Dad, I needed to tell her something so badly, but I just kept putting it off. I was just too busy."

I got in my car and drove down to Madison to the funeral home. The place was crowded; no one knew me. I made my way through the funeral home and to the casket. I saw Mrs. Ferrell;

she wore a pink dress with white lace and a corsage. Her Bible was in her hand. Her hair was as white as the drifting snow.

As I looked down into that casket, tears ran down my cheeks. I could still hear her say, "Bobby Lee, Mrs. Ferrell loves you, and Jesus loves you too."

I wanted to tell her that her life was the first life where I saw Christ, but I had procrastinated—and now it was too late.

As I stood there, I prayed, "Dear Lord, I don't know if it's possible, but is there some way You could tell Mrs. Ferrell how much I loved her and appreciated her showing me Jesus Christ through her life? I want to thank her for being a faithful witness to this 'little mountain boy.'"

MY DAYS AT SCOTT HIGH SCHOOL

I continued through elementary and high school. I went the way of my peers. In high school I was probably the most undesirable student, enduring the struggles and embarrassment of growing up in a drunkard's home. People would snicker and laugh when they called Dad's name. He came to ball games and got into fights because he was drunk.

When I was sixteen, I personally got into a fight with a teacher because he called my dad a "drunken sot." I went across the table with a stick in my hand and let him have it "upside of his head." I was expelled from school because of this. I became consumed with bitterness.

I believe I really wanted to hurt my dad; I wanted to get back at him because he had hurt us so. I thought I could out-drink him; I thought I could out-fight him, and there would be a day when I would see him broken. In my dreams I saw him conquered and hurt. He would get what was coming to him. Oh, I was so wrong to feel this way about my dad, who would have given his life for me; but I was hurting inside.

I tried to play basketball and football, but by this time we had moved far back in the mountains again, and it was hard to participate in school with no transportation. Practice would go late, and it was hard to walk eight to ten miles or catch a ride home.

Many times I would stay with friends for two, three, and four weeks at a time in the city. I stayed with the wrong crowd (my buddies) and wouldn't go home. The bad influence was too strong, and it made me more bitter and resentful of my poverty. I never had any money. If we wanted to go to some event, we just sneaked in or crawled over the fence.

One night after a late ball practice, I came in very tired and my chores still had to be done: bringing in the kindling and coal, feeding the pigs. I remember my mother told me that she had already done the chores that night because she knew I would be so tired.

"But, Mom, why did you do that?"

"I just knew you would be tired, and I wanted you to know that I love you. I wanted to make it easy on you if I could. I know how badly you want to play ball."

I went off and wept because I knew how much she loved me.

THE FOUR ROSES

I hooked up with three young men who became my buddies in school. They had the same family background as mine: either a broken home or a drunkard's home. We had something in common: we were all eaten up with anger inside, and we were going to get back at the world.

I almost ruined my life with these wrong companions. We were known as the "Four Roses"—not because we were so beautiful, but because it was the name of a brand of whiskey. Every time you saw us, we were working on getting a bottle of Four Roses. It became a weekly and then a daily affair through my teenage years—trying to get some money for the weekend so we could stay drunk. We drank beer just like our dads who staggered around our homes, but we handled it like men. We four young men were the talk of the mountains. Of course, we liked the attention and did ridiculous and outrageous things just to get people to talk about us. We thought it was smart to "live on the edge." No challenge was too great for us to accept.

One member of the Four Roses was Hoppy Walker—the town drunk who died in his own vomit. The last time I saw Hoppy, he was drunk on the street and looked like a ragbag. He had not shaved for months. He was a frail, sick, anemic man, and he died in a drunken stupor.

Another member was Richard Paxton; he was killed in a barroom fight.

Another member was Johnny Harless; he is serving two life terms in the penitentiary without parole for two murders he committed while in a drunken stupor.

The fourth member is a preacher, by the grace of God. To God be the glory; great things He hath done! There is a loving and forgiving God!

CHAPTER 4:
Married Life

THE GIRL I MARRIED

I dropped out of high school for my junior year. My parents moved two hundred miles away to Moundsville, West Virginia. I went with them and got a job working in a glass factory. I missed my friends, so I went back to school, living with my Uncle Siegle and Aunt Freda. It was during that year that I matured a bit.

I discovered a girl I really liked—she was the prettiest girl I ever laid eyes on! I fell madly in love with her at first sight, and I told myself (and some of the boys), "I'm going to marry her one day." Her name was Lenore Justice.

Actually, I had made up my mind as we played "Spin the Bottle" at a birthday party when I was fourteen (she was thirteen). Someone would sit in a circle and spin the bottle; if the bottle stopped at a girl, the spinner got to kiss the girl. Or if he sat in a chair and a girl sat down, he could either kiss that girl or "snub" her. Everyone wanted to kiss that little thirteen-year-old Lenore.

I thought, "My, doesn't she think she's something. I'm going to sit down in that chair."

I sat in the chair, and when she sat down, I snubbed her! All the boys wanted to kiss her, but I said, "No, I'll not do it. . . . It was good enough for you because you thought you had all the boys, but I'm determined you aren't going to get me." But down in my heart I always wanted to kiss her. And I did, later!

We began to date our senior year. We helped each other by listening to each other's problems. We became the best of friends. The next thing I knew we were engaged. We graduated from high school in June 1953 and married that August. This was one of the best things that ever happened to me.

Lenore's mom and dad have always been very precious to me, but they didn't always feel the same about me! After he found out Lenore and I were serious about each other, A. P. Justice, Lenore's father, did a background check on me and my family and found out the kind of reputation we had. The Justices were determined that their daughter would not marry "that hoodlum."

Mr. Justice told Lenore, "I've done a background check on him, and his family is no good."

He told the truth, but I believe that made Lenore more determined than ever to marry me.

Mr. Justice asked me, "Son, how much money have you got? Where are you working?"

"Well, I'm going to get a job in Columbus, Ohio. I don't have a dime right now, but I'll make it."

We were married August 31, 1953. This mountain boy had gone through some rough water to woo Lenore's parents. Ruth, Lenore's mother, was always one of the sweetest and kindest women I've ever known. She always wanted the best for Lenore and her three sisters.

It took me a while to get adjusted to a family with four girls; I came from a family of four boys. Lenore and I lived with the Justice family for a while, and the girls, all younger than Lenore, thought that I was a plaything. When I'd come in from work, Sandy would jump and hang on my neck, Angie would scream like an Apache and grab me by the ankles, and Aileen would jump on my back. They would wrestle me to the floor, while Lenore jumped up and down saying, "Mommy, make them stop! Make them stop! They'll hurt him!"

I didn't know how to act because I had never been around a family of girls, but that soon changed. I never had a baby sister, but Lenore's sister Aileen has become the sister I never had. She even came to live with us for a time. Yes, the Justice girls have become sisters to this Bell boy.

A. P. (we called him Pate) and I became great friends and hunting buddies. We hunted constantly; he knew where all the "furry critters" lived. Pate was a good shot and a great hunter, and it always tickled me when I was able to out-hunt him and bring home a better kill.

There is one story in particular he loves to tell. Even at the age of ninety-two, he still claps his hands and smiles, as he spits his chewing tobacco and tells about the time we went turkey hunting.

I shot down a big, black "turkey" and carried it around all day. As I came in that evening, he saw the black feathers sticking out of my pouch. Pate said, "I knew if anyone would get one, you would. Let's see what you've got."

"Oh, it's just an old 'gooney bird' I've got here."

I didn't know what a wild turkey looked like. I had never seen one in the woods before. When I pulled it out of my sack, he clapped his hands, shaking with laughter. "Son, you got a turkey all right! But it's a turkey buzzard!"

Here I had been carrying around an old buzzard all day, thinking I had killed a big turkey. The laugh was on me. I made Pate promise he'd never tell that story, but I believe he's told it to everyone in West Virginia. When I went into work the very next morning, they all said, flapping their arms, "Here's Rod—the great turkey hunter!" I've had a hard time living that one down!

There have been a few times when I've outsmarted ol' Pate, but I'll save those stories for another time. I would like to take him fishing one more time, though, and see him catch a big ol' bass so I can do to him what he did to me. (That's a private joke!)

We've had a wonderful relationship over the years with my in-laws. The rough waters became smooth. One of the best times with them I've ever had was when I sat by Ruth's bedside and we talked about heaven, the Lord Jesus, and her home-going. That day I spent with her, watching her as she got ready to "cross over," was one of the most precious times in my life. I thank God for allowing my path to cross with that of the Justice family.

THE DEATH OF OUR FIRSTBORN
~

We were barely eighteen and nineteen, fresh out of high school, with no job, no direction, no blueprint for a successful marriage, and no foundation to build upon. Needless to say, we had no promise of a happy marriage in our future. In the first month of our marriage, Lenore and I moved from West Virginia, determined to tackle the world. I had no fear; I had no doubt. I knew we would make it. We moved to the little town of Baltimore, Ohio, where I got a job working in the aviation industry. Lenore worked in a bank.

We had been there about a year when she became pregnant with our first child. She had some complications, and we had to move back home to West Virginia for a year. When the baby was born at Glover's Clinic, I remember so vividly the doctor coming out to tell me the baby was dead. I beat the wall. I wept and cried. "There can't be a God in heaven who would do this to a little baby? Why would God take a little baby? Why doesn't He pick on somebody His own size?"

I was heartbroken and once again wondered about this great big God who was supposed to be in heaven, supposed to love people. Why would He allow this to come into our life? If He did exist, why didn't He speak to me?

In reality He was speaking, and I was not listening.

That night I went home with my father-and mother-in-law, and I saw a Bible beside the couch. I picked it up and opened it. My eyes fell on Romans 8:28, "All things work together for good to them that love God."

As I read it, I thought about the phrase "to them that love God."

I thought, "I don't love God, and I don't even know that God loves me."

My heart was so broken and I was filled with such bitterness and anger that I threw the Bible down and, once again, walked away wondering if there really was a God.

The baby's funeral was preached by a pastor from my wife's church. I was in such a state that I couldn't remember anything he said at the funeral, only that he gave some good words.

After the funeral I went to him and said, "Pastor Tate, I want to pay you for preaching my baby's funeral; how much do I owe you?"

"Rod, you don't owe me anything. Son, I would love to be your pastor, and I would never take money for preaching a baby's funeral. I never take money for preaching any funeral. I love you, and I'd love to see you saved."

I thought, "Now, that's different."

I thought that was the way he made his living, by preaching funerals. But he said he loved me and he longed to see me saved. God, in His sovereign grace, was beginning to work in my heart.

Part 2:

A Mountain Boy Educated

CHAPTER 5:
Conversion and Call

CONVICTION COMES

My wife tried to get me to go to church, but I did not want to go. I was afraid to go to church because I knew if I went, I would have to get saved. Many nights I lay awake, afraid that if I were to die I would go to hell. I had felt real conviction for many years.

I never will forget one time when I went to church and Preacher Tate seemed to preach right to me. Everything he said was for me, and I felt I was the only person in the church that night. I thought any minute he would call my name, and I said to myself, "Lenore has told him everything I've done; she's set me up. When I get back to the car and we get home, I'm going to give her a 'knuckle sandwich.' I'm tired of this."

I was furious, and I vowed that if I got out of that church, I would never go back again. As I got in the car, I said to my wife, "Lenore, you set me up; you told that preacher everything that I've been doing, and he embarrassed me; he humiliated me. He told everything I've done. He even pointed me out."

I never will forget the tears flowing down her cheeks as she said, "Rod Bell, I never told him anything about you. You're just under conviction about your old, wicked sin, and you need to be saved."

"If you never told him anything, how did he know?"

Little did I realize that there is a God in heaven that reveals secrets. God was convicting me, and I saw myself as a wicked, hell-bound sinner. That great God that I had been questioning, wondering about, and thinking about—that great God was speaking to my heart.

SALVATION

Days of conviction dragged on into months and years of conviction. I could fight it no longer; I had to do something for relief. I tried everything I could think of to get away from the conviction. I couldn't walk down a street without feeling terrified, afraid that a big truck would go out of control and hit me and I would wake up in hell. Many times I broke into a cold sweat, trembling with fear.

Suddenly, it came to me. "I know what I'll do! I'll go see a movie and forget about God dying for me and forget about my sin. I'll just forget about this heaven and hell business!"

I went to see a new Roy Rogers and Trigger movie. It was just getting interesting and I had forgotten about dying and facing God when, suddenly, I looked up. Directly over my head was a huge chandelier! It must have weighed a few hundred pounds. Immediately, I thought, "If that thing falls and hits me, I'll die and go to hell."

I jumped from my seat and ran out of the building, terrified. I just knew I was going to die. It was church that made me feel this way. I surely would never go back to church. But God was convicting me and drawing me to Calvary. Thank God for His sovereign grace.

My wife and I had been in a fuss and a fight. She had gone to her home; I went to mine. A week went by, and on Saturday night we got together to try to work things out. I said to Lenore, "Let's clean up the house."

We were waxing the floor about 9:30 that Saturday night, January 19, 1957, when Bill Tate, my wife's pastor (and a Bob Jones University graduate), knocked on the door of our little apartment. I did not want to see him; I would rather have seen the devil.

As I opened the door, I said to him, "The floor is wet, and we are busy."

Before I knew it, he had stepped inside my living room and was sitting on my couch. I began to talk with him. My wife had gone into the back bedroom. He talked to me about everything: he talked about fishing, he talked about my job, he talked about my car, he talked about everything.

And I relaxed. I did not see a Bible, and I thought, "He's not so bad; he's not trying to cram salvation down my throat." So I relaxed.

Suddenly, out of the clear, blue sky, he asked me, "Rod, when are you going to get saved, Son?"

"Pastor Tate, I don't know how to be saved. I'd like to be, but I don't know how."

He reached into his pocket and pulled out a little secret weapon, a New Testament. For the first time in my life—I was twenty-two-and-a-half—I was pointed to Jesus Christ and told about that great God who created the heavens and the earth. That great God who loved me, so loved the world that He gave His only begotten Son. That great God died on a Roman cross to pay the sin debt, and He died for Rod Bell. He shed His precious blood, was buried, and rose again. He stands with outstretched arms and says, "Come unto me, all ye that labor and are heavy laden, and I will give you rest."

The first time I heard this and understood the gospel, I bowed my head and received Jesus Christ as my Savior. I ran up the white flag of surrender and I met that God whom I, for so long, had only thought about.

Back when I was just a lad looking up into the face of the starry heavens, I had asked the questions, "Is there a God? Does He exist? Does He love me?" When I met Jesus Christ, I met that God of whom I had gotten a glimpse through creation and through a teacher's love and through the love of a mother. The creature met the Creator that night, and He changed my life completely. He gave me a joy and a peace that the world does not understand.

The pastor said, "If you died right now, where would you go, according to the Word of God?"

I told him, "According to the Word of God, I would go to heaven."

My wife came out of the bedroom, and with tears running down my cheeks, I said, "Honey, I got saved."

She looked at the preacher, asking, "Did he?"

I said, "Honey, *he* didn't get saved; *I* got saved!"

She couldn't believe it.

It was about 10:30, and I said to the pastor, "Let's go tell my mother-in-law and father-in-law."

We climbed into the car and away we went—up the road, through the mountains, and over the hills. I knocked on the door; they were already in bed. My mother-in-law peeked out the window; she already had her "night cream" on, greased up for the night, with her curlers in her hair. She came out on the porch. There was that no-good son-in-law, the pastor, and her precious daughter.

I opened my arms to receive her and said, "Mom!"

She went past me and right to Lenore, "What has he done now, Honey?"

I said, "Mom, I got saved, and I want you to forgive me for being such a low-down, sorry, no-good rascal."

She looked at the pastor. "Did he?"

I said, "Mom, I got saved."

I grabbed her and hugged her.

About that time, my father-in-law came out. "What's going on here?"

"Papa, I got saved, and I want you to forgive me. I had to come and tell you I got saved, and I wanted you to know."

"Well, how did this come about?"

I told him how the pastor had come and told me I was a sinner, and I got saved.

"Was it that easy?" he asked.

"It was that easy, Pa."

This was Saturday night, and by this time it was almost midnight. I looked at the preacher and said, "Let's go tell my mom and dad."

Oh, the burden was lifted at last! The light had dawned; the darkness was gone. Joy flooded my soul!

We got in the car and went down to my mom and dad's. I will never forget it—I knocked on the door and got them out of bed at midnight. I thought they'd be happy because I'd been saved. I told them I had received Christ as my personal Savior and that I wanted to see them saved. They weren't too happy that I got them out of bed; in fact, they weren't too sure I was real. But in my heart I knew I had experienced something that was real. I told them I was going to church tomorrow and that I'd love for them to join me.

I went home happy, got up early the next morning, and went to church. At the invitation I went forward and let the church know I had been saved. I went forward Sunday night and was baptized and joined the church.

Monday morning when I went to work, I told everyone in the office that I had been saved. I told every mechanic, every employee, every customer that came in that I had been saved. I can remember telling the parts manager that I had been saved. "Man, guess what happened to me?"

He said something so dirty and vulgar I can't repeat it.

I said, "Oh, no! I got saved! You know, He'll save you too. Jesus is a wonderful Savior."

He said to me, "Why, I'm saved; I'm a deacon at the First Baptist Church."

I replied, "You couldn't be saved. How could you be saved? You've got that old, dirty, nude picture of Marilyn Monroe hanging on the wall there. I've gone down to the whiskey store and bought liquor for you. You couldn't be saved. But God will save you, if you will let Him. He saved me."

I didn't realize it then, but my co-workers would do everything in their power to keep me from serving the Lord. I didn't fully realize what I was doing, but I had to tell everyone about my salvation. I told my employer. I told one man, the head of the paint department, and he said, "Rod, I'm glad you got saved, but you've told me five times already today!"

I cannot express the fullness of joy that was flowing from my soul like an artesian well of peace. I wanted to climb the highest mountain and tell the world I had been saved. I went to church somewhere every night for almost a year because I would go to *any* kind of church. As long as it said "church" and services were in session, I went. Women preachers, snake handlers, Assembly of God, Church of God, Baptist, Methodist, Lutheran, Catholic—I went to everything because I was so hungry. I just wanted everything God had for me.

There was such a drastic change in my life. I recall my wife saying, "Well, you're certainly not the man I married."

She almost left me because I had gone so crazy over this new-found salvation. Talk about extremes! My family said religion had "run me crazy." The whole county knew I had been saved!

I went to the mountains and prayed all day and all night because I felt God calling me to preach. I carved on the trees, "Rod loves Jesus; Jesus loves Rod." The Creator of the heavens *is* real; He *does* speak to me; He *does* love me. Oh, the burning reality of that first taste of His love!

When it dawned on me that my loved ones were lost and that they were going to spend eternity in hell, my burden for them became so great that I could not sleep. I lost my appetite and became a desperate man seeking to win my loved ones.

I remember preaching in a little mountain church in West Virginia about six months after I had been saved. Someone came running into the church and shouted, "Your daddy just shot your mother."

I did not dismiss the service; I just ran out the door and down the road until I reached the crowd of people standing in the road about two hundred yards from our house. They were all neighbors.

"What's wrong? What's wrong?" I asked.

"It's your mother. Your daddy shot at your mother."

I thought they had said, "Shot your mother"; but they said, "Shot *at* your mother." He had shot at her and the blast had blown the end of the bed off, but he had missed her. I saw my mother shaking, scared and frightened, and people were trying to console her.

"What's wrong?" I asked her.

"Well, your daddy's drunk and gone crazy. He must be drinking 'white lightning' again."

"Well, I'm going to get the gun away from him."

"No, you can't do that. We've called the sheriff, and the sheriff is coming to take the gun."

I knew there would be trouble if the sheriff tried to take Dad's gun away, so I left, determined to reach him first. I knew my dad had bragged that he would shoot me someday because I thought I was so religious and pious. He said he would put me in my place. As I pulled away, my family and neighbors cautioned me. "He'll kill you. He's drunk; he doesn't know what he's doing."

"Well, I've prayed that if it takes my life to get my daddy saved, then that's what it will be."

I wasn't really brave; I was scared, weeping, and burdened. I was already emotionally drained by the time I walked up the path to the house. I could feel the bullets ripping through my body any moment—I knew that I was going to be shot. I walked onto the porch and opened the door. There sat my dad with a shotgun and two shells.

"Give me the gun. I love you, but I'm not going to let you kill anyone."

Dad began to weep, and I took the gun and shells and went out the back door. As I came around the front of the house, I met the sheriff and his posse. I assured them that everything was under control and that Dad was all right now. I told the sheriff, "We can handle it; thank you for coming."

"Okay," he said, and they all left.

Later, I learned that Woody had once again run interference for me. Dad had threatened to kill himself, but Mother had hidden the shells. Woody threw two shells to Dad, saying, "Go ahead, and do a good job while you're at it."

"I only need one," Dad said.

"Do a good job. The way you are, the whole family would be better off."

Woody packed all his clothes, and on the way out turned to Dad. "Bye. You'll never see me again. I'm leaving."

My big brother had made it easier on me again, and I didn't realize it until years later. I also found out later that the gun had discharged accidentally, barely missing Mom.

That was the beginning of God's working in my dad's life. God continued to deal with Dad all through that week. Dad came where I was working in a garage. I saw him coming and said, "Oh my, I don't want to see him." I turned my back and continued working, but Dad spoke to me.

"Son, I want your God."

We bowed and prayed there in public, and Dad began to weep. "I have accepted the Lord."

He told all of his neighbors and all of his friends that he had gotten saved, and he asked them to forgive him.

I asked him, "Dad, would you go with me to church tonight?"

"All right. What time will you pick me up?"

"6:00," I told him. I knew he wouldn't be ready, but he was! He went with me. They always asked for testimonies in this mountain church, and Dad was the first to give his. From that day until he went to be with the Lord, he grew by leaps and bounds and was one of the finest dads and greatest Christians I've ever known. He was completely changed and sold out to Jesus Christ. His testimony was, "I am just an old sinner, saved by grace."

THE CALL TO PREACH

I will never forget the first person I led to Christ, the man who worked in the parts department. I pushed across the counter four boxes of parts I had stolen and told him, "I've stolen these. I've got to make restitution because I've been saved." Little did I realize that God used that act of restoration to convict him, and I was able to lead him to Christ.

Within a year, I was struggling with the call to preach. I asked my pastor how to know when God was calling you.

He said, "Brother Rod, if you can keep from preaching, you're not fit to preach."

I thought, "Dear Lord, I've got to do it. I want to do it so bad. You've done so much for me, and I long to do it. I cannot keep from doing it."

One night the pastor preached from Isaiah 6. I saw the Lord, I saw myself, and I saw a lost world. Who would go and tell them? That night, I died to myself and said, "Here am I; send me." I looked up and saw a sign on the church wall: "Only one life, 'twill soon be past. Only what's done for Christ will last."

The word traveled all over Boone County—"Rod Bell's got religion! He's gone crazy!" I would go into the mountains and pray all day and many times into the night. My family and neighbors said, "Religion has driven him crazy; we may have to commit him to the insane asylum." They found my "praying ground" and discovered the big oak tree where I had carved "Jesus Loves Rod."

Thank God, it was not religion that had "gotten hold of me" but the reality of the resurrected Christ and a changed life.

At that time I had more zeal than knowledge. I have since learned that balance is the key to the Christian life. Zeal without knowledge is dangerous, and knowledge without zeal is dead.

I reported for duty in the little mountain church. I sold out and went into business for the Lord. I was a debtor to all men. I knew a call to preach was a call to prepare. I told my pastor, my wife, and everyone that God was calling me to be a preacher. One fellow said, "How do you know? You've not been to school; you're not educated. You know, I felt that way once, when I was first saved. But after a while, I got over it, and so will you! Calm down, Son. You've got responsibilities; you'd better be sure."

I remember the phrase he used, "But after a while, I got over it, and so will you." I said to myself, "But I don't want to get over it!"

These thoughts drove me to the Word of God, and God confirmed my call in John 21, when He told Peter, "Feed my sheep." I had developed the daily habit of reading my Bible, and this passage shone like a light from heaven for me. "Yes, Lord. I'll be a shepherd and feed Your sheep." Oh, how many times I've failed to lead them into green pastures since then, but He has always been faithful.

I asked the pastor, "Can you tell me where I can go to school? I need to prepare." I thought that since this man had a burden for souls, I wanted to be like him because he came and told me about my need of the Savior. I was sure the school that trained him would be a good school to go to.

He recommended Bob Jones University, and he took me to visit the campus in Greenville, South Carolina. I found that training preachers is what Bob Jones University does best. I surrendered to preach and told my boss that I was going to go to school.

"Oh, that's wonderful, Son. I'll do anything I can to help you. You let me know when you get ready to go to school, and I'll pay all your expenses. I'll pay your expenses through your undergraduate work, and if you go to get graduate work, I'll pay your expenses there too. Just let me know; I'll take care of it and pick up the tab."

I went home and told my wife that I knew God was in it now because Mr. Priestly had told me he would pay my way. She felt more secure because of Mr. Priestly's commitment.

I sold all my furniture; I was getting all my bills cleaned up. I sold my car; I was getting ready to go to school. After paying all my bills, I had about $168 left. I went in to tell Mr. Priestly I was getting ready to go to school and would be leaving within thirty days.

"Now, Son, when you get to Alderson and Broadus, I will make arrangements for you."

"But sir, I'm not going to Alderson and Broadus."

Alderson and Broadus was an American Baptist Convention school in West Virginia, and Mr. Priestly was on the Board of Trustees there.

"I'm not going there; I'm going to Bob Jones University in Greenville, South Carolina."

"Son, you're not going to our school? You go to that school and you'll never be heard of. They don't turn out anything but radicals and revolutionaries down there. You want to go to our school. We'll take care of you and see that you are properly trained."

I tried to explain, "But I feel God wants me to go to this other school."

But Mr. Priestly said, "Now just think about it. You'll have all your expenses paid if you go to our school, so that must be of the Lord."

I left his office that day very sad. His parting words were, "You pray about it." And I left sad because I felt in my heart that God wanted me to go to Bob Jones University. I had my heart and soul set on going to Bob Jones University.

I went home and told my wife, and she said, "Well, maybe the Lord wants you to go to this other school. He's providing for us, and we don't have anything down at Bob Jones. Maybe the Lord *is* in it."

I went through my first struggle of walking by faith. "Honey, I don't have peace about going to this sort of school, and the more I pray about it, the more I think God wants us to go to BJU."

Meanwhile, Mr. Priestley sent the Association's missionary to see me and try to convince me to go to "our" convention school. He was an elderly gentleman, a good man, but he was sold out to the convention. "Now, Son, let me help you with this decision you're going to make. If you go to *our* school and become one of *our* preachers, you'll pastor one of *our* churches. You'll have a parsonage to live in. Mr. Priestley's going to pay all of your expenses and all of your tuition. You'll draw a salary from one of *our* churches; you'll have a good annuity program, and they have a good retirement program. All you have to do is be one of *our* preachers.

"If you go to that school in Greenville, South Carolina, you will have nothing. Besides, you have a small baby, and you need some security. Now, here's what I want you to do. I have an application here for you to fill out. All you have to do is just sign it, and we'll see that everything is taken care of."

I drew a deep breath and said, "With all due respect to you, sir, God does not want me to go to *your* school, and God does not want me to be *your* preacher. God wants me to go to Greenville, South Carolina, and I'm going to be *God's* preacher and do what God wants me to do. I'm going to Bob Jones University, and I'm going to trust God."

"Now, Son, you don't have any money."

"That's right," I said, "but my God will supply all my needs."

I made the decision that day; I burned the bridges behind us.

After Mr. Priestly saw that he could not persuade me to go to his school, he demoted me to washing cars and being the janitor. He embarrassed me and, needless to say, it was humbling, especially when the other employees came by. "You'd better listen to the Old Man," they'd laugh.

I was learning to walk by faith. The day came when we loaded everything we had in our car and left for Greenville, South Carolina. All our belongings fit in the car and on top of the car, with sacks of "potaters" on each fender. We had $168 to go to college and study and prepare for the ministry, but Philippians 4:19 was in our hearts. This was God's "scholarship"—where He leads, He feeds; where He guides, He makes a way!

My family talked me into leaving our daughter, Niki, who was about eight months old, with them until we could get a job. Lenore and I "beat the bushes" all week long looking for a job and came up empty-handed. We had a little two-room apartment in Campus Park. That Saturday I told my wife, "Let's go back and get our baby. We're a family. If we're going to starve, we'll starve together. We're not trusting the Lord by leaving her behind; it's not right for us to be separated."

So back we went. We got our baby and came back on Monday. That Tuesday I got a job working in a service station at night, and Lenore got a job working in a bank during the day. God honored that step of faith. All I knew was that I had a deep, burning call from God that could not be extinguished.

CHAPTER 6:
College Experiences

COLLEGE DAYS
~

College days were exciting days. When I arrived on campus at Bob Jones University, my academics were not the best. I had a D-minus average in high school, and it had taken me five years to finish. I had never learned to read well. I found out later that I had a form of dyslexia. I was not typical "college material."

I met with my advisors, who suggested I go to the Institute of Christian Service, a two-year program. When they said "Institute," I thought about some kind of "institution" like the one my family had threatened to put me in. I refused to do that. I begged and pleaded for them to give me a chance to go to college because I wanted to give the Lord my best. I knew that none of my people had ever been to college, but many of them had been in those institutions, and I was determined not to go to an institution. I wanted to go to college and work on a degree. I was ignorant, unlearned, and hadn't the faintest idea of what it was to study in a formal, Christian university. I was soon to find out.

Thank God they gave me a chance. I was placed on academic probation and given only twelve hours the first semester. I took every "help class" they offered: I took reading clinics; I took speech clinics; I took English clinics. I took every clinic I could find. I had so many deficiencies, I thought that was my major. I was scared, but I found godly concern and care in a faculty who truly loved the Lord and me.

My mind went back to Mrs. Ferrell, the first time that I ever saw Jesus Christ in the life of a teacher. Once again, I saw that same concern and that same love. I thank God for a faculty and staff that really cared enough to invest their lives in me. They helped me and spent extra time with me over and over again. I will be forever indebted to them, and to this day, my heart is filled with gratitude for a faculty that cares.

I didn't have much time for campus activities while I was in school, but my literary society, Phi Beta Chi, elected me the chaplain. Whenever they let me preach, we usually had more outside in the hallways and on the sidewalk listening in than we had in the room. I was asked if I could tone it down because it was causing traffic jams; I was happy to comply. I enjoyed my society, and I especially enjoyed being the chaplain because I got to preach.

When we came to school, we brought everything we owned in an old Chevrolet car. The running board of that car was hanging loose, and a piece of wood held the floorboard together. We had to park at the top of a hill and roll down so it would start.

I remember sitting in the library one day studying. As I looked out the window, I saw my car go by. Nobody was driving it! I had parked on a hill and forgotten to put a rock under the wheel. I watched it roll down the hill and crash into another car before it stopped.

Words cannot express the experiences we endured through school and how God answered prayer. . . from having food to eat, to paying bills, to remembering material for exams, to seeing souls saved, to starting churches, to sending out missionaries. Truly this was "boot camp" for what has proved to be a blessed lifetime of service.

GOD ANSWERS PRAYER—WITH $12.57

While in college I often learned more *outside* the classroom than I did in class. I learned to walk and talk with God. I remember one time I could not pay my school bill in order to take my exams. I owed $12.57. My wife said, "Honey, do you think Dr. Johnson would let you take exams if you just go talk to him?" (Dr. Johnson was the school's financial director.)

"Well, I'm sure he would. But when we get out in the Lord's work, we're not going to have Dr. Johnson. Are we in God's will?"

"Yes."

"Have we done everything that we possibly can do to get the money to pay our school bill?"

"Yes."

"Do you believe that God will supply? He said He would supply."

"Yes."

"Then let's take God at His Word and watch Him supply."

We got on our knees and claimed Matthew 18:19, "Again I say unto you, That if two of you shall agree on earth as touching any thing that they shall ask, it shall be done for them of my Father which is in heaven." We asked the Lord, "Lord, if You send us $12.56, You didn't answer our prayer. If you send us $12.58, You didn't answer our prayer. We need 12 dollars and 57 cents."

We waited at the mailbox, waiting for God to answer prayer. Several days later, we received a letter from Lenore's mother: "Dear Children, I feel strangely burdened of the Lord tonight to send you all the money that I have." It was a ten-dollar bill.

Then we received a letter from Sandy, Lenore's sister: "I feel strangely burdened tonight to send you some money. We have looked through everything we have. We've robbed the piggy banks; we've robbed the couches. We turned the couches upside down." Glued with Scotch tape to a piece of gray paper was some change: a 50-cent piece, pennies, and a couple of dollars. We counted it—$2.57!

God answered to the penny what we needed! To God be the glory! God's telephone number: Jeremiah 33:3, "Call unto me, and I will answer thee, and shew thee great and mighty things, which thou knowest not." That God I had wondered about as a small lad back in the hollows of West Virginia was real. He *did* care and *did* answer prayer. His promises are secure. He will provide.

AN EYE OPENER

I had some crude ways and some crude ideas about serving the Lord. I remember going home and telling my wife that we were going to have an opera. I thought it was something like the "Grand Ol' Opry."

Lenore said, "I don't think that's what it is, Honey."

I was used to Lester Flatt, Earl Scruggs and the Foggie Mountain Boys, Grandpa Jones, and Minnie Pearl.

Lenore said, "I don't think that's it."

Boy, was I in for a rude awakening! They had some woman who sang in Latin or some kind of language I couldn't understand. I was bored stiff and thought, "My, how is this going to help me preach? What does this have to do with keeping people out of hell?"

I sat and fumed. That woman began to sing and squeal; it sounded like a dying calf in a hail storm. I said to the fellows around me, "Go get the gun; I think she's got it treed."

Everybody laughed. Finally, she stabbed herself and rolled down the steps. I said, "It would have been a whole lot better if she had done that in the first act."

I was called in—called on the carpet for my behavior. I had an "attitude calibration session"! All I wanted to do was study the Bible and learn to preach. All I wanted to do was to get in, get out, and get it over with. That was my idea of an education.

But I'm so thankful the folks at BJU were patient, loving, and understanding with me. They helped me bring my life into focus and polished off most of the rough edges.

THE NIGHT SHIFT

While I was in school, I had a job working nights. I worked at the corner of East North Street and Highway 291 Bypass, running a service station and getting paid 75 cents an hour. I worked from 11 P.M. to 7 A.M. and went to school from 9:00 A.M. until 2:30 P.M. Then I would go home, take a nap, and go back to work. It was quite a busy schedule.

Working eleven to seven was called the "dead man's shift" because it sure was a killer! I would get home in time to take my wife to work, take our daughter Niki to the baby sitter, and catch my 9:00 class. We were always in a hurry, and the four years went by quickly.

Bruce Barton owned the service station where I worked. We tried to witness and win him to the Lord until he became upset with us; he wanted nothing to do with our "religion." Thirty years later, I was preaching at the Bob Jones University Bible Conference one night, and someone left a message for me to call Mr. Barton. I called, not remembering who he was. He got on the phone and said, "Are you the Rod Bell from West Virginia?"

"Yes, sir."

"Are you the one who used to work at a Shell station at East North Street and 291?"

"Yes, sir, I am."

"I saw in the paper that there was a Rod Bell speaking at Bible Conference and that he was a 'Doctor.' That couldn't be the same guy that worked for me thirty years ago because this fellow had a doctor's degree."

"Well, don't let that doctor's degree disturb you because it's just like a curl on a pig's tail—it doesn't change the taste of the pork; it just dresses up the hog."

"You must be the same Rod Bell. Look, I just had to talk to you."

"Mr. Barton, please come and hear me preach," I asked him.

He said, "I'd love to, but I can't get out. The reason I called is I wanted to tell you that I have been saved. I have to tell you what happened." And he told me this story:

"When you were working for me, I resented your witnessing to me and giving me tracts. I was embarrassed whenever you would pray and thank the Lord for your food. One time, I came by the service station and noticed that the light was on in the office. I thought, 'That preacher boy left the lights on. I'd better go by and turn them off and lock the place up.' I pulled in and got ready to lock the door. I heard you and your buddy Joe Fritz praying, 'O God, save Mr. Barton. Don't let Mr. Barton die and go to hell.'

"I heard you weeping over my soul, and I backed away from the door, got in my car, and went home. I went away from there, but I couldn't get away from the prayer. For years I heard your prayer, 'O God, save Mr. Barton.' And I want you to know that God has saved Mr. Barton, and I want to thank you for your witness."

One waters, another sows, and God gives the increase. To God be the glory!

SCHOOL BUDDIES

My school buddies are too numerous to mention, but I enjoy them all with fond and pleasant memories. One of my dearest friends, Russell Rice, has pastored a great church in Anderson, South Carolina, for many years. Jimmy Rose was another of my unique school chums. We preached on street corners and prayed together many Friday nights. He and his wife, Nancy, have been on the mission field for almost forty years.

We had all our classes together; we studied together, prayed together, and cried together. We were all "town students." We lived in Woodland Homes Apartments because the rent was cheap and it was close to the school. We all looked after each other; if one had a need, we all knew about it.

Many times we went from house to house of other students collecting groceries because we knew a friend had nothing to eat. We would leave the box of groceries on the porch, ring the doorbell, and run! Russ, or one of the other men, would tell us how an angel brought food and left it on the doorstep.

I don't know how Lenore put up with four or five men in her kitchen all night, studying, praying, and "fellowshiping." I'm sure she went to bed perturbed many a night because we would sometimes (all right, oftentimes!) fellowship more than study.

When we prayed, we must have thought God was deaf and that we had to shout at Him. We felt that the louder we prayed, the better the prayer meeting we had. Oh, isn't it wonderful to know that God can hear the slightest sigh or the quietest intent of our heart. Thank God He is not deaf!

CHAPEL AND DR. BOB SR.
~

The greatest times of the day were chapel and "Preacher Boys." I couldn't wait to hear Dr. Bob Jones Sr. He was my kind of preacher, and he gave me something that I will never, ever get away from: "It's a sin to do less than your best." And "Do right 'til the stars fall"—a philosophy I've built my life on. "Be right, be real, be ready!" "Preach, pray, or die, but do not compromise!"

I remember him preaching, red in the face, and condemning sin, condemning compromise, and having a holy heartbeat for the souls of men. He began to mold and build a philosophy in my life: whatever you have is enough to do the job God wants you to do. Find God's will and do it, and you'll stumble over happiness on the way.

I will be eternally indebted to the philosophy that was drilled into my life. He said something in chapel one time—"God never made a possum without making a persimmon tree." Being a mountain boy, I knew the characteristics of a possum. The possum finds a persimmon tree because it has delicious fruit that possums love. He'll stay in that tree until all the fruit is gone. The persimmon tree for the Christian is the will of God. Find the will of God and there's where you'll get fruit; there's where you'll want to live. There's where you'll find peace, contentment, and a life that is pleasing to God.

I made up my mind that I was going to find God's persimmon tree for my life. I was going to find the will of God and stay there. This philosophy has shaped my life to be "steadfast, unmoveable, always abounding in the work of the Lord" (I Cor. 15:58). Over the door of my office, I have a sign that reads, "Lord, what wilt thou have me to do?" (Acts 9:6).

AFRAID OF FAILURE

Studying did not come easy for me. I knew early on I did not have the ability to do great academic work, but I felt that I must get it, even if I had to study day and night. My greatest fear was that I would fail; I had never really accomplished anything in my life before this, and now I was afraid I would fail in college too. I came to the place where I said, "Lord, I'm going to do my best and do it as unto the Lord, and I'm giving You everything I have."

I approached every subject with that attitude. I can't remember one class or one test I took in all my years of college that I did not face with that attitude. Praise God, I finished with a fairly good record. I realized I was doing it as unto the Lord, and that made the difference.

When I took Greek, I was scared to death, but I knew it was an opportunity to study the Scriptures in their original language. That year I spent five hours a day, every day, studying. Those five hours a day, every day for a year, paid off, and the Lord helped me make a good grade. The next year, I tutored some of my buddies, and my living room was filled with preacher boys studying second-year Greek. English was a different story! I've never understood why I learned more English in Greek class than I learned in English class, but it seems that's the way it was. Looking back, the daily discipline I learned because of Greek class was one of the greatest lessons I took from college.

After listening to Dr. Bob Jones Sr., the chapel speakers, and the Bible Conference speakers, my heart and soul yearned to preach. There was a burning for souls. We had "extension groups" who preached to chain gangs, on street corners, and in old folks' homes in Laurens, South Carolina.

My first year on extension, I asked the upperclassmen to make a list of all the mistakes I made when I preached and tell them to me on our trip back to the University. Every Sunday morning, they gave me pages of double negatives, dangling participles, fragmented sentences, wrong verb usage, slang expressions, and incorrect doctrine. I ate it up. I needed to know; I wanted to learn. It helped me so much when they gave me that constructive criticism.

Chapter 7:
Early Preaching Experiences

CHASING A SINNER

~

I was preaching on the street in a very rough district in Laurens one night, and a man came up, put a knife to my throat, and said, "I'm going to cut your throat if you don't stop preaching."

I said, "Before you do, let me tell you that God loves you and Jesus died for you."

He started shaking, dropped his knife, and ran. I bent down, picked up his knife, and ran after him with my Bible in one hand and the knife in the other. He looked over his shoulder and saw me coming. I didn't realize I had the knife, but I knew I had the Sword in the other hand. I chased him down and told him the old, old story. He accepted Christ and was gloriously saved. We had many conversions and salvation experiences on our extension.

PREACHING TO AN EMPTY JAIL

~

While on extension, I was frequently reminded of my own home situation when I was a young lad. I had a great burden for those drunkards under the control of alcohol, and I thought maybe the Lord would call me into a mission-type ministry. But He had other things in mind.

I remember one time preaching in a jail for about thirty or thirty-five minutes when I looked out the window and saw all my buddies gathered around my car. They were laughing and looked like they were having a good time. I thought, "That bunch of sinners. Here I am preaching, trying to get people saved, and they're down there telling jokes and having a good time."

After a while, one of them came upstairs and said, "Come on, Rod, we're going."

"Just wait a minute; I haven't finished my message."

"Well, there's no one up here in the jail to hear your message, so just come on."

I had been preaching to an empty jail for over thirty minutes, so the laugh was on me. I thought I had seen someone in the back of the jail, but I was wrong. As usual, on the way home they critiqued me, and one of the first things they said was, "Be sure when you preach that you always have someone around to listen to your message!"

MY FIRST EVANGELISTIC CAMPAIGN

I experienced my first two evangelistic campaigns during my freshman and sophomore years at Bob Jones University. I was invited to come to Winder, Georgia, and preach for Gerald Bagwell, a BJU student who was pastoring in a Southern Baptist Convention church. The church was over one hundred years old, and the people were very set in their ways. Little did I know what an experience I was in for.

I jumped into my old Chevrolet and headed off to my evangelistic crusade. Halfway to Winder, the car's engine died. I was towed to an old garage in the country, but I was determined to go on. I found a bus headed to Winder, and soon I was on my way again; I felt God had a reason for me to go.

I got on the bus and sat down beside a man who had been riding from New York City. I thought, "This is the reason my car broke down," and I began to talk to him about the Lord. He had just been released from prison; he was under a burden of sin. He and his wife were separated. His mom and dad had disowned him, and he had very little to live for. "I don't know why I'm going to Winder, but I feel that I have to go; it's my home," he told me.

"Sir, I know the reason. God wanted me to sit on this seat beside you and tell you about the Burden-Bearer, the One who can calm the storms of the soul and give you life eternal. That One is the Lord Jesus. No matter who you are, no matter where you've been, no matter what your problems are, His yoke is easy and His burden is light."

I witnessed to him, and as we passed by the streetlights along the highway, I looked over and saw tears streaming down his cheeks. The Holy Spirit was convicting him, and I continued to present the glorious gospel of the grace of God to this dear man. He accepted the Lord Jesus as his personal Savior. My, did he weep! We wept and rejoiced together, and from then on, I read to him the gospel story. I read from the Gospel of John, I gave him assurance verses, and I gave him an extra Bible that I had. I told him to read it and to find a good fundamental, Bible-believing church. He was worried that no one would forgive him.

"But my wife and my children and my mom and dad—no one will forgive me."

I said, "God has forgiven you."

The joy of the story came when the bus stopped and he got off. I watched out the window as an old, gray-headed mom; an old, gray-headed dad; and a middle-aged woman with three children came running out to greet him. They smothered him with hugs and kisses. I thought of the prodigal son and said to myself, "Kill the fatted calf. God has forgiven him, Momma and Daddy and the family have forgiven him, and there's joy in the presence of the angels of God."

As we made our way on to Winder, tears streamed down my cheeks, and I thanked God for causing my car to break down. I went on to the meeting. But that encounter was the greatest victory I had through the meeting.

I went into this old, traditional Southern Baptist church that was very set in its ways. This young preacher was a novice—all I knew to do was to preach against sin and to take a stand, to tell them about the Savior and the need to separate from apostasy. So that's what I did. Every night it was like shooting a rifle into a barrel—it ricocheted around and around. The church was dead; the spirit was like icicles hanging from the chandeliers.

I said, "Brother Bagwell, what in the world's wrong here?"

"They don't like you. They don't like me. They want to close the meeting, and they want you to go home."

"Well, let me ask you a question. I've noticed the piano is sitting in the middle of the aisle, where the Lord's table is usually placed. I've noticed the stout lady who plays it with gusto. I've noticed something else: they sing out of two different songbooks. Half of them sing out of the green songbooks; the other half sing out of the red songbooks. The half who sing out of the red songbooks sit on the right side, and the half who sing from the green songbooks sit on the left side. My brother, I'm afraid we have a real problem here. Let's just keep preaching."

"Okay, let's keep on preaching."

Before I got up the next night to preach, the pastor asked, "Does anyone have a testimony?"

The stout lady who played the piano jumped up and with a bellowing voice said, "This preacher has been preaching all week about taking a stand. I'm for taking a stand. And tonight, I'm one who will take a stand. I'm sick and tired of having the piano sitting in the middle of the church aisle. We need to put the piano back where it belongs. We need to all start singing out of the red songbooks and throw the green songbooks out the window. I'm taking that stand right now, and I want everybody in this church house to know that, by the grace of God, I'll never play this piano again while it's in the middle of the aisle, nor will I play out of a green songbook."

I said, "Hold it! That's not the kind of stand I was looking for or encouraging anyone to take. That is the kind of 'stand' people usually split and divide churches over."

We never moved the piano; we never changed the song-books. That church today is just as cold and dead as can be. All they need to do now is to sing the doxology and put the flowers on that church's grave. They should have done it forty years ago. I was preaching to a Laodicean church and didn't realize it.

But I thanked God for the tears shed when the prodigal came home, when the fatted calf was prepared in his honor.

MY SECOND EVANGELISTIC CAMPAIGN

My second evangelistic campaign as a young preacher boy was in the Hatfield-McCoy country of West Virginia. Walking "where angels feared to tread," I went to another old church that was set in its ways and needed revival, if not regeneration. I started preaching on Monday and nothing happened. It was like preaching to an empty room. Tuesday nothing happened. Wednesday the pastor knocked on the door and said, "Pastor Bell, we're going to close the meeting out tonight."

"Why? What's happened."

"I found out all my deacons, all my parents, and all the leadership of the church are allowing their teenagers to go to a dance and a wild party on Friday night. I've gone to every one of my deacons and my leadership. They said it's the only right thing to do—to let the kids go and have a good time."

With tears running down his face, he said, "My ministry is finished. I don't have the backing of the church. The deacons and the leadership put a dance and a wild party before God and revival. What can we do but close it out?"

I said, "My brother, would you let me preach just one more time?"

"Okay, we'll preach tonight, then close it out."

I spent all day Wednesday on my knees in prayer. I could not get any peace about a message. I wrestled and struggled. "God, you must give me something for those parents." When I got to the church, I still had a tremendous burden for parents and families and young people. As I bowed in the pastor's study, I asked God, "Why? Why, God? What a bunch of sorry, good-for-nothing parents, who would let their teenagers go to a dance and a wild party while we're trying to have evangelistic meetings and begging God for revival."

The Holy Spirit seemed to whisper to my soul, "That's your message."

That night, I went out with all the confidence in the world. The place was packed with parents and teenagers. I preached on "Why sorry, good-for-nothing parents would allow their young people to go to a dance while we are begging God for revival."

After about an hour of really pouring my heart out and ranting and raving, I gave an invitation. Almost the entire church—parents, teenagers, grandparents—came to the altar, weeping, begging God to forgive them for disobedience and sin.

We had a touch of heaven. Thursday night the place was packed; souls were saved. Friday night, the night of the big wild party and the dance, the young people had invited their school friends and buddies to the meeting. The place was packed. Many were saved. I had to leave on Saturday to get back to my own church, but the pastor continued on Saturday, Sunday, and through the next two weeks. He told me there was a great out-pouring of the Spirit of God, and many precious souls were saved. Homes were changed; family altars were started.

You know, I've searched diligently through the Bible for that text "Why sorry, good-for-nothing parents would allow their young people go to a dance while we are begging God for revival," but I've never found it! The truth is there, but I just can't find those verses! Thank God, though, He always blesses His Word.

THE BIG TENT

The summer of my sophomore year in college, Evangelist Fred Dillon in West Virginia gave me his meeting tent if I would come and get it. I borrowed a tractor-trailer truck and went to get that tent. I left my wife and family in Greenville, South Carolina, and went on an evangelistic tour. I had just five dollars to launch my great summer crusade!

I took off to West Virginia, and a little church I preached in one night gave me $200 for a love offering. I went and got the tent, set it up in Danville, West Virginia, on a lot next door to where the Hanley Funeral Home is today. On the tent was a big sign that read "Hear Bob Jones University Preacher Rod Bell—Preaching Nightly!"

I had never pitched so much as a pup tent, let alone a tent that would seat five hundred! My unsaved Uncle Curtis came down to help me build a platform. While we were building the platform, a storm came up and started to blow the tent down. I wrapped myself around a stake, held on to the flaps, and cried and prayed. I didn't know that if I had secured and nailed down all the flaps, she would have blown down. I had left the flaps loose, and the wind just blew under and through the tent.

I began to preach on the corner in Danville. One of the pastors of the church from which I had separated came and pleaded, "Please don't cause me any trouble. I know you're from Bob Jones, and you guys are notorious for causing trouble. Just don't preach against sin; preach 'all have sinned' and leave it at that. My people are getting confused."

I told him, "If I had a pastor like you, I'd be confused too."

I wasn't very respectful, but I soon found out why he was saying that. We had over fifty from his church that were saved during our meetings! I preached there for over a month, and many hardened sinners were converted.

One woman in particular would never come into the services, but she would sit in a window across the street and listen to me preach. On the last night of the meeting, she surrendered and was gloriously saved.

Mountaineers, "rednecks," and good ol' boys came to town just to "rock the preacher" (throw rocks at us). We stayed in the tent, and when they came to rock us, we went out to meet them. We had the joy of leading some of them to Jesus Christ and baptizing them in the river.

After having over ninety saved and baptized in the Coal River, we moved the tent to Ramage ballpark for another thirty days. We preached every night. I had two local "helpers": an old-fashioned, shouting Methodist named Jay Hager, who helped me with the devotional, and Rex Workman, who helped to get the service started. We had another fifty saved, including some of my classmates and boyhood friends. Many decisions were made for the Lord. A real touch of heaven fell upon that meeting. Many were baptized in the Coal River, and the fruit remains today.

A few years ago, I was preaching in Morgantown, West Virginia, and a middle-aged woman approached me after the service with a big smile on her face. "You don't know me, but I was a little twelve-year-old girl that got saved at the Ramage ballpark back in the sixties. I just wanted you to know that the fruit remains. Thank you for faithfully preaching the Word."

I also discovered that a young man named Miller had also been saved; he's still in the ministry thirty-five years later.

Twenty years later, I went back to the little church in Madison, West Virginia, for a meeting. The place was packed out every night. Souls were saved, and many of my schoolmates got saved. I even saw one of my high school math teachers come to be saved. The preacher wanted to extend the meeting another week, so we did. It rained cats and dogs, but people kept coming. Over one hundred professions of faith were made in that meeting in West Virginia behind my old high school.

When I went back to Greenville that summer, I had five dollars—a great, fruitful campaign, but not "fruitful" enough to provide for my family. My wife had worked through the summer, and I thank God for the way she worked. I'm not too sure I fully appreciated her and her desire to help me get through school. Had it not been for her, I would never have made it through. That summer, Lenore earned her "Ph.T."—"Putting Hubby Through."

CHAPTER 8:
The Church on "Bootleg Corner"

LAYING FOUNDATIONS WITH DR. SIGHTLER

I was grounded in the Word under the ministry of Dr. Harold B. Sightler at Tabernacle Baptist Church in Greenville, South Carolina. During my school years I realized my ministry would be in a local church, so I needed to learn more about how to serve my pastor. I wanted to learn, and I felt sure he would make me his assistant pastor. After all, I never missed a service.

I asked my pastor, Dr. Sightler, if he would allow me to work in our church. He handed me 250-300 cards with names and addresses on them and said, "Run these down; find out where these people are." (Not quite an "associate pastor's job," but I wanted to learn.)

I took the job, trying to find these "lost" Baptists. Some had died, some had moved out of town, some were backslidden, some—well, even the FBI couldn't find them. I took the cards back and he said, "You mean you've gotten them all?"

"Yes, sir, all that I could get. Anything else I can do?" (This time I knew he would make me his assistant pastor. Boy, was I surprised!)

He handed me another stack and said, "Go run these down."

I was eager to work and do anything he wanted; I just wanted to serve the church. It wasn't long before I became an assistant Sunday school teacher, and then he gave me my own class—a young adults group. I learned that one must serve and honor the Lord, and then He will honor you.

When I graduated, I went to Dr. Sightler and asked him for a job teaching in the Christian school. He made me the assistant principal. I also taught fifth grade. I "burned up the phone wires" talking to Dr. Fremont, dean of the BJU School of Education. I had been taught "You can borrow brains," and did I ever need them. I helped start the Bible Institute in 1962. I was a fifth-grade teacher, assistant principal, and dean of the Bible Institute, where I also taught night classes, drove a bus, and worked as a janitor. In my "spare time," I started a church as an outreach of Tabernacle.

My time at Tabernacle was a learning experience. I learned how to do some things and how not to do some others. But all those learning experiences were valuable, and I appreciated each one.

"BOOTLEG CORNER"

In the fall of 1960, Dr. Sightler asked me if I would like to start a mission church. I was "chomping at the bit." He took me over to a district in Greenville called City View at Hampton Avenue Extension and said, "There's a dirty, dingy corner here, run down, with rotten buildings." We pulled up in front of an old service station garage and parked.

"This is where we want to start it. Here's an available building. Now, the Southern Baptists tried to start one here, and they failed. The Church of God started one here, and they failed. The Assembly of God started one here, and they failed. And there was another independent Baptist church that tried to start one here, and they failed. Are you sure you want to try to start one here?"

"If God's in it, it will not fail. I'll pray about it, and I thank you for giving me an opportunity."

"We'll pay your first month's rent ($35), and then you're on your own," he told me.

"Thank you, sir. You are more than generous. All I want is an opportunity to preach."

He paid the first month's rent. We cleaned out the grease in the service station, put some paint on the floor, and I opened up for services. The first service we had my family and two other families. The next service we had six families, and souls were saved. God began to bless.

Little did we know, however, that we were facing unseen opposition. This area was used as a depot for a syndicate that brought bootleg liquor out of the North Carolina mountains. It was an ideal distribution point because, although it was in Greenville County, it was outside both the Greenville and the City View city limits. The locals called it "Red Egypt" because of the sin and vice. The only law enforcement authority was the County Sheriff's Department, but they usually looked the other way when it came to this neighborhood.

OPPOSITION

I wasn't there long when I began to understand why the previous attempts to start a church had failed. The people in the bootleg syndicate were in the business of distributing liquor, so they would join the churches in order to infiltrate them and put them out of business. Soon I recognized some families that were trying to do the same to us.

Dr. Gilbert Stenholm of BJU was one of my chief counselors in helping me as we started the fight for "Bootleg Corner." I took a stand against the bootleggers and exposed their sin. Needless to say, they became angry! Death threats came;

threatening calls came—not just to me, but also to my family. I felt like I was reliving my boyhood, fighting with bootleggers. But this time I was fighting against the bootleggers, not for them. This time, the fight would be different!

I worked at night until it was late, but then I would go visit folks. I visited as long as I could see a light on in the community. God began to bless, and souls were saved. The opposition began to grow too. I soon learned that "a kite rises on the winds of opposition."

Some of my fondest memories are those of incidents and conversions that took place on Bootleg Corner. Every Friday night, a group of us young BJU preacher boys would meet and pray. We prayed for God to give us His power in our lives. We were filled with zeal, but it was usually "not according to knowledge." We were determined to have all that God had for us. If only we had realized that all we had to do was give God all of us instead of trying to get more of Him.

A BOOTLEGGER DOES THE PREACHING

Another chapter in the Bootleg Corner story involves a man named Bill Hughes. Bill lived at #8 Monroe Street. My wife and I had led his wife and all of his children to Christ. Bill was in the bootleg business; he drove a car to haul bootleg liquor. We tried to win him to Christ, but he only became angry and ran us off. Week after week we went back, and week after week he threatened us, each time more violently than before. "The next time anyone comes from that church to visit me, I'm going to do the preaching, but I'm going to shoot them after I'm through! You tell them that if they knock on my door one more time, they're dead!"

The next Saturday night was visitation. Two young preachers, Walt Hoover and Jim Brock, came down from the University to go on visitation. These men were fired up, begging for a challenge! "Pastor, do you have any hot prospects?"

"Yes," I said, "Bill Hughes at #8 Monroe Street is a good, hot prospect."

"Amen, let's go."

Up they went to Bill Hughes's house and knocked on the door. Bill saw them there and opened the door. They said, "We're from Mount Calvary Baptist Church."

"Come on in, preachers. I've been waiting on you."

They looked at one another and said, "Boy, the preacher gave us a good one tonight."

Bill said, "Now, you fellows sit down right over there." He reached over and locked the door. Then he opened the closet, took out his shotgun, and put a shell in the chamber, "Now, you [blankety-blank] preachers sit there 'cause I'm gonna do the preachin' tonight!"

Those guys sat there for over two hours while Bill threatened them at gunpoint and "did the preachin'." Needless to say, they were not eager to look for "hot prospects" at another house. When they returned to the church, one said, "Look, I have heart problems. That man is crazy; he threatened us. As a matter of fact, we thought he was going to shoot us any minute."

"Well, I told you he was a hot prospect."

Those two preacher boys learned a lesson in soul winning visitation that night that would help them in future ministry. Jim Brock has been a missionary in Africa for over thirty-five years; Walt Hoover is an evangelist.

My burden for Bill Hughes intensified because in him I saw my dad. Weeks went by, and I went back to visit him. "Rod Bell, I'm going to shoot you."

I put my arm around him. "Bill, if getting shot would get you saved, I'd be willing to get shot."

He reminded me so much of my dad. He pulled off his baseball cap, threw it on the floor, and stomped, "You're impossible. Why don't you leave me alone and let me die and go to hell?"

I said, "Why don't you come to church tonight and hear me preach?"

"All right, I'll be there. Then you leave me alone."

A BOOTLEGGER TESTIFIES FOR THE DEVIL
~

He came that night and sat in the back row. I preached on "For God so loved the world that He gave His only begotten Son" and gave the invitation. Nobody moved. Finally, I said something I've never said before or since during an invitation: "Some of you serve the devil so faithfully. You're giving your lives, you're giving your souls, you're giving your home, you're giving your strength, you're giving him everything. He must be an awfully good taskmaster. Maybe you'd like to give a testimony for him and brag on him—tell us just how good he is. Would you just stand up and give a word of testimony for the devil?"

I had no more said that than Bill Hughes stood up. "I want to give a testimony for the devil tonight."

"Sit down and shut up," I told him. "You didn't hear what I said."

"Yes, I did," and he repeated almost word for word what I had said.

I thought to myself, "Okay, big mouth, now what are you going to do?"

Here's the testimony he gave: "I have served the devil for fifty-some years. He has wrecked my home; he's wrecked my body; he's ruined my health; he's robbed food out of my children's mouths; he's damned my soul. I have nothing to show for fifty-some years but heartache and trouble and disappointment. The devil has stripped me of my manhood."

He gave one of the vilest testimonies I have ever heard of what Satan had done to a lost soul. When he finished, I said, "All right, now you've heard what Satan can do, let me hear somebody give a testimony of what God can do."

Brother Hal Williams stood up and said, "I want you to know that He saved me and gave me peace, gave me joy. I used to be a vile sinner like this man, but He can save him and give him eternal life if he will just come to Him."

About that time, Bill turned and, with tears streaming down his face, ran out the door. When he did, I ran after him. I told one of the men, "Take the service; I'm going after him."

I ran after him to his home, but he beat me there. I went up and knocked on the door, but no one answered. I went around to the back, and there he sat with a bottle in his hand. His head was in his hands, and he was weeping. I said, "Bill?"

"Oh, Preacher, leave me alone; I made a fool of myself. That was a terrible thing for me to get up and say."

"No, it wasn't. You told the truth, and that's what Satan can do. But Bill, I want you to know what God can do. He can save you."

I had the joy of pointing that precious man to the Lord Jesus Christ, and he was gloriously saved. Bill became one of the best soul winners in our church because he knew where the sinners were! He and I were soul-winning partners. He'd say, "I'll point out the sinners if you'll do the shooting."

OTHER BOOTLEG CORNER CONVERSIONS
~

One night I received a call from a woman who had just gotten out of the penitentiary, having served time for armed robbery and murder. She lived next door to our church. She called me and told me she was in the illegal business of running moonshine. "If you show up tonight, we will put you in a wooden overcoat, and it will be the last time you will ever preach."

The Lord burdened my heart that night. Needless to say, I was scared, but I thought, "If I'm going to 'go out,' I want to go out being faithful."

I preached that night from Mark 5 on the wild Gadarene, and my title was "The Dirtiest Gang of Buzzards This Side of Hell That Would Run Jesus out of This Community." In Mark 5 the Jews were in the illegal business of "bootlegging" pork, just like the people in our community were bootlegging liquor.

The air was tense. As I took my jacket off, I looked back and saw the woman come in the back with two of her grown sons. I told the people about the phone call and said, "They threatened my life, and now they are going to shoot me. I'm taking my coat off tonight so you can get a good bead on this white shirt. If you're going to do it, you'd better do it in a hurry before God gets ahold of you and changes your mind."

That night we had several saved, and God moved among us. As we came to the end of the service, the woman walked out the door and said, "The devil is going to get you, you old __."

I said, "Well, you ought to know and have firsthand information because you live with him."

I did not realize how desperate these people were. They continued to threaten my life and the lives of my family. One night when I was walking down the street, I heard a motor running behind me and turned, just in time to realize someone was attempting to run over me. My trench coat became caught in the bumper of the car, and I was dragged down the alley before the coat was ripped off of me. They were desperate people.

I soon learned that the God of the mountains was also the God of the valleys. We began to have all-night prayer meetings to pray for that community. Mrs. Center, known around the neighborhood as "Fat Maw," continued to sell bootleg liquor, but she told her customers, "Don't let the preacher know." One day I received a call from Mrs. Center. We had the joy of leading her to Christ, and she was gloriously saved!

I had another man by the name of Mr. Clark who, every time I went to visit him, ran me off and cursed me out. One night it was snowing and bitter cold—one of those unusual blizzards in Greenville. As I put on my coat, my wife said, "Where are you going?"

"I'm going to go witness to Mr. Clark."

"In this kind of weather?"

"Yes. If he doesn't let me in tonight, he ought to die and go to hell. I'm going to try my best to win him to Christ tonight. I feel compelled to go."

I went over and knocked on his door. When he opened the door, the wind blew the snow, and he said, "Preacher, what are you doing out there? Come on in here."

"Mr. Clark, I've come to tell you that God loves you and Jesus died for you and I want to see you saved."

He began cursing and ran me off again. I left dejected, but I had a warm heart because I knew I had done what God wanted me to do.

In about two weeks, I received a call from Mrs. Clark, his wife. He was in the hospital at the point of death. She said, "Would you come and try to win him to Christ?"

I had led her to the Lord several months before. I went to the Greenville General Hospital and stayed all night, hoping I'd have an opportunity to win him to Christ. Mr. Clark was delirious; he had a high fever. Early the next morning I went home to get breakfast and to shower and shave so I could catch my 9:00 class.

After class I went back to the hospital. As I opened the door to his room, Mr. Clark and his wife were sitting on the edge of the bed. "Come here, Preacher. Quick, come here!"

I walked over. He asked his wife to leave and he asked me to pull the curtains. I pulled the curtains. He pleaded, "Get me saved."

That was the easiest man that I've ever led to Christ in my life. He told me, "Preacher, I died last night, and I went to hell. I saw the fire; I saw eternity. I've gotta get saved. I'm lost, Preacher; I'm lost."

He was ready for the pickin' and was gloriously saved. He was in our church until he died. God still saves the hardest of sinners. To God be the glory!

I received a call from Mrs. Mary Burton one night. "Pastor, come quick. There's been a shooting."

I went over to her house, and her daughter's husband was lying on the front porch, shot with a shotgun. I tried to lead him to Christ, but he died in my arms without Christ. This incident made an impression on the family and the whole community. We had many saved as a result of that shooting. God works in mysterious ways!

A BOOTLEG CORNER TRAGEDY

~

I was preaching one night on Bootleg Corner, and I felt strangely burdened for three precious teenagers that were in the back. I gave the invitation, and I even walked back and witnessed to them. They laughed. "We have plenty of time; don't try to cram it down our throat."

And they walked out the door, got in their car, and sped away into the darkness of the night. About 2:00 A.M. I received a phone call from the mother of one of the teenagers. Weeping, she told me, "My son and two of his friends were killed instantly on Paris Mountain. They had a car wreck, and I wanted you to know."

I remembered the last words they said: "We have plenty of time; don't try to cram it down our throat."

GOING OUT FROM BOOTLEG CORNER

~

Nineteen men were ordained into the ministry from that little church in just six years. Many of them went to the mission field; some of them have already gone on to "meet their reward."

One of the men who came to our church was L. C. Easterling. He was in his late thirties when God saved him and called him into the ministry. One night he came to me and said, "I'm having an awful struggle with my salvation. Would you help me nail it down?"

On November 8 we went into a room and "nailed it down." Every November I receive a birthday card from him, celebrating his spiritual birthday. L. C. Easterling subsequently answered God's call to go to the mission field and has been in the Kentucky mountains as a missionary for over thirty-five years planting Baptist churches.

Les Ollila was another of my deacons and my Sunday school superintendent. He is now the president of Northland Baptist Bible College in Dunbar, Wisconsin. He was the kind of man whose servant's attitude was clearly evident when he was in our ministry. We had a huge oak tree that was about to fall on the church building. It was a gigantic tree, and I said, "We need to pray that God will move that tree." Little did I realize that God would use Les Ollila to answer my prayer.

One evening as I came to the church, I looked up and saw what I thought was a monkey swinging from the top of the tree with a chainsaw. It was Les; he was serving the Lord, cutting that tree down from the top to the bottom. Les was always ready to serve—any time, any place. I had only to mention something to him and it was done.

Hal Williams was the first missionary our church sent out. God blessed and met the need for Hal to go to New Guinea. We had been trying to buy a piece of property next door to the church, and through prayer God laid it on our hearts to take the money we had set aside for the property and send it to Hal Williams. God blessed, and the property owners lowered the price of the land to the exact amount we had given to Hal, and we were able to purchase it. Hal Williams has been a missionary for over thirty years.

Charlie Anderson was a Sunday school superintendent and faithful deacon. Charlie and his wife, Peg, labored with us for four years. One year, during the summer months, I wanted to take a leave of absence and hold evangelistic crusades in a tent. I asked Charlie to pastor the church while I was gone. Charlie took over pastoring the church every Sunday, faithfully teaching and preaching the Word of God.

When I returned after three months, Charlie stepped down, I stepped back into the pulpit, and we went on to serve the Lord faithfully as colaborers. Charlie Anderson was a faithful pastor for over thirty years and has gone to be with the Lord.

W. L. Fuller was a faithful member whom God called to the Bahamas to establish a church. He faithfully served the Lord for fifteen years before he was called on to glory. Recently, I was in Puerto Rico at an FBF conference when a Bahamian man came up to me and said, "Do you know W. L. Fuller?"

"Yes," I said. "He was one of my deacons from Mount Calvary. He was saved and called to preach back on Bootleg Corner."

Then he told me this story: W. L. Fuller had come to the islands as a missionary. The Bahamian was saved as a teenager when he came under Fuller's preaching. He was later called to preach and now pastors the very church that W. L. Fuller started!

"Dr. Bell, you are my spiritual grandfather," he said.

And he was right!

Fred Thompson was a servant among servants. I always depended on Fred because he would make sure things were done that nobody else wanted to do. Fred faithfully served the Lord there on Bootleg Corner and was eventually called into the ministry, pastoring in Tennessee and Virginia.

POWER OF PRAYER

Our people learned to pray on Bootleg Corner, and they saw the power of God come and take control. Just little mercy drops of revival, but I knew God was on the throne. We would pray all night and fast and beg God for the power of the Holy Ghost to come down, to see sinners converted and saints purified and renewed to their first love. God came walking on the water many times "on the fourth watch." He was teaching and preparing us for a life of service. Bootleg Corner was my seminary.

One night our all-night prayer meeting was visited by heavenly angels. We prayed one night for God to supply our need and give us power to preach. About 2:00 or 2:30 A.M., we looked up and saw three men dressed in white standing in the doorway. A holy hush came over our prayer meeting; we were sore afraid and could not speak a word. Suddenly, they turned and left.

Astonished and amazed, we began to rejoice that God had sent three heavenly angels to visit our prayer meeting. We began to tell the story on campus the next day and all through the next week. Finally the truth came out. Those three angels were Brad Dye, Joe Norris, and Don Strange—three BJU students in beige trench coats.

BOOTLEG CORNER BECOMES MOUNT CALVARY BAPTIST CHURCH

When we were building our first new building, we were going to tear the old service station down. The building cost us more than we had anticipated, and we were unable to pay our contractor. We called a prayer meeting and began to pray, asking God to supply the need.

A tractor-trailer truck came down the road, and two wheels came off it. Those wheels headed straight for our building and broke through the wall of the service station that we were going to tear down.

The owner of the truck said, "Oh, Preacher, I don't want to turn this in to our insurance company, but I will give you $5,500 for damages if we can just call it even." That was exactly what we needed to pay our contractor!

Our dream and goal was to buy the property in front of us—all the way to Cedar Lane Road—and build Mount Calvary Baptist Church on the top of the parcel of land, facing Cedar Lane. My wife and I dreamed and prayed many times that God would allow us to do it. We had made up our minds that we would spend our life on Bootleg Corner if that was where God wanted us.

Many times I had wondered why the Lord had seemingly forgotten me down on that dirty little corner. All the rest of my preacher buddies and friends were out pastoring big churches and were successful in the ministry. But here I was, stuck down on one of the dirtiest corners in Greenville County. I was discouraged and defeated many times. I still hadn't realized that God was teaching me in His school of discipleship. He was trying to mold and make a man.

Our burden for more property intensified. I asked the deacons if they would join me and pull off their shoes to march around the property in front of our building and on the side of the adjacent hill that extended all the way to Cedar Lane Road. "We'll build our main sanctuary facing Cedar Lane and use the back for parking." With shoes in hand, we claimed Joshua 1:3— "Every place that the sole of your foot shall tread upon, that have I given unto you." We claimed both the promise and the land in simple, childlike faith. We knew one day our dream would come true because God's Word is true.

One of our greatest blessings was when we finally built a new building. I wanted Dr. Bob Jones Sr. to come and preach the dedication. I asked Dr. Stenholm if Dr. Bob could come. At that time he was beginning to fail physically, and this was affecting his thinking.

"No, I don't think so," said Dr. Bob Jr. "He's repeating himself so much he'd embarrass you and embarrass himself. I don't think it would be good for him to come."

I was persistent. "Look, if you could just give him an opportunity, I will see to it that he doesn't do anything but pray the dedicatory prayer. Then he can come on back home. He isn't getting out much at all, and it would be good for him to be out on a Sunday."

God answered our prayer and my persistence, and Drs. Stenholm and Liverman brought him down on the Sunday of the dedication. I was so excited! My hero was coming to pray the dedicatory prayer. I'll never forget when he drove up in his 1958 black Oldsmobile 98 and I went down to the car to greet him.

"Hello, Rod, have you been a good boy since you graduated?"

"Yes, sir."

"Did you ever get victory over smoking and chewing?"

"Yes sir, I have, but I still dip a little snuff every now and then."

He laughed, and with a twinkle in his eye said, "They tell me that you have some bootleggers in this neighborhood. Pretty nice neighborhood!"

"Yes, sir, I've got a few bootleggers."

"Well, I'd rather have a bootlegger for a neighbor than I would a dirty, stinkin' modernist. You can never tell about a modernist, but you can always tell what a bootlegger will do. He's a good prospect to get saved."

We were fellowshiping and making our way up to the church. "Now, Son, I don't want to get on your program, all I need to do is just pray the prayer and then I'm going to have to leave. I hope you'll understand."

"Yes, sir, Dr. Bob, I understand."

"Well, I don't want to get on your program; just let me know when you need me."

As we walked into the church, he said, "That's a beautiful church here, Son. Now I don't want to get on your program, just let me know whenever you need me, and I'll be more than happy to do my part and leave."

"Yes sir, Dr. Bob."

The service started, and he looked over and said to me, "Rod, this is a beautiful church. Now listen, I don't want to get on your program; just let me know when my time comes."

"Okay, Dr. Bob." I thought to myself, "Well, you know, I'd better let him pray and go."

I got up and announced, "Folks, we're so glad to have Dr. Bob Jones Sr. with us today. He's been sick and hasn't been feeling well, and it's certainly good to see him up, see him out and about. He means so much to us, and we're so honored to have him today. I appreciate him coming. We're going to let him come and pray the prayer of dedication. Dr. Liverman and Dr. Stenholm are waiting, and we're going to have to let them take him back home. I know you'll all understand. Come on, Dr. Bob, and pray."

Dr. Bob got up and preached for thirty-five minutes. He preached a wonderful message, bragged on the Lord, preached the gospel and how to be saved and how to know you're saved. Then he looked over and said, "Now I want to give an invitation."

He gave an invitation for people to come get saved. He made three appeals: one for people to get saved, one for Christians to be out on soul-winning visitation, and another for Christians to come on Wednesday night for prayer meeting because that service is the "backbone of the church." Then he turned around, looked at me and said, "Now, Son, I want you to come and pray the dedicatory prayer."

He had preaching in him to such an extent that when he opened his mouth, he just had to preach. The amazing thing was that he never repeated himself; he just preached "Christ and Him crucified." What a joy that was to have Dr. Bob Jones Sr. at our little church's dedication, preaching what was actually his last public sermon!

CHAPTER 9:
Family Growth

THE WIFE OF MY YOUTH

If a man finds a wife, he finds a good thing. Her price is far above rubies. God has given me a great prize in my wife.

Lenore has always been a private person until you get to know her. Then she is very bubbly and a lot of fun. She's the most honest person I've ever known. If she says something, that's what she means. Her devotion to me has been only by the grace of God. It hasn't been easy for Lenore to stay with me because, when I first got saved, I went wild. I had zeal but very little knowledge. I found something that was so real and wonderful that it controlled me; I didn't control it. I was determined to give God everything I had.

When I told her God had called me to preach, Lenore didn't like it. When I told her God had called me to go to school, she didn't like it. She didn't marry a preacher. I did not use much wisdom in trying to win her, but I thank God for His patience, her love, and her endurance. The Lord has used our mountain-tops and our valleys to draw us closer together and make us a team He could use. God has used her to be a balancing force in many areas of my life. If she doesn't agree with me on a certain issue, she always explains why.

I could never have made it through my years of college, the years on Bootleg Corner, and the many years in the ministry had I not had a kind, loving, cooperative wife who was willing to find her place and serve God there. She has always supported me, though she hasn't always agreed with me. She has always been totally honest and told me exactly what she thought. When the decision was made, she would always fall in behind it and give her full support.

I thank God that she has a good mind and a good heart; she walks with the Lord. She has been a good mother and a true "help meet" through the years. Oh, the stories I could tell of the times I have messed up, yet she stood by me; the wrong decisions I've made, and she *still* stood by me. It has not always been pleasant, but they've been forty-five good years.

She was always the most popular one in school. She made all the honor rolls and was voted "Most Likely to Succeed." She was always "Who's Who," and I was simply "What's That?"

I always like to get her opinion because she can generally give me a perspective I had never considered. I can truly say that she has a close walk with the Lord. She is my best friend.

When I finally got my act together and learned how to treat my wife as a person (and not as a "non-entity"), God began to deal in both our hearts. The Lord began to give us a ministry together. When we moved to Virginia Beach, I prayed, "Dear Lord, show us both what your will is for us to do. I will not stay here unless that's what she wants to do. Show us both."

I'll never forget the night that I asked her what she thought about moving to Virginia Beach, selling our home and car, and moving from friends, loved ones, church, and school. With tears running down her cheeks, she said, "You know what we have to do as well as I do. This is going to be one of the hardest moves we've ever made, but God is in it."

We settled it, and we did it together. She's the best thing that has ever happened to this mountain man!

She has always wanted a close friend; it's almost impossible to have close friends in the ministry. I believe one of her closest friends is Beneth Jones. They seem to truly love each other in the Lord. They have a deep respect for one another and always seem to have a good time when they're together. We cherish those times together.

"Together unto the End"
by Rod Bell Sr.
May 1998

As we were thirty-one years ago,
Young at heart, determined
Never to part:

A life of service willingly embarked,
A worldwide ministry we did start.

Through storms and aching hearts,
May we finish the race as from
The start—
A loving couple determined
Never to part.

As we were, so we are—cleaving
Together: through dark valleys
And tried by fire,
Till death do us part; as we were
From the start—one at heart!

The shades of night are beginning to fall;
Our days of ministry are sinking fast.
The eternal morning is beckoning us,
To rest eternally at last.
Strong may we finish the race,
When we shall see Him—face to face.

As we were thirty-one years ago,
Young at heart, determined
Never to part!

OUR HERITAGE OF THE LORD

The Lord has blessed us with four children: one in heaven who died at birth, then Niki, Tim, and Rod Jr. All three are different, but all three are off the same tree.

Niki is my little girl, always has been and always will be. She has a very special, special place in my heart because girls are special to daddies. She was my "sunshine," and I used to sing to her:

> You are my sunshine, my only sunshine;
> You make me happy when skies are gray.
> You never know, dear, how much I love you.
> Please don't take my sunshine away.

Niki was born in 1958 at the Glover Clinic in Madison, West Virginia, where our first daughter, Terry Lynn, was born. What a joy she was to show off! I was so proud! She was the apple of my eye, my ray of sunshine. I would sing her to sleep with old mountain songs.

> Daddy's gone a huntin' to get a rabbit skin
> To wrap my baby-buntin' in . . . .

At the tender age of eight months, Niki was packed into our '52 Chevrolet, along with everything we owned, when we went off to Bob Jones University. Boxes, canned goods, sacks of potatoes on the fenders and bumpers—it all went into and onto the old Chevy. We had no job, but we had something in our hearts: the call of God upon our life and His promise (Philippians 4:19) in our heart.

Those were not easy days. Our parents and families didn't understand why, when we were doing so well financially and living better than most of our peers, we would give it all up to "live like gypsies." Through those hard years we learned great lessons.

So vivid in my mind is the memory of Niki's first day in kindergarten. We sat on the porch, waiting for the bus to come.

Niki was so cute, dressed like a little lady with her lunch box labeled "Niki." I tried to encourage her that everything would be all right, but she looked up at me with big tears in her eyes. "Daddy, will you go with me?"

I placed her on the big white bus and assured her that we would pick her up later in the day. "Niki," I said, wiping her tears away, "remember, you are my sunshine."

She waved as the bus pulled away, and Daddy turned quickly to brush his tears away too.

When the boys, Tim and Rod Jr., arrived, she became their protector and defender. Though they experienced the typical sibling "spats" (when Sister tried to tell them what to do), they generally had an excellent relationship.

One evening, we were just getting ready to sit down for a delicious supper when, all of a sudden, Niki jumped up and bolted out the door like a flash of lightening. Over our fence, through the neighbor's yard, and over the neighbor's fence she went like an Olympic athlete. As Lenore and I watched through the window, we saw Niki going to rescue her baby brother Tim. Two ruffians had him down, beating him and trying to take away his bicycle. Niki sent the bullies home with a few knocks on their head and brought Tim home with the bicycle!

"My," I thought, "I wish I had had a sister like that when I was growing up!"

Niki came in angry. "Dad, you ought to go talk to their parents. These bullies have got to be dealt with."

Under my breath, I chuckled with pride, thinking, "Boy, she's made out of the mountain material!" With a straight face I looked at Niki: "Okay, honey. I'm proud of you, and I'll take care of it."

During her college days, Niki met a young man—a "preacher boy"—and they were married. He came from a preacher's home, had good manners and a fine testimony. The marriage endured for four troubled years and ended in divorce.

Niki has been a single mom for the last seventeen years. We never thought that separation and divorce would touch our family. Of course, it's been hard for all of us to deal with; we've been through the mountaintops and the valleys together, though. The events in the life of Niki, the "apple of my eye," have been a challenge to me. When she hurts, I hurt. When she goes through fiery trials, oh, how I wish I could go through them in her place.

Her life has not been easy, but God has used these circumstances to mold and make her into His image. I have seen Niki so tired, so exhausted, frustrated, just trying to make ends meet. Sometimes she's been ready to quit, but she "keeps on keeping on," doing right when it would have been easier to take the wrong way out.

Niki gets her talent from her mother and her grit from her father. She's produced one of the finest teenagers I've ever met— her son, John Warren Frederick. Well, I might be just a bit prejudiced and sound boastful, I know! But I see him as a young man with "the mantle of the mountain man." He has surrendered to full-time service for the Lord.

As I write this, John is in college, preparing and training in answer to his calling. John's lifelong dream was to go to Bob Jones University. When he graduated from high school at Tabernacle, here in Virginia Beach, he couldn't wait to get back to Greenville. But through a series of events, his dreams were shattered and he couldn't enroll. For six long months John (I call him "My John" because I love him like a son) went through a very dark valley in his life. He came back to Virginia Beach to live with us—very disappointed—no money, no job, no hope for a college education. Nothing!

Lenore and I prayed and claimed Ephesians 1:18 for him. Nothing about school was ever discussed; he wouldn't speak of it. He tried to get a job. He filled out almost twenty applications— nothing! No interviews—nothing!

Weeks rolled into months, and we could see God working, even though John is very quiet and keeps much to himself. But I've found "still waters run deep." When John says something, he's generally thought it through, and he comes down on the right side of the issue. I believe John will be used of God to "pass the mantle" on to his generation.

Niki is truly a lady who has sterling character and determination to serve God and raise her son for His glory. Being a single parent is not easy, and we have all learned many lessons through this experience. The Lord has used those lessons to develop in us a compassion for single parents.

— I've come to realize that divorce can happen to anyone, no matter who he is—deacon, pastor, church leader. "Wherefore let him that thinketh he standeth take heed lest he fall" (I Cor. 10:12).

— Niki's experience has caused me to love and respect single parents who stay true and who learn that these are the "humps of life" that cause us to grow.

— I've developed more compassion and concern for couples who have endured the pain of divorce.

— It's caused me to love my daughter and respect her determination to do right, regardless of her circumstances.

— It's caused me to do more premarital counseling in my ministry and to be more patient and longsuffering with those having marriage difficulties.

— It's caused us to make the development of strong families a priority in our church ministry. The family and the home are the foundation of society.

— It has caused me, not to change my conviction on marriage and divorce, but to have greater compassion, concern, and empathy toward those who are divorced.

Let me make myself very clear: I believe the Scripture teaches us that marriage is "until death do us part." But God uses all things in life to conform us to His image. Our God specializes in making gold out of ashes, and I'm confident that if we trust Him, we "shall come forth as gold."

Timothy Paul is my oldest son. I named him Timothy Paul because I wanted God to use him. *Timothy* means "one who honors God," and *Paul* means "little one." He can never "honor God" unless he is little or small in his own eyes. I feel that God has used Tim's name to help mold and make a man who seeks to honor his God.

Tim had a strong but stubborn will that presented a challenge to his parents. He surrendered to God's call into the ministry but said, "I'll go anywhere you want me to go, Lord—except to the mountains."

Well, Tim, his wife, Kim, and their three sons, Corey, Gabriel, and Thomas, have been faithfully serving God in the mountains of Johnson City, Tennessee, for the last eight years. "Never say 'never!' " Kim is a godly wife and a good mom, a true co-laborer in the ministry.

When it comes to sports, Tim has always had a problem: he is 6' 5" tall, weighs 275 pounds, and thinks he is made of steel. He spent so much time in the emergency room that all the doctors and nurses knew him by his first name. I think it all goes back to when he was just a small lad, about two years old. Niki took him to the top of a slide on a playground in Greenville and was going to catch him as he came down the slide. But he got afraid and fell about twelve feet. His head hit a chunk of concrete, and he needed brain surgery. After the surgery, we all waited anxiously for the doctor.

As the doctor emerged from the operating room, he told us, "He'll be okay. Fortunately for him, he has a hard head!"

Under my breath, I said, "Thank God! He's going to be okay, and 'Amen!' to the 'hard head'!"

This was a dark hour for our little family, but God was molding and making a man. I'll never forget going in and seeing Tim with his eyes black, his head bandaged up. "Son, what can Daddy do for you? I love you. Can I do anything to help you?"

"Daddy, sing me a song."

"What do you want me to sing to you?"

"Jesus Loves Me."

And that night as the tears flowed, we sang, "Jesus loves me, this I know."

Tim and I have a special relationship. God has used him in my life. As he grew up, we had many "incidents" that the Potter used to soften us so we both could yield to His hand. One of these "incidents" occurred while Tim was in college, when he had amnesia for six and a half months. Of course, in the believer's life there are no "accidents," only "incidents" in God's sovereign plan. The outcome depends on the way we respond—we either become bitter or get better, as He conforms us to the image of His Son.

I believe the mantle is on this young mountain man also. He preaches with a holy unction and with great compassion.

Then there's Rod Jr. Lenore named him Rod Jr. even though Tim was older. I guess she named him properly because he is a "Rod Jr." Yet he is his own man with great abilities.

He also has been called into the ministry, and God is using him on the staff at Tabernacle Baptist Church as the associate pastor. He is my partner; I depend on him greatly in the ministry. The mantle is on this young man too. He preaches with a tenderness and brokenness that comes like sweet perfume from a broken vessel.

It seems as though God has always used my children to strip me of self-reliance. In 1987 Rod Jr. was at the point of death after being severely injured in a car wreck. I stayed by his bed for twenty-two days and twenty-two nights because I felt he needed me. Through that time, God once again was stripping me of self-reliance. He has used my family to show me that I am not perfect, that I have many faults. My family has always been loving, kind, supportive, and forgiving whenever I make mistakes. How I thank God for my wife and my three children. I have learned that my family is my ministry.

Part 3:

A Mountain Man's Ministry

CHAPTER 10:
Tabernacle Baptist Church

GOD CALLS US TO MOVE TO VIRGINIA BEACH

After pastoring for six and a half years at Mount Calvary Baptist Church in Greenville, South Carolina—seeing many men ordained, countless souls saved, land purchased, new buildings built, running over 250 in Sunday school—God began to speak to my heart about moving on. This happened only after I was content to spend the rest of my life on that little corner.

Through the years since we've left, God has used Dr. Jesse Boyd and Dr. Mark Minnick to develop what is today one of the leading churches in Greenville: Mount Calvary Baptist Church on Cedar Lane Road. It is a dream that Lenore and I had envisioned for many years. I had the joy of dedicating their new auditorium a few years back with Dr. Bob Jones Jr. and one of the church's first missionaries and deacons, L. C. Easterling, who has been serving the Lord in the mountains of Kentucky for over thirty-five years.

The way God moved us was to create in our heart a deeper hunger and thirst for Him. We were getting ready to buy the land in front of the church that leads to Cedar Lane Road to build a large educational building. We eventually wanted to build on top of the hill facing Cedar Lane Road, where the church stands today. These were secret dreams and ambitions. However, as we started out on our plan, God had *His* plans. He didn't want *us* to do it; He wanted someone else to do it. Today, as you look at Mount Calvary Baptist Church, you'll see God's plan has become a reality.

As we began our building plans, one of my good friends, Dr. Russell Rice from Virginia Beach, called me and asked if I would be interested in coming there to start a church.

"No, I'm not interested; I'm getting ready to build. I'm satisfied here; our church is growing, and God is blessing. I'm not interested."

Later, Bill Charnock called me and asked me if I would pray about it. Evangelist Jack Green had recommended me to them. I told him I would at least pray about it. The more I prayed about going to Virginia Beach, the more God spoke to my heart. I began to make excuses and to put out "fleeces," wanting visible signs. One such "fleece" was a request I made to the Lord that if He wanted me to go to Virginia Beach, He would give us 282 people in Sunday school. As my Sunday school superintendent counted heads that week, there were exactly 282 people in Sunday school! Still unwilling to go, I asked him to recount. I asked my wife Lenore to pray some more about this.

The following Wednesday night, another drastic incident occurred. As we were discussing the new building, I asked God to stop our building plans if He wanted me to go to Virginia Beach; it wouldn't be right for me to put the people in debt and then leave.

Some of the men said, "Pastor, we'll do anything you want us to do, but would there be anything wrong with just putting it on hold and praying about it a little longer?"

"No," I said, "maybe God's trying to show me something, and I'm just not listening."

So we stopped our building plans.

Then a third thing happened. I was supposed to give the men in Virginia Beach an answer on Saturday. The Friday night before, my wife became desperately ill. In the middle of the night, she woke me up. "Honey, I am in desperate pain. Would you please call the doctor?"

Immediately, I prayed, "Lord, if You're trying to show me you want me to go to Virginia Beach, would you please stop the pain?"

Before I could get out of bed to call the doctor, Lenore said, "It's okay honey; the pain has stopped."

I began to shake; I was so afraid because God had shown me clearly that He wanted me to go and at least preach in Virginia Beach. I got on the phone and called the men. "Look, I've never been interested in moving to Virginia Beach; I've never been interested in even *coming* to Virginia Beach. I have a good church here, but God won't leave me alone. I must come and at least preach for you. When do you want me to come?"

"Next Sunday," they told me.

I called Dr. Gilbert Stenholm and asked him if he would fill in for me Sunday; I had to go out of town. Lenore and I prayed all the way to Virginia Beach, asking the Lord to show us both the "good and acceptable and perfect will of God."

When we got to Virginia Beach, we met in the Kempsville Elementary School. There were thirty-two that Sunday morning—five families. I kept asking the Lord, "Lord, if you want me to come, would You please save some souls this morning?" The Lord blessed, and souls were saved.

I will never forget the message I preached that morning: "Rotten Boards over Hell" from Luke 16. Then Sunday night I preached from Acts 4, "A Great New Testament Church." Souls were saved.

The people came and said, "Will you come? Will you please come to our church?"

"Only if the people vote unanimously," I told them.

I've never known a Baptist church to vote unanimously on starting a church or choosing a pastor. They came back and said the vote was 100 percent; everyone wanted us to come.

"Let me pray about it; if God wants me here, I'll be here in thirty days. If God does not want me here, I'll let you know."

My wife and I went back home that night and began to pray. "Honey," I asked Lenore, "what do you think about all of this?"

"You know, we have to do what we have to do."

We both had peace that we had to go. That night I got on my knees in the middle of the night and prayed.

"Lord, please show me what you want me to do. I don't want to leave Greenville and my church and my people."

It was the Lord who spoke to me in almost an audible voice. He spoke to my heart and soul. *"Get up off your knees; I'm not going to talk to you anymore. You know what I want you to do."*

From that time forward I had the deepest peace. If someone had put a gun to my head and said, "If you go to Virginia Beach, I'll pull the trigger," I would have told him, "So pull the trigger, because I've got to go."

I am simply saying that God gave us definite peace about it. It was one of the most difficult moves we've ever made.

When I told our church that Sunday morning, it was like bursting a water balloon. We couldn't do anything but weep. The people wept. I was the only pastor they had known. Many of them had been led to Christ there. God had blessed and honored the church through those six years, and now I was leaving. But there was a peace I cannot explain; we knew God had opened the doors for us to move on.

We called and told the people in Virginia Beach that we were coming, to come and get us.

"Honey, where are we going to live?" Lenore asked me.

"I don't know."

"How much money will they be able to pay us?"

"I don't know."

"Don't you think we should find out? You've got a wife and three children. We're going to sell our home and move, and I'd really like to know where we're going."

I hadn't used much wisdom, nor had I been sensitive to her feelings. I felt that God wanted us to go, and once again she was on the move, not knowing where she was going. It seemed like we stayed on the move. We had moved out of a new home from the mountains of West Virginia, down to a little, two-room, one-bath cottage off Wade Hampton Boulevard, across from the Liberty Life building in Greenville, South Carolina. We moved five times while I was in school. And now she was moving again. How I praise God for a faithful wife.

Oh, the blessings of pastoring for thirty-two years in Virginia Beach! When we moved here, we moved into a small house—new, clean, and nice. My family was so happy. God had taken care of us, despite my insensitivity and lack of understanding for the needs of my family. I had so much to learn, and I learned most of it the hard way. Pride, self-centeredness, and stubbornness, I learned later, are as witchcraft. I finally stopped calling it nice-sounding words and started to call it the sin that it is. As I look back on it now, I was married to a ministry, not to the Master. I neglected my family, and I wish I could do it over again—I know I'd do things differently.

I was thirty-two years old when we started, and all I knew to do was preach, pray, do personal soul-winning, and try to live a pure life. God honored that. I did not go about it in the right way. It's a miracle to me how God ever did anything with me. It's a miracle to me how my family turned out to love God and honor Him when I was spending so much of my time in the new work, getting it started.

I never will forget how we went out knocking on doors, twelve to fifteen hours a day, always seeing souls saved. From May to September we saw 157 people won to Christ and baptized in the Elizabeth River. (Our church did not have a baptismal pool.)

MOM AND DAD IN THE MINISTRY
~

After I graduated from Bob Jones University and came to Virginia Beach in 1967, my mom and dad left the mountains of West Virginia. My mom said she'd always felt called to be a missionary, and she wanted to come work in our church. And work she did! She and Dad became the custodians of our church. They got a bus route and drove the buses, visited the shut-ins, and were on the staff for over twenty years, faithfully loving and serving God.

Tabernacle Baptist Church had the joy of licensing my dad to preach, and preach he did, to anyone who would listen! Old folks' homes, shut-ins, or jails—he was on fire! What a joy it was for me to pastor my mom and dad and to see them grow and mature. I knew I could always count on my dad; he was always trying to make up for the past.

I'll never forget how, when I was about forty years old, he told me he loved me. Like a bashful young boy trying to ask a shy young lady for a date, he tried and tried to get it out, and finally he came out with it. "Son, I love you."

This was the first time in my forty years I had ever heard him say that! I hugged him and cried, and I wept for over two hours as I drove down the highway going to preach in a meeting. To think that my dad had actually told me, "I love you." Children need to hear those words verbally. That meant more to me than words can express.

My mother became one of our greatest prayer warriors, and my dad became one of our staunchest supporters. There was nothing that he wouldn't do for me and the ministry; he was totally, completely, 100 percent sold out. I cherish those twenty years that I had the privilege of pastoring two of the greatest people in my life, my mom and my dad. They always affectionately called me "Pastor."

The last words my dad said to me before he went to be with the Lord were, "Son, don't you worry about your dad; I'm ready to go if the Lord calls me. You look after your mother."

Then he looked at me, and he said, "Good night, Son; I'll see you in the morning."

What a joy I have knowing that some golden daybreak I shall see him again. He asked me to preach his funeral, and by the grace of God, it was accomplished. He told me so many times, "Son, I don't want the family circle to be broken. I want to see all my boys saved." He wanted me to preach so that his loved ones could hear the gospel.

In the mountains, people come from everywhere to funerals, and I preached the gospel and told my dad's story of just being an old sinner saved by grace. My mother also asked me to preach her funeral, which, by the grace of God, I did, telling the old, old story once again. She said, "I want to try to get all my children in, Son. Do your best—I'll be watching!"

WINNING LOST FAMILY MEMBERS

Since I was the only preacher in our family, it dawned on me that I must try to win my loved ones to Christ. God, in His grace, was faithful. He allowed me the privilege of winning my grandma, Lori Baisden, who was one hundred years old, to Christ. I also had the privilege of preaching her funeral.

God allowed me to win my mother's mom and dad to Christ and the privilege of preaching their funerals. He allowed me to win my dad's mom and dad to Christ and the privilege of preaching their funerals. I had the privilege of bringing many of my uncles and aunts to Christ and of preaching their funerals.

Mountain funerals are different. I went back to the mountains to preach one of my relative's funerals. She and her son had a "falling out" and would not forgive one another. (Mountain people never forgive or forget—that would be viewed as a sign of weakness.) They were each trying to get the last word in the argument; they had not spoken for several years, and she told him, "If it's the last thing I ever do, I will get even with you."

So when we got back into the mountains to the little mountain church, three people—two men and a woman—stood up in their bibbed overalls and white shirts. With their "Jew's harps" in hand, they said, "———— has written a song, and she wants it sung and dedicated to her son."

He was sitting on the front row. It went something like this:

You wouldn't visit mother when she was alive.
Now I see you sitting here all bright and teary-eyed.
Many years I sat on the porch and cried,
Looking for you to come into the focus of my eyes.

He wept, and we all wept, because she had kept her promise. She got back at him and had the last word.

My burden was to try to get my aunts and uncles saved. I would mail them gospel tracts and tapes. My Uncle Curt bought a Sony recorder and would take my tapes and call all of the neighbors on the hollow on Sunday afternoon to listen to his nephew preach. They would have a "preachin' time" on the porch, listening to the tapes.

When I found out what he was doing, I began to pray, "Lord, he's fooling with the dynamite of the Word of God, and he's got hold of something that will get hold of him, and it will blast the Devil out of him."

I kept sending the tapes, and he kept holding the meetings—a bunch of sinners gathering together to listen to a message from their nephew. I finally received a letter from him.

"Son, I just want you to know that your Uncle Curt got saved. The last message you preached, on 'Hell's Death March,' God spoke to my heart, and I got saved."

In that message I had used the illustration of the Bataan Death March in the Philippines during World War II and the horrible, painful, humiliating thing it was for our men. I told how General Douglas MacArthur had escaped the death march by getting on a PT boat and going to Australia. I made this application: "You can escape hell's death march by getting on the

Lord Jesus' PT boat. He is the PT boat, and we don't have to go to the country of the damned; you can be saved."

My Uncle Curt wrote, "Son, I told my wife I needed to go down to the barn and shuck some corn. I went down to the barn, and I was so under conviction. I got down behind the corn crib, and I looked up in the face of God and said, 'Oh, God! Could I get on your PT boat? I don't want to go to hell! I want to go to that country that is fairer than day.' I got on God's PT boat that day."

He was gloriously saved. I had the privilege of seeing him baptized. Years later, I preached his funeral. The last time I talked to him before he went to be with the Lord, he thanked me for telling him about God's "PT boat"—the Lord Jesus.

I've had the privilege of seeing all my loved ones saved except one. The "last holdout" is my oldest brother, but God is going to bring him in. Prayers will be answered. Winning loved ones to the Lord cannot be done overnight; it takes a lifetime. I thank God for the privilege of seeing so many loved ones get saved. "Pray that the family circle will not be broken" was the cry of my mother.

PRAYING GROUND

How exciting it was to see the Lord work in the hearts of so many people in the Hampton Roads area. We never tired of having old-fashioned river baptisms down on the riverbank with a time of "dinner on the grounds" and gospel singing, with a spirit of revival sweeping throughout our community.

In the fall of 1967, I felt burdened to challenge the deacons to claim a large piece of land on which we could build our church. We began to pray.

Unbeknownst to anyone, shortly after I arrived in Virginia Beach, I had sought out a place where I could go to have a time of prayer alone with the Lord. I found an old dirt road that led to a farm. The farm consisted of a barn, a pigpen, a cornfield, and a few large trees in the middle of a cornfield, all enclosed by a barbed-wire fence. I would come down the dirt road, climb the barbed wire fence, and pray under those large trees.

One morning, Lowell Chapel, one of my deacons, approached me. "Pastor, I've found a piece of land for sale. Let's go see an old farm that's for sale. It's just off Providence Road on the other side of I-64. There's plenty of land, just what we wanted."

Lo and behold! We turned down the dirt road, pulled over, and stopped by the barbed wire fence—it was my praying ground! I paused and looked at the land, between twelve and fifteen acres, with one side bordered by the Elizabeth River. "This is perfect. This is where the Lord wants us to build our church; we'll take it." Then I reached down and took off my shoes and socks.

"What are you doing, Pastor?"

"Remember in the Old Testament when God told the children of Israel that He'd give them all the land upon which the soles of their feet trod? Well, I'm going to claim that promise right here and now. We don't have any money, but we have a great God who can supply $12.57 to a preacher boy, so I know He can provide twelve to fifteen acres for the same preacher."

We claimed Joshua 1:3—"Every place that the sole of your feet shall tread upon, that have I given unto you, as I said unto Moses." I took off my shoes, walked around the farm, and claimed the property for God. I stopped underneath the oak trees and asked God to give us a ministry around the world, a ministry that no man could take credit for, except it be for the glory of God. God has done that, by His grace and despite our failures. One of those large oak trees still stands, located near the rear of the school building. I visit it quite frequently.

Tabernacle Baptist Church began with a heart hot for souls, for the Savior, and for sending the gospel to the regions beyond. We started teaching soul winning on Wednesday night, and the Lord worked. Our whole church went on door-to-door visitation with enthusiasm and zeal, and souls were saved. When I say "the whole church," I mean *all*—everybody! We would load down two buses, take lunch bags, and visit every Sunday after church for two or three hours. By December of 1967 we were running 317 in Sunday school, and the church agreed to purchase the land from Mr. Robert Young for $39,000.

Even though our church was growing, we had no money to make a down payment on the land. Once again, I called on our people. "Let's pray that God will give us the $10,000 to put down on the property."

God gave me the assurance that He would give us the $10,000 by the first of the year. I told the people, "We have no money, but God's going to give us that money."

Everyone shouted, "Amen, Pastor Bell!"

"But wait a minute! God's going to give it to us, but He's going to do something else. He is going to use *you* to give it!"

Give it they did, and cheerfully. The congregation gave $10,000, and twenty-nine of the members each signed a $1,000-note so that we could get a clear deed. Mr. Young conveyed the deed to us, and we paid $3,000 a year, plus 6 percent interest, for the property.

On December 24, 1967, we broke ground in the snow for our new church building. That Christmas morning our little band of folks surprised me and gave me a new '67 Chevrolet. I had given my car to the building fund and was driving a small Chevette (that's *Chevette*, not *Corvette!*) with my wife and three children. It wasn't conducive for carrying three children—you couldn't get in it; you had to "put it on," and it broke down along the highway most of the time. I guess they felt sorry for me. But I appreciated their love and kindness that day in the snowstorm when they gave us a new automobile. To God be the glory!

We had made plans to build and had no time to waste. We went to Lowe's Building Supply and were given a ninety-day line of credit for lumber and building materials. We used up $35,000 worth of material in no time, with our men furnishing the labor. We worked all day and laid the foundation. It was so cold that we could not pour the concrete, but the men were determined.

117

We poured the concrete! On the backside of our property was an old dump, full of truck and automobile tires. We pulled the tires out and stacked them around the foundation where concrete was to be poured, set them on fire, and prayed for the wind to blow the heat in the right direction. God sent a strong wind and blew the heat across that foundation. Of course, the police and the fire departments came, thinking the whole end of town was burning down!

The men stayed all night to keep the fires going so the concrete would not freeze. In our first building, the concrete floor was black because of the soot! God honored the faithfulness of our hard-working men and women, who were determined to build and not be distracted come heat or cold. God honored their faith, and the floor did not crack.

When the church was almost completed, the bank appraised the property and building at over $100,000. On the strength of that appraisal, the church was able to pay off Lowe's Supply Co. and to borrow enough money to build another Sunday school building.

In ninety days (the end of March 1968), we were ready to use the new building on Whitehurst Landing Road. How had this happened? It happened because a group of people caught the vision and began to work and pray.

We dedicated that new building on May 15, 1968, the first anniversary of the founding of Tabernacle Baptist Church. Dr. Oliver B. Green was our special guest speaker. During that dedication, we had more people outside the building than inside.

We quickly outgrew this building because our church folk were praying and out knocking on doors. People were getting saved, and the spirit of evangelism and revival fires were burning. The church became packed out; people had to sit outside the building. More people were saved outside than inside, and a new wing was started immediately. But then our building program began to slow down, and I couldn't keep our people motivated to complete this desperately needed addition. I found a way to motivate everyone: I took a sledgehammer and beat down one of the walls! The cold winter air poured in on us, and the congregation said, "We'd better get that addition finished before we all freeze to death!"

The people had a mind to work, and work they did! We built two more education wings in the next two years.

Concerned about the situation in our local schools, I began spending most of my time at the public school board, fighting for our young people. Through these battles, the Lord laid on my heart a burden to start Tabernacle Baptist School. In September of 1969, the school became a reality with fifteen students in kindergarten. Mrs. June Love was our first teacher. She not only taught, but she also became our first bus driver, using her own station wagon as the bus.

In 1970 the Lord provided a new Volkswagen bus, and our driver for that bus was the wife of one of our deacons. That bus was "prayed in"—one of our members bought the Volkswagen bus and gave it to the ministry. God always had His people in the right place at the right time.

The Tabernacle Baptist Bible Institute was the result of both a need and a dream. I felt the need was evident in 1970 for a local, church-based Bible institute. A school was needed that could train the young Navy men who were being saved in our church, a place where we could get them grounded in the Word, teach them to be witnesses, and show them how to have Bible study groups onboard the ships.

We started it as an institute to train men whom God called later in life to His work. It was to be a local church school that would stand for the fundamentals of the faith and train soulwinners and preachers to minister in the military. The dream was fulfilled in September 1970 when God founded Tabernacle Baptist Bible Institute (TBBI). Our first dean was one of my "Bootleg Corner" preacher buddies, an experienced pastor and long-time friend Charlie Anderson. Little did I realize that it would grow into a Bible college and seminary, but that's the way the Lord has led over the years.

Dr. Oliver B. Green was the vice-president of our Bible Institute and a dear friend to our ministry. He was also one of the men whom God used to fill my heart with fervency for evangelism.

Once a year, for the last seven years before he went to be with the Lord, Dr. Green came to Tabernacle and preached Friday, Saturday, and three times on Sunday. During those great times, our new auditorium would be packed with up to two thousand people. It was nothing to see thirty-five to forty people saved in a weekday service and ninety to one hundred people saved on the weekend. Scores and scores re-dedicated their lives.

We now have 350 graduates that have gone out. We say, "The sun never sets on the ministry of Tabernacle Baptist Church" because God has truly put this ministry around the world. Several of those graduates are still in full-time service for the Lord. Many of them have served in one little village or community or in the hills for over twenty-five years.

We've tried to maintain the philosophy that being successful means finding God's will and doing it the way God wants it done—Just Be Right! Be Real! Be Ready! I felt the burden to send preacher boys into the Appalachian Mountains to start churches in the hills, and God has permitted our church to "birth" over sixty churches all over America and in several foreign countries.

It is truly a blessing to see our people catch the vision. Deacons, Sunday school teachers, businessmen, and students can answer the call to go out from this local church and reproduce themselves on the mission field. I feel that this is an answer to my prayers under the oak tree, that God would put this ministry around the world and let no flesh glory in it. He has. He has blessed. He is faithful.

MINISTRY HIGHLIGHTS

In the early days, we had "Old-Fashioned Homecoming Sunday" every year. Our people would dress up in old-fashioned, bibbed overalls and eighteenth-century clothes. There would be old-fashioned singing and "dinner on the grounds." Many of our folks would drive their old automobiles, while others came in "horse and buggy."

A great memory of one such occasion was when we raised three hogs in the pigpen we had on the backside of the farm. We got ready to butcher them for our church anniversary. Those hogs were large—250-300 pounds each. We had to keep them in a freezer somewhere before we started to barbecue them early the next morning. One of our men knew the manager at a local store on Indian River Road, and he allowed us to put those hogs in his freezer. About 1:00 that morning, we got a frantic call from the manager: the heat from those freshly butchered hogs had defrosted his freezer and water was running out the door! "Come and get these hogs!"

We collected the hogs and started barbecuing them at 2:00 in the morning and had them all ready for our "pig-pickin'" that Homecoming Sunday. What a day that was, and how we enjoyed those old-fashioned dinners on the grounds.

We always had an annual camp meeting in a tent, with evangelist Billy Kelly. God blessed in those services in the early days before we had our large auditorium.

The Congress of Fundamentalists began in those early days. It was started in order to raise a testimony for historic Fundamentalism and to give other Fundamentalists (who were not necessarily Baptist) an opportunity to rally with us under the principles of historic, biblical Fundamentalism.

Through the last twenty-five years, God has given us the privilege of hosting this meeting at Tabernacle. Some of God's choicest servants have come and preached: Dr. Harold B. Sightler, Dr. Monroe Parker, Dr. O. Talmadge Spence, Dr. J. B. Williams, Dr. Myron Cedarholm, Dr. G. Archer Weniger, Dr.

Bob Jones Jr., Dr. Bob Jones III, and Dr. Ian Paisley, just to name a few. These men have preached through the years to our people and encouraged the next generation, our young people, to hold high the standard of God's Word.

One of the great highlights of this annual Congress was when we "passed the torch." We called together and charged all of our young preacher sons who had been called to the ministry—Dr. Bob Jones III's sons, Bob IV and Stephen; my two sons, Tim and Rod Jr.; Dr. Paisley's son Kyle; Dr. Van Gelderen's son Jim; Dr. O. Talmadge Spence's son "H.T."; and others.

Many times our Congress has received "notoriety," such as when the Roman Catholics picketed us because of Dr. Paisley's presence. We've had bomb threats, death threats, hateful phone calls, and biased reporting in the media, all because of opposition to Dr. Paisley. The Lord has always given us great services. Whenever there is opposition and resistance, the Spirit of God blesses and showers His people with greater spiritual riches and revival.

I remember a time when we had more bodyguards and undercover policemen than we had ushers! There had been so many death threats on Dr. Paisley's life that we had Scotland Yard, the FBI, the city police, and other special agents in our services. They always heard the gospel.

We had been receiving bomb threats, and one night I felt sure there would be trouble. I spotted a man who "looked like trouble." The auditorium was packed. "Sir," I told him from the pulpit, "you'll have to sit down; no one can stand."

He motioned to me, "No!"

"I'm not telling you any more. I want you to find a seat and sit down."

Dr. Paisley saw what I was doing. He spoke up, "He's all right, Rod; he's one of mine."

He was an undercover policeman, and I had just blown his cover!

That night we had to remove a man who kept yelling, "The pope is a good man, the pope is a good man, the pope is a good man."

"Ushers, would you please come and show this man out."

I told him that this was my pulpit, and if he wanted to preach, he should "get out and start him a church" and "get him someplace to brag on the pope"; this was a free country. But he wasn't going to do it in our church!

"Ushers, come and show him out."

The ushers came and took him outside and then tried to win him to Christ, but to no avail.

BLESSING, BUILDING, AND BATTLING
~

In 1971 our church had grown, with a large bus ministry of over twenty buses. We needed an auditorium that would be large enough to serve us for a while. We began to work on one that would seat approximately fifteen hundred people. During that time, we had one battle after another with building inspectors trying to use Virginia Beach city ordinances to stop us.

Even the Southern Baptist Convention Associational missionary came to our church and told me our sign was deceptive. Our sign read, *"Old Fashioned Southern Baptist."*

"I haven't seen you at any of the Associational meetings," he said.

"No, and you won't."

"Your sign is deceptive; you're not a Southern Baptist."

"I beg your pardon! I'm an old-fashioned Southern Baptist. I didn't leave you guys. *You guys left me.* I stand where our Baptist forefathers stood down through the years; that makes me old-fashioned. I'm south of the Mason-Dixon line; therefore, I'm Southern. And I am Baptist. That makes me old-fashioned, Southern Baptist!"

He said, "We don't need a church here. The Association is going to build one over there, and we don't need one here."

"Well, you may not need one here, but God needs one here."

"You'll never build a church here."

"With all due respect, you just wait and see."

Little did I realize the influence those "ecclesiastical bosses" have on city hall. They were determined our church would not build. But God was determined otherwise! During the time the building was being constructed, our people prayed and gave sacrificially.

One night a hurricane came up the coast, and we had our backs to the wall. The building was about two-thirds finished, and we had no insurance on it yet. The insurance company wouldn't insure it because our people were doing most of the work themselves and paying as we went.

That night, the hurricane blew the new building down. I stood in the storm that night as the rain beat upon my face, mingled with tears. I could hear Satan, as if he were sitting on my shoulder, saying, "You're a fool. You're not going to build this building."

I could hear the words of the SBC man ringing in my ears, "You'll never build this church."

I cried out upon my knees that night in the rain, "By the grace of God, we will continue."

I went home that night, one of the lowest times that I've experienced since I've been in the ministry. I had people who thought we shouldn't be building, people who said that God was not in it, that we were trying to do too much, that it was evident the Lord was trying to stop us from building. Some were saying I was a dictator; others claimed I took too strong a stand against apostasy.

That night, we prayed and asked God for wisdom. I got in the car and asked my wife, "Well, Honey, what do you think?"

Lenore has always been completely honest. "Honey, maybe you'd better check your motives."

"You think my message was all right?"

"I've heard you preach better!"

Well, I didn't need that, but then again, it was exactly what I needed. I went home, and even the dog barked at me! I was so low, I could have had my devotions under the carpet. When Lenore went to bed that night, I stayed up and wept and prayed.

I opened my Bible to seek comfort from the Word of God. As I read Nahum 1:3, God spoke to me, "The Lord hath his way in the whirlwind and in the storm, and the clouds are the dust of His feet."

I jumped up and ran through the house, tears of submission streaming down my cheeks. I lifted my heart toward heaven. "Thank you, Lord. If you want to blow it all down, it's Your work, and You have the right. We want Your good and acceptable and perfect will."

I took my pen and wrote in my Bible, "Glory to God. God blew the new building down. June 1, 1971."

Then I jumped up and cried to Lenore, "Honey, Honey, Honey, God blew our new building down."

"What in the world are you talking about?"

"God just blew the new building down, and it's all right. If He wants to flatten everything on Whitehurst Landing Road, we'll meet under the tree. He says in His Word that He has His way in the whirlwind, so 'let 'er blow' if that's what He wants. I have never had such peace; we can start back under the tree."

"I'm going back to bed," Lenore said. She wasn't too excited about being awakened at 2:00 in the morning! I don't blame her now, but back then I thought she was not very spiritual.

That night I returned to my reading. I went on through the minor prophets and got to Haggai 1:4, "Is it time for you, O ye, to dwell in your cieled houses, and this house lie waste?" That was my sermon for the next Sunday morning. I prayed, "Okay, Lord, the just are going to have to learn to live by faith."

The next Lord's day morning I preached on "You live in cieled houses, and the Lord's house lies in waste." When I got through preaching, I said, "If you don't believe what I've been preaching, just look out the window and see the Lord's house lying in waste." And I sat down.

There was the brick and the mortar and the roof—the whole building—all in a pile. "God wants to do something this morning; let's let Him do it."

We have never been in a service like that before or since. God took the offering that day! People came down the aisles to get saved; people were called to the mission field; people came to give whatever they could.

One lady gave a ring, and her husband came down the aisle to redeem the ring for $2,000. Another lady gave an automobile. One gave ten acres of land; another gave two property lots. One man gave a shotgun; another gave a fishing rod and reel. Someone gave $500; another gave $1,000. Some people made pledges; others gave bonds, securities, watches, vehicles. People just kept giving, getting saved, and getting right with the Lord!

The "offering" went from 12:00 until 1:30, and then on until 2:00 and 2:30. People were getting their hearts right with one another. The blessings of the Lord were showered upon the people. They gave over $37,000 that morning, including the automobiles, trucks, tractors, and houses and real estate. I said to Brother Anderson, "Copy this down; get this on a piece of paper because I don't want any of these people to forget what they have given." You know, sometimes Baptists forget!

I told the people I would not stop the service; God started it, and God would have to stop it. They could go home; they were at liberty to do whatever they wanted to do, but I was going to stay the rest of the day and fast and pray. That's exactly what most of them did too.

That night as Lowell Chappel, the songleader, began the evening service, he began to weep. He fell over the pulpit and said, "I'm so sorry; I feel like such a hypocrite. I didn't get in on the blessings of this morning, and I want to give $1,000."

Someone else said, "Me, too. I feel I should have given."

Someone else gave $100; another gave $500; another gave $1,000.

Someone else gave, and it started again!

I didn't get to preach that night. People were getting right with God and with each other. God sent another old-fashioned offering. People rededicated their lives; others were called to the mission field.

One little boy gave his dump truck that he had brought from home. One of the deacons said, "I'll redeem it for $50; let him have it back." The boy turned around and walked back down the aisle with the dump truck. He gave that truck three times, and every time he gave it, someone redeemed it! It was the most unusual day of services I've ever experienced.

That night, God's people gave $30,000. *He* took the offering and built the Lord's house. The next day I wrote in my Bible in Haggai, "$37,000 in cash, pledges, and promises. Another $30,000 raised that night."

God gave us $67,000 in cash, plus automobiles, land, and other valuable items. The bills were paid, the building was built, and God's church marched on. There was no pressure, no gimmicks—just His powerful presence upon a broken people. To God be the glory! When *God* takes an offering, *it's taken!*

We broke ground for that fifteen-hundred-seat auditorium on April 4, 1971. We moved into the building one year later, on April 12, 1972. The building was packed for the dedication. Evangelist Billy Kelly preached. In the first service there were twenty-four saved; in the second service, twenty-two were saved; in the third service, twenty-three were saved. To God be the glory! God continued to pour out His blessings upon His people, and the fires of evangelism were burning.

Some of the battles we've been called to fight have become the highlight of this ministry. I have not enjoyed some of the battles, but after I get into one and get "warmed up," sometimes I do enjoy it! We started the Tabernacle Baptist Hour radio program in 1969. God blessed us with a forty-five-minute program broadcast over WCMS. We engaged the Commonwealth of Virginia in a battle involving the sale of "liquor-by-the-drink." Of course, it was no-holds-barred. Many of the preachers in the area rallied and preached against liquor-by-the-drink and the Commonwealth's attempt to revoke the Sunday "Blue Laws." All eating establishments and stores were closed on Sunday. The Lord's Day was a holy day.

One of the biggest battles our church fought was to keep the Lord's Day from being commercialized. As I look back on my thirty years, I believe this issue was the straw that broke the camel's back. It seems all the other vices took over whenever God's people allowed the Lord's Day to be desecrated. The impact upon society and the lives of God's people has been devastating.

One Sunday I was preaching on the radio against liquor-by-the-drink. I was talking about how it would be better for some of these churches to go out of business and for them to be blown down and used for firewood to start bonfires with because there was no fire in them. About that time, my radio tape broke, and the country-and-western station we broadcast on played a song, "Who burned the roadside tavern down? Who burned the roadside tavern down?"

I got my tape started again. "I want you to know that the Southern Baptists, the liberal churches, and the other compromisers wouldn't do anything to stop the liquor-by-the-drink."

People wrote in and asked me, "Pastor, who burned the roadside tavern down? Who burned the roadside tavern down? I never heard your theme song before, but I heard it today."

They made fun of our church because we took a stand against liquor-by-the-drink and against revoking the Blue Laws. Today, liquor is sold everywhere in almost every grocery store; and on Sunday, the shopping centers are filled with shoppers, many of whom are God's people. We lost those two battles, but we still honor the Lord's Day and still stand against liquor-by-the-drink.

We had not been in Virginia Beach long when we were called to engage in another conflict—the battle of the Billy Graham Crusade. The Billy Graham Crusade came to Norfolk Armory, and we had to take our stand.

I went to all the independent Baptist preachers. We rallied together and placed a full-page advertisement in the paper: "The Bible or Billy—Which?" It received national attention because it compared what the Bible says to what Billy Graham was doing.

Our people took their stand and accepted their losses graciously. God has honored that position. Billy Graham's ecumenical compromise with the Liberals, Charismatics, and New Evangelicals has been, I believe, the greatest curse to New Testament evangelism. His ministry has done more harm to biblical Christianity than any other "Christian" influence in my lifetime.

There were many blessings and many battles during the '70s. *Jesus Christ, Superstar* came to town, and our church took a stand, opposing this blasphemous production. The first time it played was in 1971; the second time it came in 1974, and it rained and poured. We marched around the Virginia Beach Dome; I preached, and some people carried signs stating that *Superstar* was blasphemous and any resemblance to truth was purely coincidental. Needless to say, we made the newspapers and the "bleeding-heart liberals" sad.

In 1972, the first time the homosexuals "came out of the closet," the city of Norfolk was pressured to have a "Gay Pride Day." I will never forget when I asked the mayor if they were going to have a "Gay Pride Day."

"Well, we've got pressure to have it. We have to bring it up before Council because, if we don't, we're going to have all kinds of problems."

"If you do, you're going to have all kinds of problems," I told him.

I called the chief of police and asked if I could have a permit to protest on the night the "proud gays" were coming out. Anita Bryant was also scheduled to appear at the Norfolk Scope Auditorium to speak out in opposition to the homosexuals.

The chief breathed with relief, "Thank God! Where have all the preachers been?"

We took our prayer meeting that Wednesday from Tabernacle Baptist Church to the corner of St. Paul and Brambleton. The battle was hot. I preached the Sunday beforehand, "If you don't show up Wednesday night, I'll wonder whose side you're on."

That night, we had one of the largest prayer meetings we've ever had. Our people and our signs marched around the Scope. I preached on Romans 1: "God turned them over to a reprobate mind. What you need is Jesus Christ."

The police, with their German shepherd dogs, were there. My people stood firm as they carried their signs. Anita Bryant was inside the Scope, speaking to about five thousand who had rallied against the homosexual agenda. I was "piggy-backing" her theme on the outside, with my little group of five hundred, preaching that Jesus Christ could save sinners. What these poor, blind people need is Christ. Little did I realize our stand would make news across the nation. In various newscasts, whenever they showed the position of Fundamentalists on homosexuals, they showed film clips of our protest and stated that we still believed the Bible.

The battle had just begun, and we continued the fight through the '70s and the '80s. The conflict began to intensify as we took on the homosexuals. "Why fight the Sodomites?" was the theme time and time again from our pulpit. The newspapers were filled with headlines, "Baptist Preacher Stands Against Sodomy."

We took the conflict to the City of Virginia Beach government and protested against the homosexuals using our libraries to recruit our children with their filthy literature. We placed a resolution on the ballot in 1980 to prohibit the homosexuals' use of our libraries to distribute their literature. The resolution passed 4-1!

During that time, someone came to our church during the night and shot out the windows of our main auditorium. A plaque still hangs in our foyer today, riddled with pock marks from the bullets that raked the building that night. Needless to say, our people stood firm, God blessed, and victories were won.

We have seen the heat of battle when we fought the Equal Rights Amendment (ERA) and the "women's liberators." We rallied the troops, and over five thousand went to the state house in Richmond. Little did we realize the hornet's nest we had stirred up! Over five thousand of God's people came from all over to march on the state capitol.

It all started when the Episcopalians hosted a little "tea," inviting people to discuss their differences and share their opinions regarding the ERA and the "women's liberation movement." All the politicians came, traffic was jammed all over Richmond, and the police wanted to know who was in charge. No one knew who was in charge because we didn't expect it to mushroom like that.

Finally, the preachers said, "Rod, represent us. Get up and say something."

All the politicians in the auditorium were taking turns speaking, telling us what they were running for and what they would do if re-elected. I remember how the Lord burdened my heart at that moment: I stood up and told them that I was not running for anything; I had already been elected before the foundation of the world; that Jesus Christ was the answer. What we needed to do was get back to the Bible and the "old-time religion."

The crowd went wild. We enjoyed a great day of battle and a great day of blessings as we rallied the troops again in Virginia at the capitol.

God's blessings continued when we saw the need to organize a Christian school movement in the Commonwealth. We needed an organization that could help us in our academics, athletics, and arts programs: one that would prevent the government from attempting to regulate us or encroach on our rights and that could give us recognition on a national level with the American Association of Christian Schools.

We organized the Old Dominion Association of Church Schools (ODACS), of which I was the first president. Johnny Halsey and I also organized the Virginia Assembly of Independent Baptists, and I was elected as the first moderator. God blessed and gave us men who rallied around the cause. Little did we realize that God would ultimately use these organizations to stop the Virginia Department of Health, Education, and Welfare from attempting to control our curriculum and license our schools.

I never will forget the order that came out requiring all our schools to be licensed. When I started our preschool, I requested a license because I thought it was the thing to do. After it was explained to me what the license meant, I took the license, but only after much soul-searching.

"What are you going to do?" my people asked.

"I'm taking this license to the state attorney general, Marshall Coleman, and I'm going to lay it on his desk, and he can do with it whatever he wants."

I went in to see Attorney General Coleman.

"Now, Preacher Bell," he said, "don't get involved."

"But I already am involved."

"They'll put you in jail."

"I won't be the first Baptist they put in jail for his convictions."

We marched in Richmond in 1978 on the anti-ERA rally. As a result of that, we had numerous Sons of Religious Liberty rallies. We felt that it was important for our people to be responsible in their civic duties. Our own Dr. Carl Bieber was elected chairman of the Republican Party for the second district, the largest district in Virginia. Perhaps no political battle was as publicized as the battle with the homosexual community over the *Our Own* magazine. Tabernacle Baptist Church and our young people stood firmly and defiantly for the principles and morals of the Word of God and never wavered.

During the license issue, we saw the church rally unanimously to not take a license. They voted 100 percent on June 4,

1987, on the basis of our belief that it would violate the separation of church and state. The Lord had worked in my heart and conscience to the point that I came to a conviction on the matter of state licensing of the ministry. I wrote in the margin of my Bible in Isaiah 54—"Here I stand; I can do no other. The state of Virginia will not license this pulpit, by the grace of God. I will rot in jail first."

The die was cast, and the long, hard struggle for religious liberty in Virginia began again. We were to spend the next ten years in court, fighting the machinery of Virginia's Department of Health, Education, and Welfare.

On June 2, 1978, Governor John Daulton signed a bill exempting church-run daycare centers from licensure. The bill went into effect in 1979 and was immediately challenged in court. As expected, the conflict moved slowly through the courts, from defeat to blessing, from one victory to another battle. In 1984 the United States District Court (Eastern District, Richmond Division) ruled against us, but we appealed, and their decision was reversed and remanded by the Court of Appeals. The Court of Appeals declared the new law allowing church-run daycare centers to be exempted from licensure by the state to be unconstitutional but felt that churches still deserved their day in court. They reasoned that if churches could be viewed as a distinct class of people being discriminated against, they should be able to contest certain regulations. Upon remand, the District Court ruled that churches did not qualify as a distinct class; therefore, the law was unconstitutional. In other words, the law allowing church-run daycare centers to be exempt from licensure requirements was unconstitutional, and we would be required to be licensed by the state.

By 1986, however, the District Court and the Court of Appeals still did not know what they wanted. What was clear, though, was that they both wanted the churches in a suit. U.S. District Judge, the Honorable D. Dortch Warriner, told us, "If you lose this case, then the day of the parochial school is finished. The day of the Sunday school is in danger, and the day of tax exemption for churches is gone. The day of freedom of religion is gone."

Unfortunately, Judge Warriner died, and our case went before Judge Richard L. Williams. The battle continued, hour upon hour, mile upon mile. Finally, in 1986, Judge Williams ruled that churches *were* a distinct class. All church-run daycare centers would be represented in court by four ministry organizations. We were one of the four. The judge gave us thirty days for these ministries to "opt in or out of the class."

The decision handed down by the U.S. District Court on May 15, 1987, stated, "The Court concludes that the statute, Virginia Code #631-196.3, violates the establishment clause of the First Amendment of the United States Constitution. . . . The Court finds no per se entitlement to free exercise protection for the operation of childcare centers by sectarian institutions." (See Appendix for more documentation.)

Again, we appealed the decision.

On May 6, 1988, the U.S. Court of Appeals ruled, "The judgment of the District Court declaring Virginia Code #631-196.3 unconstitutional is reversed and in junction, the issue is dissolved." What a great victory for religious liberty in Virginia!

In 1989 our foes launched an appeal to the United States Supreme Court. However, the Supreme Court refused to hear the case, affirming the decision of the U.S. Court of Appeals. After a ten-year struggle, the battle was won, but even now we know the war is not over. The secular humanists will be back. God, give us people who will stand when they come.

One particular incident in this case is burned forever in my heart and mind. It occurred when I was being deposed by the Commonwealth attorneys. I went to Richmond and got alone in the motel. I will never forget what I promised the Lord. "I am no match for these attorneys. I cannot match wits with them. I am not an attorney; I am a Baptist preacher. Lord, I surrender and submit myself to You. You promised that You will give me the words to say."

I went into that deposition and was questioned for over eight hours. They were trying to find out if we had convictions or were just in business, trying to make money through our preschool. I told them more than once that if they only looked at our financial records, they would see that we weren't there as a profit-making business.

They wanted to know what "conviction" meant. One of their attorneys asked me, "What do you mean by convictions?"

I spoke from the depths of my soul. "A person that holds to a Bible conviction is a person who has his soul anchored and chained in bondage to God's Word, and he cannot be moved. Whatever God's Word says, he believes, and whatever he believes, he practices. That, my friend, is conviction."

After hours and hours of such drilling, the Commonwealth's attorney threw his pencil down on the table and said, "I believe this preacher has biblical convictions."

During the trial, the old judge took the page out of my Bible where I had written in the margin of Isaiah 54, "Here I stand; I can do no other. The state of Virginia will not license this pulpit! By the grace of God. I will rot in jail first. R. Bell." They entered my Bible as evidence in our case, and this statement is part of the court record. The judge held it up for all to see and said, "It looks to me like this Baptist preacher means business because he would follow the tradition of John Bunyan." Thank God for judges and lawyers who know their Baptist history! God always has His "salt" in the right place.

I remember facing Virginia's governor John Daulton in his office. "Rod," he said, "if you don't accept a license, I'll have to see that you're put in jail because you're breaking the law."

"Governor, do you put everyone in jail who breaks the law? What about these prostitutes and homosexuals who break the law on the streets behind the capitol building here in Richmond?"

"Well, I can see that we're going to hit head on."

Needless to say, we did "hit head on." Our church people rallied around their pastor whenever God called me to get involved in our civic responsibilities. "Render to Caesar the things that are Caesar's, and to God the things that are God's."

When the battle cry was sounded, our people always came to my rescue. We took the conflict to the governor's office, the attorney general's office, the courtrooms, the highways, fighting for our very existence.

It was during this time that I became acquainted with John Leyland and the great Baptist heritage that God has given us in Virginia. If you could ask James Madison, "Who was responsible for the Bill of Rights?" he would say, "The Baptists."

We have a great heritage in the state of Virginia, and it has been my burden to try to pass that great heritage down to our children and our children's children.

THE GOVERNOR AND THE BLACKBIRD

We have a slogan at our church: "There is no place anywhere near this place just like this place, so this must be the place!" I will never forget the morning I received a telephone call that went something like this:

"Hello, Rod, this is John Daulton."

"Yes, and this is Uncle Sam."

Then I caught his voice and knew that it *was* the governor of Virginia!

"I'm in Virginia Beach at Back Bay for the weekend, and my wife and I and our friends would like to come and attend your church this morning."

I was speechless. Then I finally said, "Well, Governor, we'll certainly be glad to have you," and I gave him directions to our church. I got off the phone and told my wife that the governor had just called, and he wanted to attend our church this morning.

When I got to church, there was excitement in the air! I had called some of our church leaders and told them the governor was coming. As we prepared for services, what should we discover but another unexpected visitor—a huge blackbird in the sanctuary, flying from one end of the auditorium to the other!

"Let's get this blackbird out of here. Open the doors."

We had seventeen doors and twenty-one windows.

"Please get brooms, mops, towels—*anything*—and let's try to get him out."

We began to run him from one end of the church to the other, trying desperately to get him out the door, but he was determined to stay! We spent twenty-five to thirty minutes trying to get him to leave. Finally, the people started to come in for Sunday school.

"Now, folks, the governor is coming today, and we want everything to be done decently and in order. We've got to leave this blackbird alone. Maybe he'll not cause us any problems."

About that time, one of our men threw a rag up on top of the chandelier at the blackbird. I said, "Look, don't do anything else; let's just leave him alone. The people are coming in for Sunday school."

As they came in that morning for Sunday school, I began to preach on Ezekiel 38, "Bringing Russia down against Israel." In a few minutes, my wife excitedly began to point toward the ceiling; I looked up and saw that the rag was smoking.

"Now, folks, do not panic. Do not panic! There's a rag up on the chandelier, and it's on fire. One of you men go get a fire extinguisher and put that fire out."

One of my men ran and got a fire extinguisher. Climbing up into the balcony, he sprayed foam all over the chandelier and the people, and they had to move.

"Don't panic; it's out now."

About that time, there came an emergency vehicle, siren blaring and lights flashing. They came down the aisle and went into a Sunday school class beside the auditorium where, unbeknownst to me, a man had suffered a heart attack. They brought him out, working on him.

"Folks, don't panic. He'll be all right. We're going to pray that God will help get him to the hospital."

The ambulance left. No sooner did I begin to preach again than a fire engine came. The emergency vehicle saw the smoke, smelled the flames, and called the fire engine. They came in with their ladders, clanging and banging, and raised the ladder to get the smoking rag down. Just as quickly as the ladder went up, it came down, and they walked out. I thought, "Well, everything is okay. We can just go ahead and continue to preach."

About that time, the firemen came back in with a big exhaust fan and turned it on, creating a loud "swishing" noise. I told our people, "Folks, don't worry; everything will be all right. I'm going to bring Russia against Israel if it's the last thing I ever do!"

After a few minutes the firemen returned, removed the fan, and left. Again, I began to preach. Just as I was really getting into the message, one of my Bible Institute students saw that black-bird. It was sitting right on the edge of the baptistry! The student sneaked across the back edge of the baptismal pool and tried to throw a towel over the blackbird. Naturally, the student slipped and fell into the pool, and the people began to roll with laughter. I just kept on preaching, trying to get Russia down against Israel.

CONVERTING THE KLAN AND OTHERS

Over the years, we've seen some unusual conversion experiences. One such case was Rudy Wilson, a big, burly man with long hair and bibbed overalls. He came down the aisle one Sunday morning, weeping, wanting to get saved. As he bowed and received Christ as his personal Savior, he told me he that he was the grand wizard of the Ku Klux Klan. He wanted to join the church.

"You'll have to bring me proof of your repentance. Get out of the Klan," I told him.

The next week, he came back down the aisle, two more people with him.

"Did you get out of the Klan?" I asked.

"Yes, sir. I went to my chaplain, and I brought him with me today."

He introduced me to the chaplain and the chaplain's wife.

"Are you out of the Klan?"

"Yes."

"When did you get out of the Klan?"

"Today."

"When did you get saved?"

"Just a few minutes ago."

Rudy had witnessed to them and brought them both to Christ. What a joy it was when we had the privilege of baptizing them all.

One night as I sat on the platform waiting for the service to start, the phone rang in my servicemen's center. Charlie Stallings, director of the servicemen's center, said, "Pastor, I have a woman, actually a prostitute, on the phone, and she wants to come to church."

Our men had been down on the street corner passing out tracts and preaching. She had heard them, had received a tract, and wanted to come to a church service.

"What am I going to do?" he asked me.

"Take your wife and go get her. Bring her to church."

He jumped in a church van and brought her in, just as I was about to preach.

I preached the old, old story, as the soiled dove of the underworld dressed in the clothes of the harlot sat on the back row. I remember so well how she was painted up—rouge, lipstick, mascara, false eyelashes—enough paint that if you were to kiss her, you'd get the "painter's colic."

She came down the aisle, wanting to receive Christ as her personal Savior. By this time, the tears had melted the makeup, and the black "Maybelline" dripped down her cheeks. One false eyelash had slid sideways. She came down the aisle, "I want Jesus Christ as my personal Savior."

One of the ladies took her to the prayer room, and she accepted Christ and was gloriously saved.

She came back out, embarrassed because of the way she was dressed. "I'll not be dressed this way next Sunday, Preacher."

Weeks went by, and she was so faithful. She was burdened about her estranged husband. We found out where he was, and the men went after him, brought him in, and he was saved. They began to grow and develop into strong Christians.

I remember the day she came and asked, "Can we sing in the choir?"

"If anyone can sing 'Amazing grace, how sweet the sound that saved a wretch like me,' you can. Get in!"

They joined the choir and served the Lord for several years until the day they were transferred to San Diego. She and her husband stood in front of the church to tell everyone good-bye.

"Can you recommend a church to us that goes down on the street corner and passes out tracts and tells old sinners that God loves them and Jesus died for them? We want that kind of church—a church that will unite families, present Jesus Christ, and make a difference."

I recommended to them a good church on the West Coast, and they left happy in the Lord, serving Him and loving each other. God makes the difference.

I remember Dave Landers, a long-haired hippie, who came down the aisle one Sunday morning and got saved. Shortly after he came to know the Lord, David's wife was saved. Then God called them into His service. They went to school, were trained, ordained, and called to serve the Lord on the mission field of Bolivia. They have been faithful down through the years.

Sherman Davis, a man who was saved out of a motorcycle gang, came to Tabernacle and God trained him, ordained him, and sent him out. He has been faithfully serving God in the little town of King George, Virginia, for almost twenty-six years. To God be the glory!

Jimmy Modell is one of the interesting characters from our church. He used to play in a rock band, but God saved him and did a work in his heart. He loves to give a testimony for the Lord. I remember the first time he went on visitation; I took him with me, and it went something like this:

"I don't know anything about visitation. I can't say anything. I won't know what to do."

"Well, all I want you to do is just go with me and I will do the talking; you just observe."

When we got into the home and had talked for a while, I said, "Brother Jimmy, tell them how you got saved."

Jimmy gave his testimony, with tears streaming down his cheeks. That was thirty years ago, and he's never kept quiet since! He witnesses to everything. He's so enthusiastic for the Lord, I believe he'd witness to a doorknob.

There is one incident, though, that I'm sure he'd like to forget. A preacher friend, his wife, and I were sitting in the car, waiting for Jimmy to come out of the restaurant. Jimmy had this trick that he would always play—holding his throat while his elbow was hidden behind a door. It really looked like someone was choking him, and he was very clever in doing it. But this time was different. As we sat in the car waiting on him, he put his elbow behind the door, reached out, and was choking himself. As he stood there, legs shaking and "being choked," his pants fell down around his ankles! Embarrassed, he came to the car and said, "Pastor, I don't believe the Lord is in that, do you?"

"Jimmy," I told him, "I promise you I will not tell a soul unless I have a big crowd!"

I cannot say I have kept my promise, but I believe this may be one of the best opportunities to let the secret out!

These stories could be repeated over and over again as we thank God for the faithful servants He has brought through the doors of Tabernacle Baptist Church.

STORIES FROM THE BAPTISTRY

The baptismal pool has frequently played an interesting part in my ministry. One Sunday evening, church had just started. As I walked up to the platform, I looked up in amazement to see, behind the choir where the baptistry was, water just about to seep over the top of the glass. As the choir enthusiastically sang "Showers of Blessing," I got on the phone and called the deacons. "Get the water out of the baptismal before it overflows."

Two of my faithful deacons, Ken Dorhout and Milton Snell, tried to remove the drain plug but couldn't get it out. I tried to go on with the service, but I could see my people snickering, and I knew I wasn't saying anything funny. One began to laugh, then another one. I watched the faces of the congregation enjoying something other than my message.

Little did I realize that my two deacons were working behind me in the baptismal waters, trying to get that drain plug out of the pool. The remote drain-opening lever had broken, and they were down in the water, trying to dive down and pull the drain-plug out, but they kept bobbing up to the surface.

Finally, they came up with a brilliant idea. One placed a mop behind the shoulders of the other and held him under the water while he pulled out the plug. The congregation was almost "rolling in the aisles" as they watched the show.

When it dawned on me what was happening, I said we would have to put a sign on the baptismal: "Absolutely no swimming during services!"

The next Sunday as I came out I had a sign made and put on the baptismal pool that said "NO SWIMMING." It could happen only at Tabernacle!

One of the most solemn occasions in my church ministry happened one Sunday night. As I was preparing for a baptismal service, a heavyset man who was going to be baptized came running up the stairs. When he reached the top of the stairs, just before we put him into the baptismal waters, he had a heart attack. As we were working with him, I told the people to pray and to call the rescue squad for help. The deacons and I performed CPR on this dear man, but he died in our baptismal room. It was a very shocking and sobering experience. I'm thankful he was not from the Church of Christ (which requires baptism for salvation) but that he knew he was saved by grace through faith. He didn't need the baptismal waters to get him into the presence of Christ; he was ushered in by the grace of God.

We have an "educable slow" class in our Sunday school, consisting of about eighty-five precious souls. We work with them, helping them to understand they are lost and need a Savior.

Bobby Whitlow was a young black man who had been deformed and crippled from paralysis. His speech was slurred and his body was twisted. He had been saved, and now he wanted to be baptized.

That same night we were baptizing Rudy and several others. After I baptized Rudy and brought him up out of the water, the next person to come into the baptistry was Bobby, this twisted, crippled young black man. Rudy came up out of the water, made a mad rush up the steps, and picked up Bobby.

I thought, "Oh, my! This ex-Klan member is going to crush this dear little black man."

But to my amazement, Rudy turned around, carried Bobby down the steps, and handed him to me.

"Rudy," I said, "I thought you hated the black man?"

With tears running down his cheeks, he said, "Not any more, Preacher, not any more."

As tenderly as a mother handling a baby, he placed Bobby in my arms, and I baptized him in the same water as the former Ku Klux Klansman, Klan chaplain, and his wife. The Lord certainly does make the difference. If there is no evidence of a change in your life, you haven't been saved.

The people from Tabernacle Baptist Church are just ordinary people who serve an extraordinary God. They have put up with me for over thirty-two years and have been faithful, loyal, loving, giving, and sacrificial, to the point that I sometimes stand amazed at what one group of people, surrendered and sold out to the Lord, can do. Our church is blessed to have some of the most godly people I've ever known. We also have some who are weak, frail, and fragile. But God uses the bruised reed and the smoking flax. He will not be quenched. He has used this group of people to spread the gospel around the world. They have handed down their heritage to untold thousands by sending missionaries to twenty-nine countries and by starting or rebuilding sixty churches throughout the United States. These people have a burden to follow the Great Commission and get the gospel to the regions beyond. Millions of dollars have been channeled through Tabernacle Baptist Church to the mission fields. Because of their faithfulness, the "Old Lighthouse" is still sending out the light all over the world! The sun never sets on their ministry—while we sleep, they preach; while they sleep, we preach.

Chapter 11:
Preserving Fundamentalism

CONGRESS OF FUNDAMENTALISTS
〜

Let me say a word about the Congress of Fundamentalists, which we hold at Tabernacle Baptist Church each year. In the early seventies, God burdened my heart to keep historic Fundamentalism alive. I wanted to give all true biblical Fundamentalists in America, including those who were not necessarily Baptist, a rallying point where we could stand together on the great fundamentals of the faith. In 1974 we started our "Congress of Fundamentalists." We invited men who took an orthodox, separated stand on the great doctrines of the faith—independent Presbyterians, independent Baptists, independent Methodists, and others who were true Biblicists. Our church has had the privilege of hosting the conference now for over twenty-five years. It is always a great blessing to have men come and preach the unsearchable riches of Jesus Christ. Although we may disagree in some policies of church government or in minor areas, nowhere is there a disagreement on the essentials of salvation or the major doctrines of the faith. These men are true historic Fundamentalists. They are staunch separatists, carrying a vibrant testimony of biblical Christianity into the twenty-first century.

I remember one night after our church service, we were sitting and having fellowship, and one of the preachers said, "You know, we ought to do this on a world-wide scale." From that table came the impetus that produced the first World Congress in Edinburgh in 1976, then in the Philippines, then in Greenville, South Carolina, and then in London, and then regional Congresses all over the world in places like Singapore, Australia, Korea, Japan, Bolivia, Chile, and Germany. God has allowed these meetings to impart encouragement and great strength to fundamental, Bible-believing brethren all over the world. To God be the glory; great things He has done through the Congress of Fundamentalists. These kinds of meetings play a key role in passing down the mantle of biblical Christianity to the next generation.

A regional Congress was held in Arad, Romania. I was to be one of the keynote speakers, but the speaking schedule in our church was so tight I did not feel I could afford to be gone on a Sunday. I told the men I would go and speak on a Wednesday night and return Saturday so that I could be in my church on Sunday.

Monday morning I flew to New York, then to Budapest, Hungary, and from Budapest down to Arad, Romania. It was a six-hour train ride in Romania. I finally got on the right train; not knowing the language, I did a lot of smiling, a lot of nodding, and a lot of laughing!

At the border of Hungary and Romania, an interesting event occurred. We had come to Romania just after the Ceausescu regime had been overthrown. Of course, the authorities were highly suspicious of any travelers or people crossing the borders. As the train chugged to a stop, on came six Communist guards to check passports. One checked our pictures, one checked our passports, one checked our luggage, one questioned us—each had just one thing to do (I guess we would call that "job security").

As I stood there, one of the men beside me took a picture of the scene with his camera. The guards immediately snatched the camera away, removed the film, and gave him back an empty camera, enraged.

I saw the guards looking for guns. I noticed that they had detained a heavyset man; as he was being searched, they found a gun. As they inspected the weapon, the man jumped from the train and ran, trying to escape. I watched out the train window as he ran, the guards behind him. As he jumped across a ditch, the man's pants fell down, and the guards tackled him, wrestling him into submission, and took him into custody. It reminded me of the old "Keystone Cops" movies. I couldn't help but laugh— it was too funny to watch, all the Romanian guards with their long beards, wrestling the man with no pants!

I preached the next night and boarded the train the next morning for my return trip to Budapest, Hungary. Tired and weary, I looked forward to a few hours sleep at the airport motel. As I was getting a bite to eat, someone put a drug in my drink. I went upstairs to go to bed and collapsed on the bed, completely knocked out. Just as I was waking up, I was aware of someone moving quickly through the door as it closed; I knew immediately I had been robbed. All of my bags had been opened, and my things were strewn about my room. Someone had come in and robbed me of all of my money and my papers!

I immediately jumped up and went downstairs. One of the waiters could speak a little English. I told him, "I've been robbed!"

In broken English he replied, "It happens here all the time."

I went down and filed my complaint; the manager was very apologetic. I called my secretary and said, "Mrs. Borah, get me out of this place." Before I knew it, she had the papers and instructions and had made new flight arrangements. I was on my way home. I stood in my pulpit the next Sunday morning and thanked God for His faithfulness and for a good secretary who knew what to do in a crisis.

In 1986 we were in the Philippines for the World Congress. I have always been a great admirer of General Douglas MacArthur. I wanted to go and see Corregidor on the island of Bataan. As we made our visit, we saw the cemetery and memorial to all the young men who had died in the liberation of the Philippines. An old, gray, weather-beaten Filipino man was there, and I said to him, "General Douglas MacArthur was one of my greatest heroes. He was a great American hero."

He nodded and said, "He was a great man, but he's not my hero."

"Oh?" I took offense. "General Douglas MacArthur was my hero. He is one of our greatest heroes."

Again he nodded, "He was a great man, but he's not my hero."

As I looked at him, I noticed tears in his eyes. He waved his hand toward all those crosses on the graves of the young American men who had spilled their blood liberating the island. "These are my heroes."

And I had to agree. They had paid the supreme price; they had given their lives.

One of my responsibilities for the World Congress, in addition to being the chairman of the Resolution Committee, has been to help plan the congresses. I have never sought the place of leadership; I have always felt that there are many more people who could do a far better job than I. My mom always said, "Mountain folks have poor ways, but we get the job done." I have frequently been pushed into a place of responsibility and found that I love it. Challenges have always excited me, but I still approach them with fear and trembling. I guess that comes from when I was a child; there was always something to do, and one had to be responsible to see that it was done. But this matter of helping to plan the World Congresses was just out of my league. Despite my feelings of inadequacy, I could not say no; I had been asked to do it. Dr. Bob Jones Sr. had trained me well: "You can borrow brains, but you cannot borrow character."

I always tried to get men on our committee I could rely on to be good thinkers: clear, level-headed, balanced, resolutionists who were committed to the cause of Christ and biblical Fundamentalism. I would never want to "go off on a rabbit trail."

The resolutions of the World Congresses of Fundamentalists are a clear, strong testimony to the great heritage that has been handed down to biblical Christianity. If we ever stop examining ourselves and become timid about speaking the truth, taking the proper stand, or being willing to attack the enemy with no holds barred, we will hand down a weak and anemic Fundamentalism to the next generation. We are in the process of planning our Congress for the year 2000, and we want to give a clear call to the world that biblical Fundamentalism is alive and well, still standing for the Word of God and the fundamentals of the faith. We oppose any and all error that is in the world today that would attempt to rob our Lord of His proper preeminence. This is true biblical ecumenism. This is the essence of the historic Christian faith, and it is strong and vibrant in the twenty-first century. This effort will continue under the very capable leadership of men like Dr. Bob Jones III, President of Bob Jones University, and Dr. Ian Paisley, the European Chairman.

THE FUNDAMENTAL BAPTIST FELLOWSHIP

The history behind the Fundamental Baptist Fellowship (FBF) is another milestone in my life. The FBF was founded in 1920, in opposition to the great modernist infiltration within our American Baptist Convention. It is the oldest Baptist "fellowship" in America, with a history that goes back over seventy-nine years. This story is well known in Baptist circles.

In 1976 Dr. G. Archer Weniger approached me and asked if I would consider becoming the thirteenth president of the FBF. Again, I reminded myself that I was not looking for "another job"; I told him I would pray about it. Well, I prayed about it, and God gave me "another job."

We met in Chicago at the O'Hare Airport Hilton and reorganized the Fundamental Baptist Fellowship. Our first national meeting in 1976 consisted of thirty-five laymen and seventeen pastors. Now, across the nation, there are ten regions and numerous satellite, state, and local meetings. I can in no way take the credit for what God has done through the FBF; it has been His work, performed through the sacrifice of many of God's dear servants. I merely raised the banner, and men rallied around that banner. It has been a sacrifice at times and a challenge to many of God's choicest servants across the nation, who have taken time away from their churches and from their pulpits to strengthen others and be a blessing. I thank God for the people of Tabernacle Baptist Church. In no way could I accomplish what has been done and maintain a demanding schedule were it not for loyal, loving, godly, sacrificial people. They were willing to "give me up" so I could try to strengthen and lift up the hands of preachers across America.

One of the hardest things I have ever done in my ministry is to leave my people when I know they need me. I am their shepherd; I want to be with them. Often I have sat on the runway, in airports, and in motels weeping because I had to be away from my people and my pulpit. But God had shown me that this was what I must do. I felt there were so many other preachers, more capable than I, who could have done a much better job, but there was a need. When I look at what God has done in the last twenty-three years, I marvel at His extraordinary blessings upon this ordinary man. The "mantle of the mountain man" lives on. Our God is a sovereign God, who plans His work and then works His plan.

Some of the most godly men I have worked with have been those I met through our Fellowship. I've had the privilege of working with Drs. Hugh Hamilton and Earl Barnett, FBF comoderators in Alaska, who have faithfully served God there for thirty years, taking a clear-cut stand for the fundamentals of the faith. Their vision for the work established a regional FBF meeting in the frontiers of Alaska.

Dr. James Singleton of Tempe, Arizona, and Dr. David Innes, of San Francisco, California, have helped to pioneer the western region of the Fundamental Baptist Fellowship. We have crisscrossed this country together, up and down and across America, and around the world too; God has used them mightily.

Dr. Marion Fast, a brother whom I dearly love in the Lord, has been greatly used, along with Dr. Ed Nelson, to establish the Rocky Mountain region of the Fundamental Baptist Fellowship. Their mantle has been most recently shared by Dr. Matt Olsen and Rev. Jeff Musgrave.

Dr. Wayne Van Gelderen Sr. and Dr. Frank Bumpus, two of my dearest friends, now with the Lord, were greatly used of God to develop one of FBF's strongest regions, the mid-American region. Schaumburg, Illinois's historic Bethel Baptist Church has been the site of some of our greatest meetings. Then there is the mid-Atlantic region, headed by Dr. Rick Arrowood and Dr. Bennie Moran. These two men have sacrificially given of their time and talent, traveling hundreds of miles as they established the mid-Atlantic region. The Fellowship is greatly indebted to them.

In the Northeast, Drs. Gary Jones, Paul Henderson, and Chuck Phelps took the helm in the cold New England area, now one of our strongest regions. The Northeast is seeing a hunger for the purity of God, for holiness, and for God's revival fire.

In the Southeast, Dr. Walter Kirk and Dr. John Vaughn have rallied the troops behind the FBF. One of the highlights of my ministry in the FBF occurred during our seventy-fifth anniversary meeting at Dr. Vaughn's Faith Baptist Church. My message, "His Hand Clave unto the Sword," was taken from II Samuel 23:10. I had no idea I would be presented with "the sword." The FBF presented me with the "Cutting Edge Sword," a beautiful, shiny, five-foot-long warrior's sword with finely honed, razor-sharp edges. This magnificent weapon, symbolizing the "sword of the Spirit," the Word of God, will be passed down to future generations of Fundamentalist leaders.

The Caribbean region, of which Dr. Johnny Daniels is our moderator, is one of our largest regions and includes representatives from several of the islands. We have had great meetings, trying to be a blessing to the West Indies. What a joy it is to go to their islands, meet their people, preach, and help them take a strong stand for the historic fundamentals of the faith and their Baptist heritage.

It has been a distinct privilege to be a part of the Fundamental Baptist Fellowship. Though it is a ministry of sacrifice for many men, I count it an honor that God allowed me to have a small part, working with some of God's choicest servants. We are planning to open up more regions across the nation and into Mexico and Canada. It looks as if the FBF has "come to the kingdom for such a time as this." Godly men have rallied around the banner. My prayer is that we've been able to encourage the many Fundamentalists who stand alone in remote places around the world.

Frontline magazine, a publication of the FBF, is published bi-monthly and is now in its tenth year. God has used this timely publication to strengthen the hands of Fundamentalist Baptists. We have tried to make it an informative magazine, dealing with current issues and trends in such a manner as to strengthen and encourage Christian families. There is no way the FBF could have produced this publication were it not for the sacrifice of the Bethel Baptist Church, Dr. Frank Bumpus, and his staff, who gave birth to this "missionary endeavor." Despite our inexperience in this area, we felt there was a need to get this resource into the homes of Christians all over America; and by the grace of God, we just "stepped out," and God did it! Dr. John Vaughn has recently become the editor of *Frontline* and Executive Director of the FBF. He has done an excellent job, improving the quality and format of the magazine.

My people have been very understanding in accepting my schedule as I travel extensively for the FBF, various conferences, and mission endeavors. I remember one of our dearest saints who was on her deathbed. I was scheduled to speak in Tempe, Arizona, and I went to see Mrs. McDaniels on Sunday afternoon. "Mrs. McDaniels, I hate to leave you, but I've got to go speak in Arizona Monday. And I have to speak the last part of the week in Sacramento, California. But if you feel you need me, I'll be more than happy to stay."

"No, Preacher, God's opened the doors for you to preach; you go and preach. Don't you worry about me. I'll be all right. I wouldn't feel right for you to miss services."

Before I realized what I was saying, I told her, "Well, if you die, give me a call, and I'll come back and preach your funeral."

She chuckled, "That would sure be long distance because I would be in heaven."

Then, red-faced, I realized the mistake I had made. I went on to Tempe, Arizona, and as I preached that Monday night, someone told me Mrs. McDaniels had passed away. I immediately caught a plane, flew all night, and preached her funeral on Wednesday. I then caught a plane Thursday, went back to Sacramento, California, and preached Thursday and Friday. I flew back home Saturday and was in the pulpit on Sunday.

Trying to be a pastor and trying to be president of the Fellowship has not always been easy. I often wonder if Dr. Bob Sr. was right when he said, "Duties never conflict." They may not conflict, but I think they overlap quite a bit!

CHAPTER 12:
Missions

Going on mission trips has always been a vital part of our ministry. Since my life-threatening surgery in 1989, I've made more mission trips than at any other time in my life. The doctor keeps warning me to be careful, that in my condition I could catch some "bug" very quickly. But I don't know about that. The Scripture tells me, "And as thy days, so shall thy strength be." I want to do everything I can for my Lord during my "extension of time." I believe one of those things is to serve our missionaries. Many times missionaries feel alone—"out of sight, out of mind." We try to spend as much time as possible visiting those whom we have trained and sent forth.

I'll never forget the time I took Dr. James Singleton with me, and we went to visit missionaries in Thailand, Burma, Japan, and Singapore. As we went into these countries, we had some rich experiences. When we visited Burma, I wanted to see where Adoniram Judson baptized his first convert. I went down to the muddy river and had Dr. Singleton take my picture. We weren't there a minute when along came a soldier saying, "No picture, no picture." We left there as quickly as we could. Burma's government is very strict, and the country has very little religious freedom.

Another interesting incident occurred when we were in Thailand, on the Cambodian border. We had breakfast in one of the little villages. As the missionary took us out through the jungles, we saw little huts built upon stilts. We observed a woman throwing a net out into the murky water. "What's she doing?" I asked.

The missionary replied, "Grocery shopping. She's fixing your breakfast."

That reminded me of my mother up in the Appalachian Mountains, who would "grocery shop" out in the hills to feed our hungry tummies.

We greeted each other and, after a while, she pulled from that pond a luscious eel. She was dressing the eel, and she reached inside the eel and pulled out some eggs. Throwing the entrails away, she placed the eggs together with some fish, herbs, and spices into a pot. We sat under the roof of the bamboo hut, and I asked God to help me "miss" my mouth and make it look like I was eating. I thought I had seen poverty in Haiti and India, but this was some of the worst. Thank God for faithful missionaries who serve in these remote areas, men like Jim Hayes and his family in Thailand.

I almost left Dr. Singleton in the Burma airport. When I got through customs and was preparing to board the plane, the Burmese authorities took Dr. Singleton aside, claiming he had failed to have his passport properly stamped. He protested, and they whisked him away. I called back to him jokingly, "I'll see you back in the United States, Dr. Singleton. I told you you couldn't get away with this!"

He's a dear friend, and we've had so many wonderful experiences, preaching and travelling together for over twenty-five years.

My first trip to Bangalore, India, was to speak in a Congress of Fundamentalists regional meeting with Dr. Ian Paisley, Dr. Bob Jones Jr., and Dr. Jim Singleton. India is a great country, with a population of over 980 million people. It's a land that is very religious, a land of William Carey. It's difficult to explain

India's culture and its different religions, its vastness. There are eight religions representing over 338,000 gods. It is a country that needs the gospel, but it is closed to American missionaries. They say you have freedom of religion in India; you can preach what you believe, but you cannot try to make converts or preach against another religion.

Through our Bible college and seminary extension work, we have helped to start Dr. Kumar's and Dr. Franks's works. In 1997 I preached the commencement exercise in both their seminaries and Bible colleges. Each has a Bible college and a seminary—one is in Bangalore and the other in Tirpattur, about five or six hours south of Bangalore. I have tried to be a pastor to our missionaries, especially the men who have come up through Tabernacle Baptist Ministries and gone out under our local church.

I went to India in 1997 and saw the hand of God throughout our trip. One of my church members, a Christian businessman named Henry Jordan, had been saved in our church years ago. He is a dear friend and faithful servant to this pastor since my near-death experience, and he wanted to go with me to "look after me." My doctors told me not to try to make this kind of trip with my physical condition and digestive system being as it is. I have no stomach and no spleen. I could very easily get some kind of dysentery or other "bug" that would do me in, but I felt that I should go. Brother Henry went with me to "carry my bags."

From day one, everything that *could* go wrong *did* go wrong. We arrived in New York only to find our reservations to India had been cancelled, despite the fact that our tickets had been issued and were in our hands. On our way to India, we stopped off in Ireland and joined another one of my men, Hap Barko, to speak at Dr. Paisley's Easter Convention. We had great fellowship and a blessed time in Belfast.

After the Easter Convention, Henry and I went on to India. We arrived in India in the middle of the night, but our faithful missionaries were at the airport to pick us up. We were so glad to see a face that we recognized. Dead tired, we spent the night with the Kumars—Dr. and Mrs. Kumar and their children gave us their bedroom and opened their home to us. They treated us like kings and made sure that we ate nothing that would make us sick. I've never been treated better, and I thank God for their hospitality.

We met Dr. Franks in Bangalore and had great services there. We were sitting upstairs in the Grace Baptist Church with Dr. Franks, and they were encouraging members of the congregation to increase their "Faith Promise" giving. As I listened to him expound the blessings of the Faith Promise plan, Dr. Franks mentioned a missionary who was dying of cancer. It caught my attention, and I listened more closely. Unbeknownst to the congregation, this missionary was one of our graduates who had married one of our teachers. Now, Dr. Franks's people were taking up an offering to help this missionary family. Here was a little church of about thirty-five to forty members, concerned about a missionary over twelve thousand miles away in the Marshall Islands, Chuck and Beth Manyo. How that thrills my heart to see the Faith Promise plan working.

The next night we preached the commencement exercise at Brother Kumar's school. What a joy it was to see eighteen young people graduate from his Bible college and to see the great work they are doing. Next, we drove out to see the orphanage and the new facilities and campus where Shalom Baptist Church is being built. What a joy it was to see the multitudes whose hearts were stirred to stand for the Word of God and the testimony of Christ in a good, strong, separatist, Fundamentalist Baptist church. As we prepared to lay the cornerstone, it thrilled my heart to read the inscription engraved on it:

Shalom Baptist Church Ministries
Foundation Stone Laid and Dedicated by
Dr. Rod Bell Sr, Founder and Pastor of
Tabernacle Baptist Church Ministries &
President of
Fundamental Baptist Fellowship
Virginia Beach, Virginia, USA
To the Glory of the Triune God
on the 4th of April, 1997
Christ said, "I will build My church" (Matthew 16:18).

The Kumars and Frankses are very special to me. I've seen God answer prayer in their lives, and they are truly taking the right stand. One time Dr. Kumar came to the United States from India, and he had a malignant tumor on his vocal cords. God used a doctor in our church to remove the cancerous tumor, and He gave him back his voice so he could continue to preach.

Another significant incident in his life occurred during another visit to our country a few years ago. He was suffering terribly from severe migraine headaches. I took him to our doctor, who thought a tumor could be returning to Dr. Kumar's brain. "If I were you," the doctor said, "I'd get him back to India as quickly as I possibly could."

I asked Dr. Kumar if he had the money to go back to India.

"Yes, I have the ticket: I can go back. I have no insurance here in America, and my doctors told me it could possibly cost $100,000 if surgery were necessary."

We asked him to have a CAT scan, which showed two spots on his brain. The Lord began to deal in my heart about sending him back to India. I asked Brother Kumar how he felt. "Well, I'm going to leave that up to you. If they operate on me here, I have no insurance; if I go back, I have it paid for, but I don't know when I can get it done."

We got on our knees and claimed a promise, "Commit thy works unto the Lord, and thy thoughts shall be established" (Prov. 16:3). Also, in James we are told that "if any man lack wisdom, let him ask of God, who giveth to all men liberally and upbraideth not." God will give us wisdom when we commit our work unto the Lord and we don't know what to do.

That's what we did that day in the office. As we prayed, the Lord gave me peace to put him in the hospital here, not to send him back to India. After we prayed, I said, "That's exactly what we should do."

We put him in the hospital, the doctors began to work on him, and they found out he had two blood clots on the brain. They removed those blood clots; they had come from a simple "bump on the head" when Brother Kumar was building his new building a few months before. When he got on the plane at high altitude, the tissues had begun to hemorrhage. The doctors told us that if we had put him back on the plane with those clots, the high altitude would probably have caused a stroke or massive brain hemorrhage. I thank God, for He is faithful!

As I was leaving India, a man introduced himself and said he had ridden the train four days to get to the dedication exercise. He was a Roman Catholic, and I had the joy of leading him to Christ. He was one of Brother Kumar's five cousins. The next day, Henry Jordan and I left with Brother Franks. As we went back by Grace Baptist Church and preached, we were told Mrs. Franks was very sick with a fever and dysentery. It was so hot in that little upper room. I asked them if she had a fan.

"Yes, we do," they replied hesitantly.

"Well, let's get the fan for her."

"Pastor, you have her fan because we put it in your room over at the Kumars so you'd be comfortable. She'll be all right."

I never knew such gratitude as was in my heart at that moment. I was so rebuked because of my selfishness, and I thank God for the spirit of these missionaries.

The next day we left for Tirpattur with Brother Franks's daughter Leah, a missionary nurse whom we support. We went to spend the night in Tirpattur after having a meal at the Frankses' home. I wanted to preach in the Jawadhi Hills. There are over sixteen villages that are not evangelized. Brother Franks's daughter is an excellent nurse, and she kept telling me it would be best for me not to go. They explained the potential dangers: "it would take so long to get back in there, the trip is too strenuous, and you might catch a bug, and if you do, you could dehydrate within a few hours." I wanted to go so badly. I thought, "If I go and I do catch a bug, then they can just plant me on the side of a hill because I want to preach the gospel to those who have never heard."

What a joy it was to be riding over the rough, rugged hills, through roads that were almost impassable. We stopped at about 10:00 P.M. and entered the first village. The first thing I knew, there were over six hundred people around us, sitting on the cold, damp ground with their children. For two hours they listened to us preach and tell the story that two thousand years ago there was another hill called Calvary. And on that hill, God's Son died for their sins. I told them I was also a mountain boy who heard that old story, and I believed it. And someone else believed and told another. How my heart beat with joy to be able to tell them of His grace.

A little boy from back in the mountains of West Virginia now had the privilege to travel twelve thousand miles to tell them the same story. My mind went back through the tunnel of time to when that little boy on the side of a hill would get out behind his house, look up in the face of a starry heaven, and say, "Is there a God? And does that God care? And would that God, in the middle of the night, accept my thanks for being introduced to the Lord Jesus Christ?" He put a burden in my heart to tell the story.

I went back to Dr. Franks's home and spent the day getting ready to return to Virginia Beach. That night, Henry Jordan became very ill. As we got on the plane, he was stricken with severe dysentery. We arrived in Bombay and were told we'd have to wait until 4:00 the next morning, but we'd get our tickets to go back to New York.

We returned at 4:00, but no ticket, no reservation. They had bumped us. They told us they had bumped about three hundred passengers, and it was one of the biggest messes I'd ever seen in my life! I looked at my buddy; I knew he was getting sicker and sicker. "We'll get out of Bombay tonight; if anything leaves for London, we're going," I told him.

We caught Air Canada into London and finally arrived in New York. Henry was very ill. We got him into Norfolk and put him immediately in the hospital, where he was treated by several exotic disease specialists brought in just for him. After five or six days, he was on the mend. I look back over that trip and thank God for the love of a church member who loved his pastor and looked after him. Thank God for the love of those missionaries, the Frankses and the Kumars. Thank God for the blessing of their concern, trying to make sure that I did not get sick. Thank God I did not! Mrs. Franks got sick, all the missionaries got sick, their daughter (the nurse) got sick. But to God be the glory, He is faithful! He protected me, and I did not get sick. I made it back and had a greater burden for the Jawadhi Hills and a greater burden for India. Oh, that we might train some young men to take the gospel into that country and tell the people the old, old story.

Part 4:

A Mountain Man Remembers

CHAPTER 13:
Great Men of God

FRANK BUMPUS

Frank Bumpus was my lifelong friend from college days. I've seen Frank go through the fire and come out as pure gold. Frank was known by his friends as one of the most compassionate yet firm preachers in Fundamentalism. He was a man of conviction and was affectionately known as the "Bulldog of Fundamentalism." Frank had lost one son (killed in an accident); another son is a paraplegic. I have had the joy of spending many hours of fellowship with this dear brother. I thank God for the great church and the great testimony he maintained over the years in mid-America. His wife, Ruth, and their daughter and son-in-law, Brad Smith, are like family to us. Frank went to be with the Lord on March 5, 1999. I had the privilege of preaching his funeral. Despite a frigid Midwest blizzard, the two-thousand-seat auditorium was packed to overflowing with people wishing to remember and honor this great man of God.

Frank had been diagnosed with leukemia in 1993. I made three trips to Schaumburg to check on him and preach for him, to meet with his staff and deacons, and so on. He had a huge building program. He was a modest man of very few words. He told me once, "I don't want to go to heaven and leave my people in debt. Let's pray that God will pay off this huge mortgage before I go." He and I sneaked around the corner into an unfinished room and prayed. We claimed Matthew 18:19—"If two of you shall agree on earth as touching anything that they shall ask, it shall be done for them of my Father which is in heaven." I asked God to let Frank live until he got the building paid for. That was about six years ago. The building was almost paid off when he went to be with the Lord.

They say you can count your true friends on one hand. Frank Bumpus was one of those I count as a true friend. I never will forget the night I received a call from Dr. Bumpus. "Brother Rod, I need someone to pray with me."

He was going through deep water with one of his sons who was at the point of death.

I got on a plane and flew to Chicago. Frank picked me up, and we drove in the rain all night, up and down the streets of Chicago. Tears streamed down our faces as the rain ran down the windshield. We were struggling with the will of God—Frank's loss of one son in an accident and his other son lying at the point of death. The Charismatics were accusing Frank, claiming that these trials were a curse from God brought on after they (the Charismatics) had turned his family over to the Devil for the "destruction of the flesh." These people had been voted out of the church for speaking in tongues. It was one of the most trying times my preacher buddy had gone through. But as we drove through the dark streets of Chicago in the rain, a verse kept coming to my mind, "God is faithful." And our God *is* faithful—He honored Brother Bumpus and used him in a great way to build a church whose testimony reaches across the nation and around the world.

After the night of prayer and driving up and down the streets of Chicago, Frank took me back to the airport. I got on the plane and flew home, with the assurance in my heart that God is faithful. He's too good to do wrong and too wise to make a mistake.

BOB JONES JR.

What can I say about Bob Jones Jr.? What does a scholar, a teacher, an author, a poet, an orator, a great Shakespearean actor, an art collector, a mentor—one of the twentieth-century giants of Christianity—have in common with a mountain man? I spent over ten years under his tutelage, starting my freshman year at BJU in 1957. God took me from a poor drunkard's home in the mountains of West Virginia and allowed me to become friends with Dr. Bob Jr., who was not only my friend but also my "father in the faith." He did not always tell me what I wanted to hear, but what he thought. You did not ask Dr. Bob a question if you didn't want to hear the truth! I miss his voice, his wisdom, and his counsel so very much. He helped me when I needed help. He came to my aid when no man stood with me. I would look around and there stood my "father in the faith"—Dr. Bob. I've heard him say so many times, "We always seem to come to the same conclusion." With a twinkle in his eyes, he continued, "You know, it may be because we believe in the same Book!"

I'll never forget the first time Bob Jones came into our home. My two boys, Tim and Rod, were just little fellows, maybe four or five, and we had given them strict orders—"Dr. Bob Jones is coming, and I want you boys to behave." Before we knew it, Dr. Bob sat down, took off his shoes, crossed his legs, and was giving my boys a horsey-ride while they sat on his foot! The boys taught Dr. Bob an old mountain song:

> *Bill Grogan's goat was feeling mighty fine,*
> *He ate three sheets from off the line;*
> *He coughed them up with a terrible hack,*
> *And butted the train right off of the track.*

Lenore and I smiled at each other, charmed by the sight of our little boys playing with Dr. Bob in our living room.

The other day I looked through my files at the letters I had received from my "father in the faith." As the tears streamed down my cheeks, I still cannot believe that God allowed me to have a friend like Bob Jones Jr.—I still have to say it was all of God's grace. Oh, how many times he encouraged me when my back was "against the wall." So many times I would call him for advice, just to "run something by him." What do you think about this or that? And he would always give me his opinion.

"Son, you pray about it. Don't you do it because I said to do it. You pray and get God's mind on this thing. Do what you feel God wants you to do."

I thank God for that kind of spirit and attitude he had. He passed a great legacy down to us younger preachers—a legacy we must pass down to the next generation.

Not only was he a man of compassion, he was a man of conviction. He had conviction that the Bible was the authoritative Word of God, divinely inspired and absolutely without error. The Bible was God's authoritative voice. He had convictions about separation from apostasy. He denounced the apostates and attacked the wicked, politically corrupt system of our day with the fire and the fervor of a young man, even though he was twenty-five years my senior. He had such keen discernment and insight; I believe he could smell compromise and error. If there were ever a man with a brilliant intellect and keen insight, it was Dr. Bob.

I listened with amazement every time he stood to expound the Word of God. Like a master artist, Dr. Bob painted word pictures in our minds when he preached and made the Book come alive.

"Lazarus! Come forth!" he preached with the trumpetlike tones of authority.

You could almost see the flesh coming back on Lazarus's bones, the grave clothes being unwrapped.

When he preached about God and Adam walking through the garden, you walked alongside them. You could smell the sweet fragrance of Eden in the air, you could touch the stones, you could feel the soft breeze as his words wafted across your soul.

When he preached Christ, you could see Christ's wounds at Calvary, you could feel His pain and the agony of Gethsemane. You could hear the shouts and jeers of the crowd. When he preached, you saw Christ, not Bob Jones.

I'll never forget the time he was getting ready to preach and his front tooth (a crown) fell out. Here he was with nothing but a steel peg in his mouth where the tooth had been! He looked at me, "What in the world am I going to do?"

"Just hang on, my brother, I'll fix it."

I got some "Crazy Glue." Dr. Bob looked at it and at me. "Just be careful; don't glue my mouth shut! If you do, the modernists will love you, and some Fundamentalists might too!"

I was very careful as I tried to put the glue on his tooth and then work that tooth back onto the peg. We had just finished and it was time to go preach. I sat there and watched him preach, with the Crazy Glue holding the tooth in place. I didn't get much from the sermon that day; I was praying that the Crazy Glue would hold!

My, how he exalted Christ and lifted up the living Savior. I loved to hear him preach and brag on Christ. He was a Christ-centered preacher and always stirred our heart to love our Lord more. When I was growing up as a young preacher, I determined to "hold myself accountable" to five men of God, of which Dr. Bob Jr. was one. I took Dr. Bob Sr.'s advice, "You can borrow brains, but you cannot borrow character." I always sought the counsel of Dr. Monroe Parker, Dr. G. Archer Weniger, Dr. Bob Jones Jr., Dr. Ian Paisley, and Dr. Gilbert Stenholm (who was like a "walking encyclopedia" regarding issues and trends in contemporary theology). I praise the Lord for these men. With the exception of Dr. Paisley, they are all gone now, and I miss them so. I count it such a privilege to have walked with these men and many others, too numerous to mention.

Dr. Bob Jr. and I were preaching on a street corner in Belfast to a mighty crowd one evening. To hear that clarion call to the gospel ring out from the Chancellor's lips and watch him preach on the resurrected Christ—my heart beat with joy just to be able to stand by him and then take my turn and preach. On another occasion, he and I were in Northern Ireland getting ready to make a visit to Victoria Hospital, which was located in the "bad country" in an Irish Republican Army (IRA) stronghold. The IRA murdered many of the patients in that hospital. We had two jeeps full of policemen—one in front and one behind us, while we were in armored cars. There were twelve to fifteen policemen with us while we made the hospital visit. As we exited the armored car, soldiers formed a ring around us, shoulder-to-shoulder, as we walked into the hospital, up the stairs, and into the room. We were there to visit the Reverend Wiley, one of Dr. Paisley's friends who helped him get started in the Free Presbyterian movement. You could feel the tension in the air because, many times, the IRA would come right into the hospital and shoot people. But like Elisha, we were surrounded with a "ring of fire" (the soldiers).

I watched Dr. Bob climb into the back of the jeep with the soldiers with machine guns, as we made our way back from the hospital, and I thought, "What if we preachers in America required that kind of protection before we could make a hospital visit to one of our people?" Such a thing here in America is almost beyond comprehension. But our experience in Belfast shows the awesome power of the IRA terrorists. These people are bloodthirsty, brutal murderers, willing to shoot you down right in a hospital.

On another occasion in Northern Ireland we went out with Dr. Paisley to the "badlands" on the border, to dedicate an Orangemen's (a Protestant fraternal organization) Hall. We had been told not to go to the dedication out there because it was extremely dangerous. As we marched down the road with bag-pipes playing, we could see camouflaged soldiers with paint on their faces, hidden along the roadside. We had "angels unaware" guarding us! It is quite an experience to try to preach under those conditions. Dr. Jones and Dr. Paisley taught me that nothing can stop God's man until God is through with him. God has a sovereign purpose and plan, and we are His merchandise until He is finished with us and takes us home.

Many times I've had the privilege of preaching with Dr. Bob in Alaska at our FBF meetings. One time while we were preaching, a moose came up to the door and looked in the window. Everyone was distracted from Dr. Bob's sermon, watching the moose. Dr. Bob said, "Don't get your eyes on that big moose on the outside, but watch the mouse on the inside!" Everyone chuckled, and he controlled the crowd while the moose went from window to window. Dr. Bob kept us spellbound. He could turn chaos into calm.

Another time, we were touring in Northfield, Massachusetts (home of D. L. Moody). Dr. Bob and I bowed at Moody's grave and prayed that God would never allow the campus of Bob Jones University to become like the modernistic, liberal, heathen school that Northfield has become. We prayed that God would destroy BJU first, without one stone left upon another, rather than allow it to become like Northfield—they didn't even know who D. L. Moody was. Dr. Bob walked into the place, and I could see tears in his eyes as he saw the sorry shape the school was in. We found Moody's letters strewn here and there and Spurgeon's Bible (which Spurgeon had bequeathed to Moody). I picked the Bible up and had my picture taken with it behind Moody's pulpit. I cherish that moment—to have a time of fellowship with God's dear man.

Whenever I preached at the various World Congresses, before several thousands of people, Dr. Bob would pat me on the knee and say, "Let 'er rip, Rod. Be yourself, and preach." That was such an encouragement to me because I knew I could not preach with the eloquence of Bob Jones or with the doctrinal expertise and theological oratory of Dr. Paisley. I just had to be myself—that "old crooked stick" God had saved back in the mountains. But God covered us with the same blood from the same cleansing stream called Calvary. We were in the same family, brothers in Christ. There was a closeness between a mountain boy and a member of British and European Parliaments, standing shoulder-to-shoulder with Bob Jones, Chancellor of BJU, one of the wisest men I've ever met.

He was a "man of steel and velvet." Often he joked, "Rod, you are a perfect example that even God can make a silk purse out of a sow's ear!" In other words, "You can take a man out of the mountains, but you can't take the mountains out of a man." He was a most compassionate, kind, understanding, and gentle man—truly a man who lived for others. I praise God for the privilege of allowing our pathways to cross, whether in the jungles of the Philippines or the blazing heat of Mexico on our way to help a missionary.

Dr. Bob and I took our wives to Puerto Rico on the Joneses's fortieth anniversary (Lenore and I were celebrating our twenty-fifth anniversary). We were preaching at a meeting in Puerto Rico, and we decided to take our wives to St. Thomas (a neighboring island) and go shopping. Dr. Bob said unenthusiastically, "I'll go, but I won't enjoy a minute of it!"

That's what I always liked about him—you always knew what he was thinking. He didn't mind telling you. So we went and stayed about thirty minutes. He looked at me, "Do you like this place? You've seen one old dusty island, you've seen them all! Let's go. They can come back when they want to!"

So we caught a plane back and enjoyed the rest of the evening together in a nice, cool, air-conditioned room!

Had it not been for Dr. Bob and his wise counsel, I would have gone off on many an extreme position. He is a man God used in my life to give me balance—to know where and when to "draw a line in the sand." I'll always be grateful for the balance he gave me, and the love and patience with which he developed me. He didn't have to do that, but he did.

I've thought so often, "What does a mountain boy from the slums of a tarpaper shack and a bootlegger's den have in common with a Shakespearean actor, scholar, educator, statesman, orator, preacher, a man of a hundred talents?" It still baffles me that he was my friend, and I know he was my friend. He loved me, and I loved him like a father, and I miss him. He filled a place in my life that no man could ever fill, and when I heard that the Lord had taken him to glory, I cried like a baby. Lenore and I loved him as a father. We will always cherish that week shortly before his "home-going" when, in God's providence, He allowed Dr. Paisley and me to be in Greenville together. We had been asked to join Dr. Alan Cairns for the twenty-fifth anniversary celebration of his Free Presbyterian Church there in Greenville. Dr. Bob called Dr. Paisley and me together and told us he wanted to see us every day, that we were to be his "chaplains." His mind was crystal clear; he had his usual wit and a sparkle in his eye. He talked about the things of the Lord, about the good things of Christ, and how the Lord had taught him so much.

"Ah, blessed thought! Just to think that, throughout eternity, we will get to know Him. It will take all of eternity just for us to get to know Him," he said.

I thought, "What fools we are, to think that we know something about Christ, when we know so very little. We've only scratched the surface."

He put a thirst in my heart to know Him, not just about Him.

I count those moments the greatest privilege I've had in my sixty-four years. I was so humbled to be asked by the Jones family to represent all the preachers from all over the world, to speak on their behalf, at Dr. Bob's funeral.

I keep remembering Dr. Bob as he would say, "Be yourself, Rod. You can do it." He was a real encourager, a real Barnabas to me. We shared many private moments and personal thoughts together. He was my mentor, my friend, my teacher; he helped guide me and gave me a balance I never had before. I saw a side of Dr. Bob that few people see—I saw compassion and tenderness, a childlike honesty, a transparency, a humble, contrite heart that loved and sought souls for Jesus. He was every inch a man after God's own heart. I count it one of the highlights of my life to have traveled around the world and to have preached alongside this mighty man of God on hundreds of occasions.

I appreciate his counsel and wisdom; you learn so much just by watching and listening as you're with these giants. I told them I would "carry their old socks" just to be around them. I remember one time, during a political campaign, Dr. Paisley had walked so much that he had blisters on his feet, and his feet were rubbed raw. I washed his feet, dressed them with ointment, and put white socks on them. He preached that night in house slippers. Of course, no one knew because his feet were behind the pulpit. But I count it an honor just to be around these great men of God. Every time I've been with these two men, my heart has been stirred to study the Word, to love the Lord, to have a greater prayer life, and to stand courageously for the fundamentals of the faith, regardless of the consequences. I will be forever in debt to them.

I feel that one of the best ways I can express my appreciation for Dr. Bob Jones Jr., my friend and my father, is to share the eulogy that I gave at his home-going:

DR. BOB JONES, CHANCELLOR
MEMORIAL SERVICE EULOGY
Psalm 91:1-2

We are not here today to deify a man, but to glorify that man's God. The best way to do that is for the world to see his good works and glorify his Father which is in heaven.

I am greatly honored to have been asked to represent the Fundamentalist preachers. What can be said to pay proper tribute and honor to a man like Dr. Bob Jones, Chancellor? Dr. Bob was a fundamental, Bible-believing, Christ-honoring preacher. He preached Christ crucified; he magnified the Blood, the Book, and the Blessed Hope.

He stood without apology "for the old-time religion." He was a separatist, and he cried long and loud against apostasy and the ecumenical movement. He constantly warned against that movement and pseudo-Fundamentalists.

His voice caused the modernist to tremble. It caused the soft preachers to check up and take stock. It caused the worldly religious system of Babylon to hate and deride him.

Among Fundamentalist preachers, Dr. Bob was our champion, our leader, our voice. The church has not reproduced his equal in this century. His passing marks the end of an era, as it was with Moses.

He was the giant among giants. He was God's giant "redwood," yet he treated us "saplings" as his peers. His shadow has passed through the lives of thousands of preachers. It has been a great privilege to have known him; to have known him is to truly love him; our lives will never be the same. Dr. Bob was a man of character, conviction, and compassion.

How can mere words fully express our heartfelt, godly love for the Chancellor of this great University? He was a man recognized for his many abilities and talents, but in his heart he was a preacher—an uncompromising proclaimer of redeeming grace found only in the Savior's blood. Yes, he was first and foremost a preacher! Whether it was in the bustling city of Seoul, Korea, or on the street corner in Belfast, or in a country church in the North Carolina mountains, or in the Ulster Hall in Edinburgh, Scotland, you could find him preaching the gospel with trumpet tones. He truly was a twentieth-century, circuit-riding, Fundamentalist preacher, and the world was his circuit.

To thousands of us preachers, he was a father who offered advice based upon deep biblical insight. He entreated and loved us as sons. When we needed encouragement, he was there. He taught us how to contend without being contentious. When in the heat of battle our backs were to the wall, he was there. We always felt free to seek Dr. Bob's counsel and gain his wisdom. His heart was tender and compassionate. He could be as hard as flint when it came to compromise, but tender and compassionate when it came to sinners and those in need. He was truly a man of "steel and velvet." We are going to miss him as a father to us all.

Then he was a friend to all those who feared God and kept His commandments. It made no difference what kind of denominational label a man wore. If he was a true biblical Fundamentalist, a true separatist, Dr. Bob was his friend. And if Bob Jones was your friend, he was your friend until the end.

He would stand by you when you were hardest hit. He was there, being identified with you and taking your kicks. He said to me one day, "Rod, you younger men are going to have to pay the price! I just regret that I will not be here to take your kicking for you."

Not only has Dr. Bob been a father and a true friend to thousands of preachers, he has also been faithful. What an example he has left for the younger generation. From the hot, burning sun of India, the humid heat of Mexico, the bumpy roads in the Philippines, or on the dusty islands of the sea, we would find Dr. Bob encouraging a missionary. While most eighty-five-year-old men would be enjoying a comfortable retirement, not our Chancellor, not our Dr. Bob. He looked for no easy way, but for the right way and the best way. Not sparing his physical strength or energy, the word *quit* was simply not in his vocabulary. He was faithful to the end. As it was said of Mary of Bethany, so it can be said of Dr. Bob, "He did what he could."

He was our example of one who knew how to finish the race, and he finished it well. He was a living example of the exhortation, "Be ye steadfast, unmoveable, always abounding in the work of the Lord."

I have had the privilege of preaching around the world with our Chancellor. Whenever I was with him, I always had a greater desire to pray more earnestly, a greater desire to study the Word of God more deeply, and a greater desire to love the Lord Jesus more dearly.

For Dr. Bob, the battle is over, the good fight has been fought, the Faith kept, the race is run, and the course is finished. His sword is sheathed; he is in the presence of the Lord whom he has served for over eighty years, and the Savior will reward him with a crown.

In Joshua 1:1-2 we read, God was giving Moses' eulogy, "Moses my servant is dead; now therefore arise, go over this Jordan." God has buried His worker, but His work must go on.

We must now pick up that sword and continue to do battle, following the example of our great "Comrade in Arms," until we, too, hear either the heavenly call to celestial rest or the sound of the trumpet when the Lord Jesus comes. Press on, weary saints! Some golden daybreak Jesus shall come, and we shall drop this old flesh and rise and seize the everlasting prize, and shout, while passing through the air, "Farewell! Farewell, sweet hour of prayer."

God help us preachers to be faithful. Numbers 23:10, "Let me die the death of the righteous, and let my last be like his!"

I am a man most fortunate to have known the Chancellor, to have had the opportunity to be trained and tutored under him, one-on-one, on hundreds of occasions as we've crisscrossed this country preaching. His kind has never been equalled in this century, and I'll always cherish those precious moments with this giant redwood.

IAN PAISLEY

I have had the privilege of "walking with giants." I feel greatly blessed to have been in the presence of great men like Dr. Bob Jones Sr., Dr. Gilbert Stenholm, Dr. Bob Jones Jr., Dr. Bob Jones III, Dr. Harold B. Sightler, Dr. Noel Smith, and Dr. Oliver B. Greene. So often I feel like a "wee sapling" among the giant redwoods. The influence of great men upon my life has had a dramatic effect. I've seen such men in all types of situations.

One of the biggest giants to me is Ian Paisley, from Ulster, Northern Ireland. I first became acquainted with the Free Presbyterians and Dr. Paisley while I was a student at Bob Jones University. Dr. Bob Jones Jr. had this bombastic, big man who had been in jail to come and preach in chapel. I was fascinated not only with his stature and his accent (his Northern Ireland brogue), but I was especially intrigued by this man's message. It was the freshness of heaven upon his life, in the reality of the resurrected Christ whom he magnified, that won and captured my heart.

I thought, "This man must be an independent Baptist because no Presbyterian preaches like that. Presbyterians in our country are dead, cold, fossilized, and apostate."

But when I met him, he said, "I am a Free Presbyterian; I've been set free from all of that, my brother."

Most people in the world do not know the Ian Paisley that I know. The world doesn't know the compassionate, hard-hitting, Christ-honoring, loving, honest man I know. The press has always tried to make Dr. Paisley look like a villain, but I've found that every time they try to make him look bad, God makes him look good. He has the spirit of the reformers and the prophets of old. I've enjoyed being with him and Dr. Bob Jr. in India, the Philippines, Singapore, Korea, Hungary, Australia, and Canada. What a joy it is to have traveled with those two "giants" and just be a tag-along.

I've had the privilege of being with him in the heat of the battle. He's allowed me to stay in his home, and his family has treated me as one of their own. His precious wife, Eileen, has a wit and humor that sustains her through the tremendous stress and pressure she withstands because of the situation in Northern Ireland. She supports her husband 100 percent; she is truly a "helpmeet" to him. He could not do the job he's called to do without her beside him.

You learn much about a man's family when you stay in his home and see his children. All the Paisley children love the Lord and are faithfully serving Him in various capacities. His twin sons, Kyle and Ian Jr., are a blessing to be around. Ian Jr. is an astute, intelligent politician with the wit and conviction of his dad. Kyle, a preacher, has the keen insight and expository genius of his dad. I believe Kyle will be a great leader in the Free Presbyterian movement. I've had him to speak in our Congresses several times, and I've had the privilege of speaking in his church. We've traveled and preached together in South America. It is clear to me that Dr. Paisley's "preaching mantle" has fallen upon Kyle.

I shall never forget the first time Dr. Paisley came to our church in 1970. Our new auditorium was packed, and there had been bomb threats because of Dr. Paisley's visit. The ecumenists were angry because we tried to take a stand for the Word of God and the testimony of Jesus Christ. One evening, I answered the phone; the caller said, "The hatemonger from Northern Ireland will not live to get out of Virginia Beach."

I immediately called the police. The next thing I knew, we had the city police, the state police, the SWAT team, and the FBI come. There were six or seven undercover policemen assigned to Dr. Paisley. They chauffeured him wherever he went and checked for bombs under the cars using dogs and special mirrors. They sat and guarded his hotel room all night. I went down to pick him up the next morning and as I started to knock on the door, some policemen stepped out from behind the bushes. Before I knew it, I was "spread eagle"! They made me identify myself, and I told them I was the preacher, Rod Bell. I had to show them some identification before I could get my speaker. This was the beginning of a long and fruitful relationship with one of God's choicest servants. I have never been around Dr. Paisley or the Free Presbyterians that I did not develop a greater hunger for the Word of God, a greater desire to pray, and a greater love for the Lord Jesus.

One of my first trips with Ian Paisley was to find the first missionary who came to America, who landed on Virginia's Eastern Shore. I asked Dr. Paisley, "A Presbyterian, Calvinist missionary? Coming as a missionary to win souls?"

"Ah, yes. He's here somewhere. We've got to find him."

Early one morning we got in the car, crossed the twenty-five miles across the Chesapeake Bay Bridge to Virginia's Eastern Shore, and traveled to Accomack, Virginia. We spent several hours inquiring in the town, but no one knew anything of a

"Francis Makemie." Finally, we found an old Presbyterian librarian.

"Yes. There's a marker, way out in the countryside here, but I doubt you'll be able to find it."

Dr. Paisley, like a bloodhound on the trail of a criminal, said, "We'll find it."

Off we went, out through the countryside, down trails, through the undergrowth. We found an old Presbyterian grave-yard. As we walked around through bushes and twigs, it was like a jungle; we found a statue of the first missionary the Presbyterians ever sent to America to evangelize the colonies. The man's name was Francis Makemie, and the inscription gave the town and the date.

We prayed, and Dr. Paisley prayed for God to keep evan-gelistic zeal and to give us a heart for souls like Makemie. Rod Jr., a lad of just fourteen, said, "Dad, I'll never forget this day." We stood there in the rain, where the history of this great man had almost been forgotten. Someone had taken a rifle and shot off half the face from Makemie's likeness on the statue.

Paisley said, "That's the devil's crowd. Even though he's dead, they're still taking shots at him! That's what they'll do to you and me too, Rod, after we pass through this vale of tears and sorrow. They'll still take potshots at us. "

Another time, Dr. Paisley and I met in Washington, D.C., for an extremely important appointment with Senators Strom Thurmond and Jesse Helms. Our appointment was for 4:00 in the afternoon, so we had the whole day to sightsee. I asked Dr. Paisley where he'd like to go.

"I'd like to see the Arlington House, Robert E. Lee's home, and the place where he stood when he made his decision to fight for the South instead of the North."

"I don't know if there is such a place."

"Oh, yes there is. I've read about it in the history books. Let's go, Son."

We got on a bus to Arlington Cemetery and went over to the Arlington House, made our way through the crowd, went to the caretaker, and asked him if there was such a place.

"Yes," he said, "There is one window where it is said that Robert E. Lee stood where he could look across the Potomac River and see the White House and up Pennsylvania Avenue to the Capitol."

Dr. Paisley asked, "Would you mind if I just went over there and stood for a few minutes?"

"Of course. Please do."

Doc usually got to do what he wanted to do because of his public stature—people knew who he was. They let down the rope, and he went over to the window and stood, with his head bowed. He stood in silence; I could tell he was praying. After a few minutes, he came back, and we viewed the rest of the house. Later in the day, I asked him, "Doc, why was that the place you were most interested in?"

"I wanted to stand in the footsteps of a man who had courage, and who had enough courage to turn down the opportunity to become the Chief Staff Officer of the United States Army and go with the Confederacy—not because it was popular, but because he had convictions. I always admire a man with convictions, and I wanted to thank God for a man named Robert E. Lee who had convictions. God, give us men today who, like Robert E. Lee, have convictions."

I've had the privilege for over twenty-five years of speaking at the Great Easter Convention at the Martyr's Memorial Free Presbyterian Church in Northern Ireland. What a privilege to be identified with a man and people who are not ashamed of the gospel of the grace of God, who have such a great zeal for souls and a world-wide mission outreach and who stand without apology against the one-world church and the mother of harlots, the Roman Catholic system.

The highlight of the Belfast Easter Convention, of course, is always what I call "Dr. Paisley's state of the union address." He preaches in the afternoon and gives the "challenge" for another year. The first time I saw the closing service of the convention, there were three thousand people standing and singing "God Be With You 'Til We Meet Again," waving white handkerchiefs. A sea of white handkerchiefs and cold germs—the most unsanitary service I've ever been in, but one of the most blessed.

The Free Presbyterians are a praying people. During my darkest peril, my son Rod Jr. called Dr. Paisley and told him I was in a bad way and that the doctors were not expecting me to live. Dr. Paisley went to the Lord in prayer. The next day, he called my wife back and told her that God had given him the assurance that I was going to live. The Lord gave him the assurance from the Word of God: "Epaphroditus, my brother . . . was sick nigh unto death: but God had mercy on him; and not on him only, but on me also, lest I should have sorrow upon sorrow" (Phil. 2:25-27).

The Free Presbyterians took me to the Lord in prayer. I received phone calls, letters, gifts, cards, and encouragement from all over Northern Ireland, Canada, and Australia from Free Presbyterian brethren who were praying. Still today I see them, and they tell me that they have held me up in prayer daily. I believe it. The power of prayer is evident in their lives and ministries.

In April of 1990, after my recovery, I again had the joy of speaking in the great Easter Convention. How wonderful it was to be able once again to preach and fellowship with our brethren of like precious faith! It was unusual the way that I felt through that time of recovery. I thought that if I could just get together with the brethren of like precious faith—if I could get around good, fundamental, Bible-believing men who love the Lord—I would be better, I would be stronger. God taught me a lesson: we draw strength one from another. We need to be encouragers and encourage those who are going through times of difficulty. I thank the Lord for that experience.

The schedule of the Easter Convention is not one you cherish. It is one that keeps you on the go and one that causes time to go by quickly. Those involved seem to forget when to go to bed and when to eat. We have enjoyed many good Chinese meals in Mrs. Paisley's kitchen, brought from the Chinese deli at 1:00 or 2:00 in the morning after services all day.

Dr. Ken Connolly and I had the privilege of speaking in the Cumberland Road Prison. There were over twelve hundred prisoners, all in for murder. This is the prison where Dr. Paisley had been incarcerated. He showed me his "suite" as we preached in there one Sunday morning. To see these men raise a hand for prayer and to see the power of God resting upon Dr. Connolly and Dr. Paisley as they preached was a unique experience. I had the joy of preaching in the prison from Matthew 11:28-30— "Come unto me, all ye that labor and are heavy laden, and I will give you rest."

Preaching on the street corners and in the city square at Belfast is one of the joys of going to Northern Ireland. As the accordion plays, songs are sung and testimonies given; then the Word of God is preached. There is a solemn stirring among the crowded streets of Belfast. The first time I preached there, the policemen instructed me, "If a motorcycle comes by and there are two men on the motorcycle, the one on the back will be the one to do the shooting, so hit the deck!"

Then they turned me loose and told me to go ahead and preach.

I thought, "Dear Lord, how can I ever get my mind off the motorcycle and on the Master?" But God enabled me to preach, and I had a great time and great liberty.

I honestly believe that I have been in every old bookstore in the British Isles and Northern Ireland. If any town has an old bookstore, Dr. Paisley knows where it is. We were in a bookstore in Northern Ireland, in Ulster, during a time when terrorism was rampant and bombings were frequent. We were on the floor, looking through the books, and a great blast went off down the street. People began to run and look to see what was happening. I got up and headed toward the door too.

Just then, Doc said, "Look, Rod. I think I found a good book. Look here!"

He found a volume for which he had been searching a long time. "There may be another one or two here."

We kept searching while everyone else was scampering to see what the bomb blasts were about. Here was a man who was more interested in books than the blast! I can't say I was ever that excited about a book. All I wanted to do was to get out of there in a hurry! But I never showed my concerns to him; we just kept looking for books. Later, we found out that the IRA had blown up a nearby car.

During one trip to the Easter Convention, I had just arrived when we went visiting together. Doc always visits his parishioners. We visited a policeman whose arms had been blown off by an IRA terrorist bomb. We visited with him in the hospital— a young man who had been maimed for life because of the brutality and senseless killings of the IRA.

The same day we visited the family of another man who had been blown up by a bomb. Paisley went to give his condolences. One of the constables came and said, "What are you doing here, Doc? Don't you know this is not a good place to be? This is not a secure place!"

Doc said, "These people are in my political district, and I always come to pray and offer my help to the bereaved."

The constable persisted, "Don't you know that that man was making a bomb to blow you up, and it exploded prematurely and killed him?"

"His family needs the prayer far more than I."

We prayed, and Doc prayed that God would save the family of this man.

The thing that has impressed me most about Dr. Paisley is that he always tells the truth. He is known as a man of his word. There's not a hair on his head that has even a hint of compromise. "The Big Man" (as they call him in Ulster) tells the truth, unlike our politicians today. The reason Dr. Paisley is so popular among his constituents, even the Roman Catholics in his district, is that they know he always tells the truth.

He is a man of great prayer, and he walks with the Lord. The modern media recently named Dr. Paisley the "Villain of the World"; they named Pope John Paul II the "Most Popular" and Billy Graham and Bill Clinton as the "Most Admired." We have, in my sixty-four years, seen the truth become a lie and a lie become the truth. Right is wrong, and wrong is right. The Deceiver is capturing the hearts of men. Truth is slain in the streets.

But thank God our God is faithful, and He will send revival: "if my people, which are called by My name, shall humble themselves and pray." As I heard the cry of the old-timers in Northern Ireland when they bowed to pray, "Oh, God! Remember '59. Remember '59," so may we cry out for revival. The great Fulton Street prayer meeting swept across the nation, and gave birth to the Second Great Awakening. It was an awakening of prayer because of the great economic and apostate conditions that existed in that day. May we get our heads out of the sand and beg God, "Do it again, Lord." As we face the twenty-first century, it is our only hope.

We were in Enniskillen, which is on the border and the home of one of the most notorious IRA men, who had been bragging that week that Dr. Paisley would die. We had a big tent pitched there, and we were preaching every night. The security was extremely tight. Needless to say, there were tense moments. The guards and policemen and the military were on the alert.

Dr. Paisley preached one night to a packed-out tent on "Whosoever shall call on the name of the Lord shall be saved." We saw many saved in this evangelistic service. On the last night, he preached on Revelation 17-18, the "Mother of harlots" (i.e., the Roman Catholic Church), and I never sensed such power in the atmosphere—it was electrifying.

He left that night and went back to Belfast; I stayed in the motel in Enniskillen because someone was going to pick me up at about 3:00 A.M. to catch a plane at Shannon. I went to bed about 11:00 P.M. I was trying to get to sleep, and all of a sudden, the door opened in my room, and I saw a silhouette of a man with a machine gun in his hand. I rolled out of bed and hit the floor.

"What do you want?" I asked.

I was scared to death; my heart, I know, was beating out of me. I thought that the IRA had me.

"I'm sorry, Dr. Bell, I thought you had gone to Belfast with Dr. Paisley."

It was the innkeeper standing in the door, and the "machine gun" turned out to be a broom in his hand.

"I'm sorry, go on back to sleep."

How in the world could you go back to sleep after you had been scared to death? Needless to say, I did not sleep any that night. I got up and got my clothes ready for my 3:00 pickup.

During one of my trips to Northern Ireland. I preached for Reverend Jim Beggs in Ballymena; my wife and I enjoyed being there and had a great time of blessing. Jim Beggs is Dr. Paisley's brother-in-law; he has a tremendous ministry and honors the Lord. I dedicated a new building in Toronto, Canada, for Dr. Frank McClellanden, another of my Free Presbyterian brethren. The blessing of God is on this work. I also had the privilege of preaching with Dr. Alan Cairns on the twenty-fifth anniversary of the Free Presbyterian church in Greenville, South Carolina. Those men have preached in my pulpit many times, and I have great respect for both the men and their message. They are God's men—faithful men; I count it an honor to have them as friends.

I preached in Glasgow, Scotland, for David Cassels at the Jock Troop Memorial Church, and I was introduced to Mrs. Jock Troop. As I was closing the service, she began to praise the Lord, saying how I reminded her of blessed Jock, her husband, a famous evangelist in Glasgow. I considered that to be a great honor and tribute coming from her.

I have had the privilege of preaching with many men in Northern Ireland and have always been treated with the utmost respect. My wife and I enjoy being with the people of Ulster and have had an open door there ever since 1976. Speaking at Dr. Paisley's Easter Convention has been a great blessing and challenge to me. I thank God for the spirit of brotherly kindness and fellowship and the sincere desire to serve the Lord in that fellowship with my Free Presbyterian brethren.

We have enjoyed countless hours of fellowship, traveling through Europe, India, Australia, Singapore, the Philippines, and across America, preaching together and fellowshiping one with another.

In 1983 we went to the Philippines. I discovered (the hard way) that I was allergic to mango. I broke out all over my body from an allergic reaction to mango juice. I was absolutely miserable and felt like Job, who scraped himself in the trash heap. Dr. Bob Jr. and Dr. Paisley came to my room to check on me. I was one large welt. They looked at me, then looked at each other.

"Well, I don't think it's cancer," said Dr. Bob.

"No, I don't believe it's cancer. What do you think it is, Bob?"

"I believe he has leprosy."

Dr. Paisley shook his head, "Yes, it's a sure case of leprosy, and maybe it's because of the friends he's been keeping!"

I thought, "All I need is some more jokes and encouragement from these guys!"

They had a good laugh; I didn't feel much like laughing, but their friendship and presence did make me feel better.

One year we held our World Congress of Fundamentalists in Sydney, Australia. The security was so tight they had to hide Dr. Paisley out in a farmhouse. I got a phone call: "Rod, I've got to have some steak!"

We went out and got something to eat. The security had become a burden instead of a blessing. The authorities would not let us use the huge amphitorium we had reserved because of the threats against Dr. Paisley. The World Congress of Fundamentalists was covered by the press with contempt. One newspaper headline stated, "A Vicar of Hate Met at Airport with Dogs." As we arrived and saw the headline, we felt this would be an unusual meeting. The Communists and the Catholics worked hand-in-hand, demonstrating and picketing against our meetings. But God blessed, souls were saved, the Lord Jesus Christ was honored, and a testimony was upheld despite the efforts of the ecumenical, one-world church. God's truth marched on!

In 1976 I was privileged to speak at the World Congress of Fundamentalists held that year in Edinburgh, Scotland. What a joy to see some of God's choicest servants from all over the world band together for the sake of Jesus Christ and to study the Scriptures. The theme of that Congress was from I Samuel 15:22—"To Obey Is Better Than Sacrifice." It was at this Congress that I became acquainted with the Free Presbyterian movement—the Fundamentalists of the British Isles and Europe, a group of men who have paid the price for their faith.

After the Congress, my wife and I rode on a train from Edinburgh down to Glasgow. As we rode on the train, we sang the old songs of the faith. We crossed the North Channel (between Scotland and Northern Ireland) by ferry. When we arrived in Belfast, buses took us to our respective lodgings.

I had the privilege of preaching with Rev. Stanley Barnes of Hillsboro, Northern Ireland. This was the beginning of a long friendship with my brethren in Ulster, Northern Ireland. I went back through our family history and discovered in County Antrim, Ulster, my "family roots." My family (the Bell clan) emigrated to the United States from Ulster. I have a solid kinship with these brethren; the Scotch-Irish blood runs deep in our veins.

I participated in my first "Cow Pasture Rally" with Dr. Paisley in Northern Ireland. When we arrived, I was thrilled to see a huge crowd of about ten thousand people waiting to hear God's man preach. As I walked through the cow pasture to the platform, I was told, "Watch out for the land mines!" I was looking around to see if I could find one when, suddenly, I stepped in one. Of course, the joke (as well as the "land mine") was on me because I had already been cautioned that the "land mines" were everywhere.

As we made our way to the platform, I saw army troops posted on each corner of the pasture and policemen on guard with machine guns up in the trees and around the cow pasture.

Needless to say, Dr. Paisley waxed eloquent, presenting a clear gospel message about the risen Lord, denouncing Rome and magnifying the Lord Jesus Christ. His cry rang out clearly, resounding through the valleys of the Ulster countryside. After a few minutes, he looked down to me and said, "Come up on the platform and give a word for our Lord." I felt I would surely make a good target for the terrorists, but I jumped up and, with fear and trembling, did the best I could do and told the old, old story.

One of the events that takes place in Northern Ireland every Easter is the street meetings, where we preach the gospel in front of Belfast's magnificent and historic city hall. It's quite a moving experience to go into a city besieged by terrorists and see firsthand the bombings, the senseless murders, and the ravishing of the young and innocent by the hand of the pope's "underground army," the Irish Republican Army (IRA). It is, indeed, frustrating to see the people in Northern Ireland suffer at the hands of terrorists, while the ecumenicals and the news media portray the terrorists as "the good guys."

My trip with Dr. Paisley to India in 1984 was an adventure of a lifetime! We were on our way from the Easter Convention to meet Dr. Bob Jones Jr. in Bangalore, India. Dr. Paisley was the final speaker, and he closed the convention late that night. We flew to London and took a motel room there so we could get a fresh start for our early morning flight to India. What an experience that was—driving in armored cars, having bodyguards with automatic weapons, eating and sleeping while bodyguards stood outside our door twenty-four hours a day.

As I walked with Dr. Paisley through the airport, one of the guards approached me and asked, "Are you naked?"

I thought, "What kind of character is this Paisley traveling with?"

Unbeknownst to me, the guard meant, "Are you carrying a gun?"

"Am I naked?!"

Dr. Paisley laughed, "You know, he's a Baptist preacher, and I wouldn't allow a Baptist preacher to have a gun around me." He gave the guard a big slap on the back, and we made our way through the airport to get on the plane.

We landed in Rome, Italy. We fueled up and took off again, landing in Kuwait in the middle of the morning. As the Arabs came onboard with their headdresses, I felt sure we were being hijacked, but then I realized these men were cleaning our plane.

When we landed in Bombay, it was mass confusion, to say the least. A small, dark man approached and ordered, "Give me your passports." We, like fools, handed the passports to him, not knowing who he was. As we stood there, it dawned on both of us that we had just given this stranger our passports in a strange country.

"Do you know that man?" I asked Dr. Paisley.

"No, I thought you knew him."

"I have no idea who he was."

"I didn't know him, either."

In a few minutes, the man returned.

"Come right this way." He took us through customs, and we were immediately on the plane to Bangalore. To this day, I believe this was very much an "angel of whom we were unaware," looking after two preachers in that foreign land. Only God in heaven knows!

We made our way to Bangalore and asked the taxi driver to take us to a nice motel. We were taken to one of the worst "flea bags" I've ever stayed in, with creepy-crawlies everywhere! We were eaten alive that night. We got up the next morning and tried to find Dr. Jones. He was right around the corner in a nice, five-star hotel! It always pays to plan.

We had the privilege of preaching in a Fundamentalist Conference in Bangalore. We drank no water but plenty of "limca" (a delicious lime drink), and we ate lots of rice and curry. The most important thing was that we got to preach the gospel and encourage God's people to stand for the fundamentals of the faith.

I will never forget one night when I was preaching against "Mary, the Mother of God." I had no idea that I was getting us into trouble with the authorities; I could have been deported for preaching against another religion. Dr. Jones and Dr. Paisley bailed me out, and I was able to stay in the country.

We preached in a tent, in 100-degree weather, for the graduation exercise of the preachers at Dr. Chelli's school. Seeing India that week was an unforgettable experience. Dr. James Singleton (of Arizona) and I were greatly honored to be in the presence of two giants, Dr. Bob Jones Jr., Chancellor of Bob Jones University, and Dr. Ian Paisley.

When we got ready to leave Bangalore and fly back to America, Dr. Bob Jr. took us to the airport. Dr. Paisley was late, and we thought he would miss the plane. The minutes ticked away, and we waited. Just before the plane was ready to pull away from the gate, there came Dr. Paisley, rejoicing. "Hallelujah! I just won my first Hindu to Christ!" He had been out sharing the gospel with our tour guide from that week.

We all rejoiced because we were leaving far richer than when we came, with a greater love and determination to stand for Christ. The greatest lesson I learned that week was how blessed America has been. When I see the poverty, the hundreds of thousands of false gods, and the religious confusion in the land of India, I can't help but thank God for our blessed land.

His Family & Background

right:
Rod's birthplace at Low Gap
below:
"The happy couple"
Dr. and Mrs. Rod Bell Sr.

below:
Great-grandfather Ball, with Great
Uncle and Great Aunt

below:
Great-grandparents - Laurie and
Lewis Baisden. Laurie died at age 104.

right:
Rod's basketball team, Danville
grade school, Danville, WV
from left to right:
back row: Mac Bell, Mike Star,
Jim McClure, Coach White,
front row: Aston Barker, and
"Bobbie Lee" Bell (Rod)

left:
Grandpa "Hen" Bell on "Old Jim"

above:
Raymond and Sybil Bell,
Woodie, Rod, Dennis, and Jim

below :
All the Bell clan, including the
dog (Maggie), Christmas 1995

left:
The Bell boys: Woodie,
Rod, Dennis, and Jim,
1942

below:
The Justice girls: Lenore J.
Bell, Angela J. Pharr,
Sandra J. Hoffman, and
Aileen J. Toler

below:
Bell and Jones families on TBC's
30th anniversary

His
Training
&
Early Adult
Years

left:
Rod (Dr. Bell), age 17, in
West Virginia State Gold Key
He had to borrow his uncle's suit and shoes
below:
Rod's graduation day from BJU, with Lenore's
parents, A. Peyton and Ruth Justice

below:
Pastor Bell receiving honorary doctorate

above:
Danville Baptist
Church, Rod and
Lenore married here,
1953 (Church has
since relocated)

right:
Lenore Justice, 1953,
in Carolyn Lee
Miller's home,
Madison, WV

His
Ministry

left:
Protest rally against
homosexuality in
downtown Norfolk

right:
Bootleg Corner
building used for
nursery 1958
The start of Mount
Calvary Baptist
Church in 1960

left:
Tent meeting, 1960
Danville, WV

above:
Ramage, WV, one-room school-
house; later a church
right:
Mt. Calvary, new auditorium,
1964 and Bob Jones Sr.'s last
earthly sermon preached here

left:
Baptism in the
Coal River near
Ramage Ball Park

above:
Drs. Bell and Paisley with Easter Conference speakers,
Belfast, Northern Ireland

above:
Dr. Bell with the first
missionary that his
church sent out,
Guy Smith.
left:
Dr. Bell receiving
"the sword" (FBF)

child: for more are the children of the desolate than the children of "the married wife, saith the LORD.

2 Enlarge the place of thy tent, and let them stretch forth the curtains of thine habitations: spare not, lengthen thy cords, and strengthen thy stakes;

3 For thou shalt break forth on the right hand and on the left; and 'thy seed shall inherit the Gentiles, and make the desolate cities to be inhabited.

4 Fear not; for thou shalt not be ashamed: neither be thou confounded; for thou shalt not be put to shame: for thou shalt forget the shame of thy youth, and shalt not remember the reproach of thy widowhood any more.

5 For thy Maker is "thine husband; "the LORD of hosts is his name; and 'thy Redeemer the Holy One of Israel; The God of the whole earth shall he be called.

6 For the LORD hath called thee as a woman forsaken and grieved in spirit, and 'a wife of youth, when thou wast refused saith thy God.

7 'For a small moment have I forsaken thee; but with great mercies will I gather thee.

8 In a little wrath I hid my face from thee for a moment: but "with everlasting kindness will I have mercy on thee, saith the LORD thy Redeemer.

9 For this is as the waters of Noah unto me: for "as I have sworn that the waters of Noah should no more go over the earth; so have I sworn that I would not be wroth with thee, nor rebuke thee.

10 For the mountains shall depart, and the hills be removed; but my kindness shall not depart from thee, neither shall 'the covenant of my peace be removed, saith the LORD that hath mercy on thee.

11 ¶ O thou afflicted, tossed with tempest, and not comforted, behold, I will lay thy stones with fair colours, and 'lay thy foundations with sapphires.

12 And I will make thy windows of agates, and thy gates of carbuncles, and all thy borders of pleasant stones.

13 And all thy children shall be taught of the LORD; and great shall be the peace of thy children.

14 In righteousness shalt thou be established: thou shalt be far from oppression; for thou shalt not fear: and from terror; for it shall not come near thee.

15 Behold, they shall surely gather together, 'but not by me: whosoever shall gather together against thee shall fall for thy sake.

16 Behold, I have created the smith that bloweth the coals in the fire, and that bringeth forth an instrument for his work; and I have created the waster to destroy.

17 No weapon that is formed against thee shall prosper; and every tongue that shall rise against thee in judgment thou shalt condemn. This is the heritage of the servants of the LORD, and "their righteousness is of me, saith the LORD.

CHAPTER 55

HO, every one that thirsteth, come ye to the waters, and he that hath no money; come ye, buy, and eat; yea, come, buy wine and milk "without money and without price.

2 Wherefore do ye 'spend money for that which is not bread? and your labour for that which satisfieth not? hearken diligently unto me, and eat ye that which is good, and let your soul delight itself in fatness.

3 Incline your ear, and "come unto me: hear, and your soul

870

above:
Street-preaching with Dr. Paisley in Belfast
right:
75th anniversary, FBF, in 1997 at Faith
Baptist Church, Taylors, SC. Dr. Bob
Jones Jr., Dr. Bell, Dr. John Vaughn, Dr.
Bob Jones III
below:
Dr. Bell, Virginia Governor John Dalton,
and other Baptist preachers who helped in
the cause (Church licensure issue/victory).

right:
Tabernacle Baptist Church
below:
Bells and Joneses trapped in cave in Barbados

below:
Drs. Bell, Paisley, O. Talmadge
Spence, Ken Connolly

right:
"Mountain Man" on horseback in
Bolivia, South America

CHAPTER 14:
The Darkest Hour

I know that my people love me, and they certainly know I am not perfect. They pray for me and follow my direction, even though sometimes I don't give the clearest of signals. I feel I sometimes take them for granted, and the Lord has dealt with me in these areas. The people whom God allows one to pastor are like sheep: they can be a blessing to the shepherd, or they can be a problem to the shepherd. But the blessings have always outweighed the problems. The "sheep" at Tabernacle have always followed me faithfully, which thought often frightens me. I must never disappoint or mistreat them.

I have seen my people rejoice in the spirit of giving—giving their automobiles, their homes, land, money, diamond jewelry, all their personal possessions—to get the work done and get the gospel out. I've seen them go to the bank and borrow money, mortgage their homes, and take out loans just to support God's work. This is evidence that the people have, first of all, given themselves to the Lord. No wonder God has used Tabernacle to get the gospel to the regions beyond our shores.

However, a crisis does not make character; it reveals character. The character of the people of Tabernacle Baptist Church was most clearly revealed during the darkest peril of my life.

One of the most difficult years of my life was 1989. It was the darkest chapter of my ministry. It brought out the true character of Tabernacle's people, and the love of Christ was manifested through them. It was the time that I entered into "God's school of discipleship." It has been good for me to be afflicted.

January of 1989 started out with the death of one of my dearest friends, Dr. Roy Harrell, an old soldier of the cross. I had promised him I would preach his funeral, but when he went to be with the Lord, I was sick from the news of his home-going. I felt like I had the flu. I certainly did not feel like driving six or seven hours to preach the funeral and then driving six or seven hours back home. So I asked two preachers to drive me, and I rested in the back of the car. Little did I realize I was also in trouble physically—I was hemorrhaging internally. I returned home and saw the doctor on February 10, 1989. He found that I was hemorrhaging and put me in the hospital immediately. After three or four days, they still could not find the source of the hemorrhaging. They discovered later that the lining of my stomach was dissolving.

After several tests and several specialists, I was placed under the care of Dr. Juan Montero. I had no idea that over the next several days I would be taken to the extreme limits of my Christian experience.

I had taken for the year 1989 a verse as our church's motto: Luke 11:1—"Lord, teach us to pray." Little did I realize what the Lord had in mind—that this was the means He would use to teach us. In January our church had studied the Lord's prayer life, and now He was going to put it into practice in the life of our church and family.

I could not pray for the Lord to stop me from hemorrhaging. I never did, and I never have. Every time that I would feel like maybe I should, I was quickly rebuked by the Spirit that I should pray, "Not my will, but Thy will be done." I could not pray for my healing, although I'm sure hundreds of others across the nation and around the world did. There was no doubt that people were praying.

I remember the night Dr. Montero came in and said, "We have to remove your stomach—a total gastrectomy. This is the only way we can save your life." I signed a piece of paper, giving them the okay to proceed. I had already been through one operation, and it had failed to correct the problem. This was the "first installment" on my registration fee into God's school of discipleship; I enrolled that night.

THE SURGEONS' ACCOUNTS

My Patient: The Reverend Rod Bell

The following account was provided by the surgeon who was responsible for my care in the operating room that night in February 1989.

"Reverend Rod Bell has given us the ultimate challenge in surgery."

The above statement was the opening line of my office progress notes dated March 8, 1989—exactly three weeks after Rev. Bell's two emergency major operations, both of which occurred on February 15, barely fourteen hours apart.

I will never forget St. Valentine's Day of 1989. I spent most of the afternoon and evening trying to make a decision of when NOT to operate. This is the most difficult time experienced by any surgical consultant. Once the decision to operate is made, it seems like someone has taken a heavy load off the surgeon's back. Such was the scenario in Rev. Bell's critical hours in the intensive care unit.

On February 13, I was consulted to see a mildly obese pastor who had upper gastrointestinal bleeding and a history of peptic ulcer diathesis which needed blood transfusions in the past. His parents and siblings had had a similar problem. He had been taking non-steroidal anti-inflammatory drugs over the past several months for musculoskeletal pains which he had attributed to a car accident. Upper gastrointestinal endoscopy performed by the gastroenterologist revealed massive gastritis with no definitive ulcer craters and with marked amount of blood clots throughout the stomach. He continued to bleed within that twenty-four-hour period in spite of the most intensive medical management. After a total of nine units of blood transfused since his admission on February 10, I reached the difficult decision to operate in the wee hours of February 15. I learned from my surgical training never to let a patient die from exanguination or obstruction without at least an option to operate. The relief of the decision to operate was short-lived.

Findings in the operating room showed no bleeding ulcer craters to suture, ligate, or resect. Instead, I was confronted with the dreaded finding of massively bleeding diffused stress ulcers throughout the stomach. The picture is that of a gastric mucosa (the lining of the stomach) practically sweating with blood. After I opened the stomach and started scooping out blood clots, I knew I had to make a quick decision as to what was the best treatment option. At that setting there were only two choices: one was a less radical parietal cell vagotomy, which is the highly selective form of cutting off the acid secretory region of the stomach. The other option was to do a total gastrectomy, removing the entire stomach. This is the most radical of procedures and usually fraught with many side effects and complications. I decided on the first option, hoping that the newer anti-ulcer medications along with the vagotomy would control the bleeding.

It was not meant to be. Fourteen hours later, we were back in the operating room, with Rev. Bell in severe shock. My good friend Dr. Prudencio Mendez, who is an ear/nose/throat specialist and a close friend of Rev. Bell, was kind enough to hurriedly come and scrub with me for the operation. We reopened the incision in a few seconds and readily saw a huge, markedly dilated, bluish stomach filled with blood. We knew then that we were left with one option if we were to give Rev. Bell a chance to live. The odds were so against him at that particular moment. We ended up removing the entire stomach and also the spleen. The patient, with massive blood transfusions, continued to be in shock. We continued to work feverishly, with silent prayers interspersed during quiet moments.

When a patient's stomach is completely removed from the distal end of the esophagus to the first portion of the small intestine (which is the duodenum), one has to reconstruct a new food conduit or pouch. There are various ways to do this, utilizing the loop of the small intestine. In Rev. Bell's situation, time was of the essence to get him out of the operating room in the quickest possible manner, not with the fanciest procedure. This we were able to accomplish by just pulling a loop of small intestine, anastomising it to the esophagus, and making a small opening alongside the loops for the passage of bile. I purposely bypassed constructing a pouch to save precious time. Eleven units of blood were pumped in during the two-hour procedure. What doth it profit anyone with a perfect operation and a dead patient?

The gamble paid off. Never in my wildest dreams would I have thought to hear Rev. Bell brag at his first office visit that he had already been to his favorite Chinese restaurant a few times, enjoying and keeping down every bit of his food and drink.

For a human body to fully recover after being subjected to such stress within a fourteen-hour period is truly remarkable and makes you wonder how thin a line separates life from death. Sometimes that line is just the width of a scalpel blade. I believe God still has great missions ahead for the Reverend. In my select patient gallery, he is an authentic "Hall of Fame-er."

Juan M. Montero II, M.D., F.A.C.S.

Chesapeake, Virginia

My Pastor and Patient

The following account was provided by a member of my church, a surgeon, who assisted in the operating room that night in February 1989.

Pastor Bell has graciously asked me to write up a testimonial concerning the 1989 incident when he was taken to

Chesapeake General Hospital because of a severe episode of gastrointestinal (GI) bleeding.

Pastor Bell's problems started in 1989, a few months after his automobile was rear-ended, leaving him with severe neck pain that required potent analgesics.

After several months of treatment with non-steroidal anti-inflammatory drugs (for which one of the potential side effects is gastrointestinal bleeding), Pastor Bell began to experience severe gastric problems, including bleeding. He was admitted to the intensive care unit at Chesapeake General Hospital. Needless to say, he looked as if he were a guinea pig undergoing massive testing with all kinds of tubes going into his veins, into his stomach via his mouth and nose. Such viewing was impressive to say the least. The specialists were trying to stop the GI bleeding using iced water as well as laser techniques, but unsuccessfully. Dr. Juan Montero (Juanny), a Chesapeake General Hospital general and thoracic surgeon, was in charge of the surgical aspects of Dr. Bell's condition.

Dr. Bell continued to bleed so severely that a decision was made to emergently take him to the operating room. I participated in that decision-making as if I were making such a choice for myself. I knew Pastor trusted me fully. I was in prayer almost all the time, so I knew the Lord was in charge, not us! I knew that if we did not take him to surgery, he would be with the Lord in no time. I was also aware that the Lord still needed Dr. Bell on earth, so it was inevitable to sense that the decisions were definitely God-directed.

After Dr. Montero started operating on Dr. Bell, the bleeding continued, but in amounts I have never ever seen before. Blood was coming out faster than it was going in, which meant that a negative fluid balance was perilously present. I was in tears and praying as hard as I knew. Juanny had to practically press down on the aorta to stop the blood flow into Pastor's stomach organ while we were transfusing blood into him. Pressing down on the aorta was a desperate move by Juanny to control the massive blood loss from every site of the stomach lining. And that was a smart move by Juanny. Pastor Bell had received at least forty units of blood when I lost count.

I went out to talk to Mrs. Bell and those with her several times during the surgery to update them, but I did not want to worry them more than necessary, so I was skeptical in letting worrisome information out. I knew the Lord was in charge, so I was not worried.

Finally, as a last resort, Juanny removed Dr. Bell's stomach. The bleeding finally stopped, and Pastor miraculously was still with us. "What a great God we have!" came out of my mouth so loudly that everyone in the operating room laughed in obvious happiness. I immediately came out to give Mrs. Bell the good news about stopping Dr. Bell's blood loss.

From there on, Dr. Bell has been doing great, and to date, he feels superb. His diet is almost normal, and his bowel is working fairly well, which probably is not typical for patients undergoing surgery of this sort. Now he can truly say that he can't "stomach" things any longer! Praise the great Lord we have who allows us to undergo serious illnesses to show His great power. I can sincerely believe in my heart that there is nothing more powerful than prayer.

May the Lord continue to bless Pastor Bell, his ministry, and his family. He knows he will always have a friend and a brother very close to his heart. To God be the glory!

Prudencio Mendez Jr., M.D., F.A.C.S.

RESOLUTION OF APPRECIATION

In appreciation for the outstanding skill demonstrated by these two professionals, the FBF lovingly passed the following resolution:

We, the members of the board of the Fundamental Baptist Fellowship, would like to express our appreciation to Dr. Juan Montero and Dr. Pru Mendez for the wise and incisive medical skills they employed during the recent physical crisis of our beloved colleague and esteemed leader, Dr. Rod Bell.

The skillful hands and abilities of these surgeons were providentially used by God in preserving the life of our beloved brother during the most critical hours of his recent physical perils. We are grateful to God for their invaluable skills and labors. Going beyond the call of duty, they gave themselves unreservedly to help sustain our brother's life.

We would like to thank them again for their timely assistance in an hour of desperate need, and we wish them continued success in their medical endeavors.

Unanimously passed by the Board
69th Annual Meeting of the
Fundamental Baptist Fellowship of America
Schaumburg, Illinois—June, 1989

* * *

The doctors told me later that I was clinically dead, that they had lost me a couple of times. I can remember at least one of the experiences, but I don't want to "magnify" an experience; I wish only to magnify the grace of my God. I remember telling my family good-bye, and then I remember being all alone, by myself, waiting to see the Lord, knowing this was the end. It was all over—the tears, loved ones left behind, emotions I cannot explain ran through my mind. Then a peace, which I cannot describe, swept over my soul, a calm in the midst of the storm. I thought, "The God of the mountains is the God of the valleys." The peace, the joy, the ecstatic rapture of His presence washed over me, and I could hear His voice saying, "All is well. It's okay, Son." I heard the most beautiful music and saw a peaceful valley that is beyond description. I cannot explain the peace and joy of my Lord that I experienced—the indescribable joy and the ecstasy of His presence. He was going with me all the way.

As I look back on it now, I realize that God was stripping me of my self-reliance. That backbone of pride had been broken. All my life, I had been very self-confident—I did not really need anyone or anything; I could handle the situation myself.

Everyone around me, including me, thought I was completely surrendered to Him. But God was peeling off the old shell of "self" layer by layer, like peeling an onion. It comes off one layer at a time; it brings tears and is very painful, but it is very profitable in the end. Pain in a Christian's life is a process with a divine purpose. The many times before in life when I'd reached the end of my rope, I would tie a knot at the end and hang on with "bulldog tenacity." I was determined to get through this hard spot. Somehow I'd make it. This was the pride of the mountain man—self-willed determination. In reality, it was merely pride.

I learned some valuable lessons while going through God's school of discipleship. The tuition is high, and it accepts no money. It costs not *anything*, but *everything*. The cost of tuition is a totally surrendered life. Only then do we come to the end of ourselves. Perhaps that's the greatest lesson I learned through my darkest peril: "Without Him, I can do nothing." This realization gave me a different perspective on the things that are important. It caused me to focus on the Master instead of the ministry. It brought into focus the things that are eternal, while understanding that the temporal will soon pass away.

As we went into Discipleship 101, God began to teach me many lessons. These lessons were taught to me in the darkness of that valley so that I could share them with others later in the light. This time was probably the greatest "postgraduate" course I've ever taken. God was carefully molding and making a better pastor, a better husband, a better father, and a better man. There are still many warts, knots, ugly blemishes, and rough edges, but God is patiently refining and molding. He's not through with me yet!

For several days I was in the Intensive Care Unit (ICU), not knowing much of what was going on. Some lessons during that time taught me so much. I learned how much I needed my mate, Lenore. I completely depended upon her and drew such strength from her presence. She rose to the occasion: I saw her as a real help meet, a "rib" to protect me from areas of my life where I was vulnerable. I saw the need of my family and the importance of being the right kind of father and the right kind of husband. Things that seemed unimportant before suddenly became extremely important to me. I saw the need to be a better pastor and a better servant of the Lord.

Most of all, I saw the Lord in a different light than I had ever seen Him before. I saw Him as my Lord and my Master. I realized that when you are dead, your earthly ministry is over— finished. I began to pray that after I recovered and left the hospital, the Lord would give me an extension of time, an infusion of power, and an enlargement of coast. In a measure, God has answered those prayers.

I look back and see the lessons that were taught and that I am still learning, and I know that these were some of the greatest days of my life. I had finally come to the place of desperation regarding revival; I had an unquenchable thirst for the power of God in my life. I felt that I needed Him more than I needed life itself and that if I couldn't have His blessing and power, I wanted to die.

There were some precious incidents during this crucial time. About six months after the surgery, my wife came in and gave me a green piece of paper with scribbling on it. "I think you can probably handle this now," she said.

I looked at it and could see my handwriting. I had scrawled the words, "Will I ever preach again?" I don't remember writing those words, but I remember so many times thinking them. I thought I was finished, that God was through with me; that's not a pleasant thought for a preacher. But God, once again, was molding and making a man. He was through with the life of selfishness and stubborn, strong wills. But, thank God, He wasn't through with the man who would be yielded to Him. And that's what I wanted more than anything.

The next class in God's school of discipleship was one I had never experienced before: I was about to enter one of the most depressed times I have ever gone through in my life. I had never been "depressed" in my life—I always took things in stride and could work them out. But this time was different. I became so depressed: I imagined I would never again eat a hamburger or drink a Coke. I imagined I would never walk on the beach with my wife or preach again. I was at the place that I was totally, completely whipped; I knew I was finished. In my mind, I felt "it is all over." I found I could not even watch a television commercial of a man and his family enjoying a vacation or walking together or playing together because I knew I would never do that again. I knew I was going to be a "vegetable," that I would become a burden to my family and my church. The battle against depression would become the greatest battle I've ever fought.

I received strength from other preachers, from God's men who came in to give me a word of encouragement, and from letters and cards. I received strength from the Scriptures, from listening to tapes, from the promises of the Word of God. I came to the place where I told the Lord I would be the best vegetable that He had, but I was going to work as long as I could, if He would give me the strength. That's when I asked God for for an extension of time, an "enlargement of coast," and to be endued with His power.

The need to have a "Barnabas spirit" during this time of traumatic experiences was indelibly impressed upon my heart and mind. It caused me then, and still does to this day, to reach out to those who are hurting, to those I can help in some way. I remember Paul Hawkins, one of my preacher buddies, coming into my hospital room to encourage me. He told me that I would preach again, that I would use this experience to help others, and that it wouldn't be long until I'd be back in the pulpit telling the old story again.

I often thought, "If he only knew what I know." But he kept visiting me and encouraging me, almost daily. How I thank God for that Barnabas spirit. Russell Rice and Walt Coles were such an encouragement to me too. Dr. Bob Jones Jr. called and said, "If you are going to lead preachers, this may be the price of leadership."

My doctor, Pru Mendez, would come in every morning, bend over my bed, kiss me on the forehead, and say, "I love you, my Pastor." He then would pour out his heart at the foot of my bed, asking God to give him back his pastor. God answered his prayers. I remember our little Filipino nurse, one of our church members, Fely Manzo. Every day she would have prayer with me and encourage me with the Scripture. Tears rolled down her cheeks as she wept, praying for her pastor, asking the Lord to give her pastor back. All the church was a prayer meeting: they didn't just call a prayer meeting; they were a prayer meeting.

I thought, "Lord, I have never been able to pray that you would heal me and raise me up."

I can remember my deacon and his wife, Ken and Helen Dorhout, praying and weeping, asking God to give them back their pastor. Through the years, these two servants have been such a help to their pastor. I recall so vividly John Mendoza and John Jennings coming to the foot of my bed at the midnight hour, pouring their hearts out to God, asking God to raise up their pastor.

So many came to pray and encourage me; I cannot begin to put all their names here. One night I remembered the verse I had taken for that year, "Lord, teach us to pray." That was exactly what the Lord was doing, and I didn't realize it! I had asked Him, and He was teaching not only the pastor but also his people to pray.

I will always have a very special place in my heart for all the people who came to me during those dark days, who gave me a word of encouragement. From Mike Phillips's nightly backrub to Bill Hill's visits, to the old Nazarene preacher who came in with a songbook in his pocket and said, "Brother Bell, you've always been such a blessing to me. I just thought it would be good for me to come in and sing you a song." I didn't want to hear a song; I was too sick for a song. I didn't want to talk; I didn't want to sing; all I wanted was to be left alone. He reached in his pocket, pulled out a songbook, and sang the old song,

By and by when I look on His face,
Beautiful face; thorn-shadowed face;

By and by when I look on His face,
I'll wish I had given Him more.

By and by when He holds out His hands,
Welcoming hands, nail-riven hands;
By and by when He holds out His hands,
I'll wish I had given Him more.

More, so much more.
More of my life than I e'er gave before--
By and by when I look on His face,
I'll wish I had given Him more.

In the light of that heavenly place,
Light from His face, beautiful face.
In the light of that heavenly place,
I'll wish I had given Him more.

More, so much more.
Treasures unbounded for Him I adore--
By and by when I look on His face,
I'll wish I had given Him more.

By the time he had finished, I was so glad that he had come—it was just what I needed that day to get me through. God spoke to me through that dear brother. *"When I look upon His face, His wonderful face, I'll wish I had given Him more."*

When my two sons went through their incidents (not *accidents*, but *incidents*), I told them God was making a man. All they had to do was yield to the hand of the Potter and let Him make the vessel. It dawned on me, when I was going through my incident, that I had better practice what I was preaching. During the first two years of this darkest peril of my ministry, God was stripping me of self-reliance. I've always been a very confident person; I knew I could do it, I could make it happen. God showed me I was just to be a channel, that I needed to be clay in the Potter's hands.

Tim's incident occurred in March 1984. He was studying for the ministry at Bob Jones University and was hurt while playing basketball. His injuries resulted in amnesia, which lasted six months. God taught Tim many things from this incident, but at the same time, He was teaching me. Many times God touches us in places we least expect. He knows the cord that is around our heart; whenever He pulls it, He pulls us to our knees, making our heart bare and naked to His Word. The time of Tim's amnesia was one of the hardest I've had to face in his life because I knew Tim had a good mind, and I knew Satan was trying to destroy him, to stop him from serving the Lord.

There were times I felt that the Lord had forgotten us. I spent many nights searching each area of my life, asking God to help me be right, wondering if I were really serving God from the heart, doing it to be seen of men, or for the advancement of my ministry. Was I married to a ministry or married to the Bridegroom? So many things went through my mind as I searched, asking God to show me His good and acceptable and perfect will. While I tried to help Tim with his memory, praying daily that it would return, God was stripping me of my self-reliance. I realized my inability to handle this situation; I was not in control. I needed to surrender to the Master's hands.

These were deep, dark valleys, but I would not trade anything for what God has done through this incident in Tim's life. I think it made him a better preacher; I feel it has made me, to some degree, a better dad and pastor. Truly, good Gethsemane experiences make good Calvary preachers. It has provided an opportunity whereby we can feel for others. God was showing me that I needed to be sensitive to others and that I needed my family and friends. It pulled us out of ourselves and toward our Lord, forcing us to deal with our feelings toward each other, toward the ministry. It caused us to talk, to pull down walls I had erected because of the lack of communication with my family. I realized that at times I was in love with the ministry and not in love with the Lord.

It's amazing how God can teach us so many things when we stop and wait on Him and enter into His school of discipleship.

I thank God for that incident in Tim's life. I never want to repeat it, but it was a class in Discipleship 101.

Rod Jr.'s incident occurred in 1987. He, too, was studying to become a preacher at Bob Jones University and was an assistant pastor in Georgia. I received a call that he had been in a car wreck. He had been hit head-on by a big truck, and they had to cut him out of the automobile. The doctor said, "If I were you, I would get here as soon as possible."

My wife and I and Tim jumped on a plane and flew to Greenville. Bob Jones III met me at the airport and gave me his car. I never will forget the Jones's compassion in helping me through this incident. We spent twenty-two days and twenty-two nights at the foot of Rod Jr.'s bed. Each time as I was reminded that Rod had less than a 5 percent chance to live and that we could lose our son, we began to pray more earnestly. I searched my soul; I did as I had been told by Ken Hay of The Wilds, "Don't ask *when* am I going to get out of this trial, but ask *what*, and make yourself available to let God teach you." God, again, was stripping me of my self-reliance.

One night I was on my knees praying, and God gave me Psalm 118:17—"I shall not die, but live, and declare the works of the Lord." I got peace that it would be all right. If the Lord wanted to take Rod Jr., He could take him. If He wanted him to live, he would live. And God was teaching me to hold loosely those things we tend to clutch so dearly; it only causes more pain if He has to pry them from our fingers.

I was supposed to be in the Caribbean that week, preaching in the Dominican Republic with Bob Jones III and other preachers. I called Bill Wingard, and he took my place. During those times, God was again stripping me of self-reliance, showing me my need to minister to my family and spend time with them. I was pulled between trying to reach into the islands, trying to reach the world, trying to reach the city, trying to do everything, but I was trying to do it in my own strength and not by waiting upon the Lord. Therefore, I felt that Rod Jr. needed me, and I was determined to stick by him through this darkest peril of his life.

I thought back to when he was thirteen or fourteen years old: "Dad, I've got a real problem."

"What is it, Son?"

"I'm jealous of God because God is always taking you away from me."

I did not understand at that time that Rod needed me and that I needed him. It was hard for a young lad to see his dad gone all the time and not have him there when he needed him. I was determined to stay by him during this difficult time, and I did. I told Rod I would leave the hospital when he left, and that we did. I slept in his room, at the foot of his bed, for almost a month. I helped where I could, but the most important thing was just being there for him. The day finally came, and we flew home together. It was a time when we both understood that God was once again teaching us. This course in God's school of discipleship was a sobering one: Pastors neglecting their own while trying to save the world can lose their own in the process.

The Lord has used these incidents to show me I have a real partner in the ministry. God has made Rod Jr. a vital part of Tabernacle Baptist Church. We have so much in common; at times, we're so much alike. Though we don't always see things eye-to-eye on administrative matters, he's always most gracious. I've learned that whenever Rod Jr.'s made a decision, he's thought it through, prayed it through, and pulled out all the loopholes. Most of the time, he is right. I feel that God's hand is upon him, and God is going to use him in a great way. What a privilege it has been to labor together with him at Tabernacle. He may be a "Junior," but he is definitely his own man.

I am truly thankful for all the incidents that have taken place in the lives of my family. Dad cannot be on the Potter's wheel without the entire family also being affected. We grow from glory to glory. This treasure is in an earthen vessel, but God has to break the earthen vessel before His light can shine in. I have never known a man to be used to his fullest potential for God until that man has been broken.

I've learned that Romans 8:28 is a soft pillow for a tired heart. What we have learned through the night, we can tell in the light. The sweetest perfume comes from a crushed rose. We need to humble ourselves; we need to let God mold us, make us into His image. I have learned to quit trying to make it happen; I cannot do it myself. The Lord is the "Energizer."

It's always amazing that when we enroll in God's school of discipleship, God always begins by getting our attention and showing us our heart as we really are in the light of His glory and His grace. When God gets our attention, we begin to see what fools we really are and have been, trying to do a supernatural work in the energy of the flesh. Then God begins to show us that it's not the temporal things that really matter, it is the eternal. Generally those things that He wants us to deal with are the things that we take for granted, day in and day out, week in and week out. They have no price tag; they cannot be purchased because they are priceless. We never take inventory and stop to count our blessings. It's really our home, our children, our relationship with our family, our attitudes—it's the little foxes that seem to spoil the vine. Not being the right kind of pastor, not being the right kind of preacher, not building a relationship with Him, not being open and transparent and naked to the eyes of a holy God, but living a façade, living a life of make-believe, and not being real. God generally shows us how unreal we are. The need to be right and real is the proper focus. But we cannot be right until we see Him in all of His righteousness, all of His glory, all of His grace, all of His holiness, to see Him as He really is.

I prayed three prayers during the darkest peril of my life: I asked for an extension of time as God had given Hezekiah, an enlargement of coast, and an endowment of power. Through the physical incidents God has brought me through, my doctors tell me I am making medical history—that I should not be doing what I am doing physically. I am reminded every day that time is so important in serving the Lord. We go this way only once; we must redeem the time we have before we reach eternity. "The night cometh when no man can work." We must redeem the time and work in His strength while it is day.

CHAPTER 15:
God Answers Prayer

AN EXTENSION OF TIME

Psalm 90 teaches us to number our days. God has given me an extension of time. Having gone through the valley of death's shadow, I realize how valuable time is. God gives us an allotted time to serve Him and occupy until He comes. We dare not be slothful but diligent, faithful stewards of His time. In my mind and heart, I have realized that every day could be my last day. It behooves us to serve God sincerely, as if every day will be our last; for tomorrow we might be in that city that is fairer than day, looking upon the One who loved us and gave Himself for us. What really matters is living day by day to His glory and knowing Him in a more intimate, personal relationship. How my heart is filled with gladness and praise to Him because He has given me an undeserved extension of time. He has been so good and so great to give me a few more days to labor in the field. I want to be working in the field when the sun sets. I praise God for an extension of time.

AN ENLARGEMENT OF COAST

God has enlarged the coast of ministry since we entered His school of discipleship. I had no idea what God was doing and what God had in mind when I bowed beneath the old oak tree in 1967, asking God to put this ministry around the world. It would be a ministry for His glory; I had no idea that I would ever see what God has done through a handful of people who were willing to serve Him. Laban told Jacob, "God has blessed me because of thee." God has blessed Tabernacle Baptist Church, the Fundamental Baptist Fellowship, and the various Congresses of Fundamentalists. God has blessed me because He has given me some of God's choicest servants to help me. I am indebted to so many people. The Lord has allowed the FBF to grow from just a handful to over five thousand Fundamentalist Baptist pastors. I know it is not because of me; it is in spite of me. He has enlarged our coast around the world through the Fundamental Baptist Fellowship and the Tabernacle Baptist Church missions project.

Missions is the heart of God. A church that is not mission-minded is not a spirit-filled church. We have been privileged to see scores and scores of preachers ordained and sent through the local church, carrying the gospel of the grace of God to the regions beyond: from Ball Fork Hollow, West Virginia, to India, China, Russia, and the islands of the sea. I have always had a burden for the islands of the sea, especially the Caribbean. We prayed for over twenty-five years that God would open a window of opportunity there. Despite numerous setbacks, in the last ten years, we have seen God open up the West Indies through men who have the same burden to reach the English and Spanish-speaking islands in the Caribbean. God has used men like Dr. Johnny Daniels, Mike Casillas, and others. These men have had servants' hearts, sacrificing time and effort to open up these islands for a sound witness. God has given a leader—Dr. Johnny Daniels—to the West Indies preachers. Scores of native pastors are rallying to the Fundamental Baptist Fellowship in the

Caribbean region. These are native pastors who are standing true to the Word of God and need a helping hand. We have seen the region grow, from Puerto Rico to Santo Domingo, through the islands of the sea into Barbados and Grenada. God has greatly encouraged our hearts in opening these doors. Indeed, He has enlarged our coast.

About twenty years ago, I was in the Dominican Republic, back in the mountains with a missionary and a native pastor. We were in the back of an old truck, coming down through the trail on the dirt road, and a tire blew out. We stopped, of course, and were trying to fix the tire. As we jacked the truck up and placed rocks under it, we found the tires were slick. A tusk from a pig's tooth had run through one of our tires. The natives began to gather around as we worked to fix the tire. I thought, "What a great opportunity to give out gospel tracts and have a witnessing and preaching time."

Using the missionary as interpreter, we preached, and several accepted Christ. About twenty years later, I was back in the Dominican Republic and saw the native pastor. He asked me if I remembered the incident with the truck tire.

"Yes, I do."

"We have a church there in that valley now called Pig Tooth Baptist Church! There were some people saved that day, and we started a mission church in the valley."

I never cease to be amazed at how God takes an insignificant thing, like the tooth of a pig, and does His work. Thank God for the faithful native pastors carrying on God's work in those remote villages; I think they are God's choicest servants.

We now have an official invitation to go into Cuba with the Fundamental Baptist Fellowship. There are "underground" Baptist churches there who have remained true under the regime of the Communist dictator Fidel Castro. We are praying for God to enlarge our coast in that area. We must be ready for this door as it opens.

Another example of how God has enlarged our coast occurred approximately thirty years ago, and the effects are still being felt today. Little did we realize that our burden to help the Fundamentalist cause would give birth to the Congress of Fundamentalists. One evening as we relaxed after a preaching service at Tabernacle's 1973 Annual Congress, our moderator and co-moderator, Dr. Paisley and Dr. Jones Jr., suggested that we attempt to have a worldwide Congress on a one-time basis to try to strengthen the hand of Fundamentalists. That idea grew until it became a reality in Edinburgh, Scotland, in 1976. Our coast has been enlarged by men rallying around the cardinal doctrines and fundamentals of the faith and being true separatists.

The enlargement of the coasts of the Fundamental Baptist Fellowship is another example of God's goodness. Dr. John Vaughn, the FBF's Executive Director, and Dr. Bob Whitmore are writing the history of the Fundamental Baptist Fellowship. For the last twenty-two years, the hand of God has been upon this Fellowship in an unusual way. I remember meeting Dr. Weniger in the Hilton Hotel at O'Hare Airport in Chicago. "Rod, if you would take charge of the FBF, the board would be pleased."

"If it's merely the pleasure of the Board at stake, the answer is 'No' because my hands are full already. I have more on my plate than I can eat now."

He asked me to pray about it, and the more I prayed about it, the greater the burden became. I could not understand why; I thought there were so many more men with far greater ability than I. I recommended others to take it, but we met again after much prayer. As we met in O'Hare Airport in the Hilton Hotel in the fall of 1976, I became the president of the Fellowship. We reorganized the Fundamental Baptist Fellowship into five or six regions, appointing moderators over each region. I have always had one desire: to raise the banner that has been faithfully proclaimed down through the years and allow those who have a "kindred spirit" to rally around it. I have, through the years, tried to maintain a proper balance and make the FBF an organization that would be a voice, not merely another bureaucracy or "convention."

I started traveling every week, and Tabernacle Baptist Church paid the way. We brought speakers with us into the churches, trying to rally preachers around the Word of God and strengthen their hands. It took me away from my church quite a bit, and I will always be indebted to our people for not complaining and bellyaching about their pastor's being gone so much. The hardest thing I've ever had to do was to leave my church and my people, but I knew I had to do it. To this day I can't explain why, but I just knew I had to do.

Our coasts have been enlarged through the Tabernacle Baptist missions program. Churches have been started in Mexico by Dr. Julio Torres, in Indonesia by Dr. Suhento Liauw, in Singapore—all graduates of our seminary. Others of our missionaries have started churches and seminaries in India through Dr. Franks and Dr. Kumar. Dr. John Gunter has helped start over fifty churches in South America. What a blessing to see these ministries flourish.

Sometimes I get into trouble because the young men who come from these countries to attend our seminary ask me if I will come to their country and help them lay the foundation stones for their new buildings, churches, Bible colleges, and seminaries. "Of course, you know I will. I'll be happy to!"

A few years after they graduate, I get a call, and I have had to travel all over the world because I've given my word. I've given my word to Khan Mung, who will graduate with his doctorate and go back to Burma. I have given my word to Isaac, who will go back to Ghana with his doctorate and start a church. What a blessing it is to see God bless His Word and enlarge His coast.

AN ENDOWMENT OF POWER

I have seen God answer prayer in our forty years of ministry. I have experienced the reality of His presence many times. I know that we serve the true and the living God and that our God is real. He will do what He says He will do.

I have been so burdened for revival. I began to read the histories of great revivals. I thank God for the burden that has been quickened in my heart to have a great outpouring of the Holy Spirit in true revival. We are living in a nation and generation that has never seen a nationwide revival. The average church member does not know what revival is. He thinks that if you put a sign on the wall *"August 17 through 24:* **REVIVAL!***"* and have some special singing and a good preacher, the folks at least can say they had a revival. This, I found, is not revival; this is an evangelistic endeavor.

You can have evangelism and not have revival, but you cannot have revival without evangelism. Revival is what God does *in* His people, and evangelism is what God does *through* His people. A mighty working of Holy Ghost revival is what our church needed and what our country needs. I cannot explain the burden that was upon my heart for real revival. *Revival* means "to rekindle or to stir." This is a work that is not done of men but is done by a sovereign God in the hearts of His people. Matthew Henry said, "When God intends great mercies for His people, He first sets them a-praying." For years in our church I tried to use the methods of Finney; I tried to make it happen. But God began to work as I enrolled in God's school of discipleship with a naked, open, and transparent heart, wanting our God.

When I went in 1976 to preach in Edinburgh, Scotland, I was challenged to have a greater burden for true, Fundamentalist, Bible-believing people. I saw men there who loved the Lord, who had a prayer life and a hunger for real revival.

Going to the prayer meetings in Ulster, we would hear the old saints of God pray and ask the Lord fervently, "Oh, God! Remember '59. Oh, God! Remember '59."

I had no idea what they were talking about. They were talking about the great revival that swept Ulster in 1859. Our Second Great Awakening in America in 1857-58 jumped across the Atlantic Ocean, and over one hundred thousand souls were saved in Ulster. The '59 revival started in Antrim County in Ulster, when four young men began to pray. I began to hunger and thirst for revival.

CHAPTER 16:
Revival

MY EDUCATION IN REVIVAL WITH MY CLASSMATE DR. PAISLEY

I knew little about true, Holy Ghost revival sent by a sovereign God. Oh, I had read many books about the First Great Awakening and the Second Great Awakening. But it never really came alive as a burning reality until I was touched by the life and ministry of Dr. Ian Paisley. I feel I have been brainwashed by an American mentality regarding evangelism and revival. I have learned there is a great difference between evangelism and revival. Evangelism is simply a campaign to witness and share the gospel: to win souls. You can have evangelism without having revival, but you cannot have revival without having evangelism. Dr. Ken Connolly has given the finest definition of *revival:* "Revival is the sovereign, sudden, selective, sensational operation of the Spirit of God. It descends amid prayer, produces purity, and reaches the perishing."

Revival became a reality to me when I was in Northern Ireland and saw the desperate religious and political situation. Here were a handful of Bible believers who had their backs to the wall, and unless there was a divine intervention, they would be crushed under the heel of Rome's tyranny. As I traveled through England, Scotland, Wales, and Ulster and became educated by Dr. Paisley about revival, I became engrossed and totally consumed with the need for revival in America. We *must* have revival in America, or else we will perish.

I believe it started with hearing Dr. Paisley speak about the Great Revival of 1859 that swept throughout the British Isles. Seeing history come alive started that thirst in my heart as I visited the land of the Welsh revival—Spurgeon, the Wesley brothers, Whitefield, Knox. I began to realize that no man has a monopoly on God. If God would do it for these men, God could do it again, even for a mountain boy from West Virginia.

Dr. Paisley and I decided to visit the New England areas where the First Great Awakening took place under Jonathan Edwards and George Whitefield. We got up one morning at 2:00 A.M. and caught the first flight out of Norfolk. Landing in Boston, we were on our way.

We had arranged with librarians, historians, and others well acquainted with the Great Awakening to visit these historic places. We saw the remains of the foundation of the church where Jonathan Edwards preached his famous sermon "Sinners in the Hands of an Angry God." We sat and listened intently to the historian's lecture. We looked at Edwards's sermon—the small piece of paper, yellow with age, now kept in a vault. The historian told us that Edwards had held this piece of paper with black scribbling on it close to his eyes because his eyesight was failing and just read the sermon out loud. But oh what mighty power was there! Souls cried out, fearful that they were falling into the pit of hell. Great revival came.

I asked the caretaker if I might just be able to touch the notes; he told me I could touch them, just not take them! I just wanted to touch the notes of the man who was in touch with a sovereign God.

We visited the grave of David Brainerd and followed his trail as he ministered to the Indians with such fervency. The man had been quite sick, but he gave his all to Christ. One of the guides told us how the Indians had planned to kill him. Coming upon him, they heard him pray with such fervency, and they observed that as he prayed the snow was red with blood from the effect of disease on his body. The Indians decided that any man who had that kind of burden for them should be spared.

We sang at Northfield, where Moody had preached in the great auditorium. We had to kick beer cans out of the way because the night before, a drunken party had taken place. Our hearts were broken as we saw the results of the apostasy that has overtaken this place. We asked one of the students if he knew who D. L. Moody was.

He looked a bit bewildered. "No, I don't believe I do. Is he a student here?"

"No. He's the man who founded this school."

The school today is only for the elite, the children of our foreign ambassadors. God is seldom mentioned. We went out to his grave and asked God to never allow this to happen to our own ministries. We thanked God for the burden this great man had for souls and for the work God had permitted him to do because he was willing to give his all to Christ.

As we left there, we went to Moody's house. We saw the rostrum of all the great speakers who came to Northfield's campus—what giants they were. We asked if we could see the bedroom where Moody died. The caretaker showed us the bedroom. Dr. Paisley asked if he could see the inscription of Moody's dying words.

The caretaker replied, "Oh, we don't have anything like that around here."

Dr. Paisley persisted, "Yes, it's here. I read it in a book. It's around the fireplace somewhere."

On his knees, crawling around, Dr. Paisley looked up and saw where Moody had written his last words. "Ah, here it is."

He dusted the spot off with his handkerchief, using a tender, almost sacred touch. "*Earth recedes. Heaven opens before me. . . . It is beautiful. It is like a trance. If this is death, it is sweet. There is no valley here. God is calling me, and I must go.*"

"I never knew that was there," the caretaker said.

Paisley replied, "I knew it was there because Moody said it before he entered the pearly gates."

That was a memorable day. We visited cemetaries; we prayed and sang songs everywhere we went. There is a tape somewhere in Dr. Paisley's collection called "Songs from the Sepulcher." We made our way across the state until we got to where Whitefield preached his last sermon. We kept calling ahead to ask the caretaker if he would please wait for us. We were coming but we were behind schedule a bit, enjoying the rich experience of walking in the footsteps of these giants.

We finally arrived at the place about 2:00 in the morning. The caretaker and his wife were still waiting for us. We saw the pulpit where the great Whitefield had preached. I asked the caretaker if this was the place where Whitefield had preached his last sermon.

He said, "Yes, this is it."

"Why is it all roped off?"

"Well, the platform is old and may be dangerous. We don't want folks climbing up there and perhaps getting hurt."

"Listen. This is my friend Dr. Ian Paisley. Would it be all right for him to get up there and just say a few words?"

"Oh, no. It's too dangerous."

"But he's a member of the British Parliament and the European Parliament. It would be nice if he could just say a few words from there. Besides, he has a Bible college named after Whitefield back in Ireland."

"No, no."

"But he's the pastor of the largest Protestant church in the British Isles. He's God's man, and he's come all this distance just to see this place. Wouldn't it be all right if he could just say a few words?"

About that time, I had an idea. I reached into my pocket, withdrew a $50 bill, and placed it in his hand. "Don't you think it would be okay for him to get up there and just say a few words?"

"Oh, I think it would be all right!"

Dr. Paisley preached at 2:30 in the morning—"Behold! The Lamb of God which taketh away the sin of the world." He preached for about ten to fifteen minutes, with three or four of us as a congregation. It was probably the shortest and most expensive sermon I've ever heard! I enjoyed every minute of it.

Then we went down underneath the pulpit, where we saw Whitefield's bust. Whitefield had been buried under the pulpit, but his body had been stolen. The bust was there in a case. I opened the glass door, reached in and placed my hand on that replica of Whitefield's head, and asked God to give me just a small portion of what this great man of God had. I promised that I would use it for His glory.

Paisley prayed, and then with a roaring laugh said, "If I had a camera, I would print this in every Baptist paper across the nation! A Baptist, with his hand on a Presbyterian's head, praying for a double portion of his spirit!"

I replied, "I'm not so sure he was a Presbyterian. I think he was a hybrid of both!"

We laughed together and made our way on to our next stop in Boston, to a large park where Whitefield had preached. It was about 4:00 in the morning, and we were singing in the park where Whitefield had preached to as many as twenty thousand without a microphone. Then I saw the Park Street Church. We dragged ourselves across the street into the hotel, two weary preachers whose hearts were leaping with the joy of the Lord, praying that God would do it again: visit Ulster and America with the old-time, Holy Ghost power of revival.

We walked where the giants had walked, and I was reminded that God is no respecter of persons. True to His Word, God *did* send the pure, sweet winds of revival to our church, in His good time.

The following is a chronology I compiled in 1992 when God so graciously sent revival to Tabernacle Baptist Church. Some of the incidents have already been mentioned, but I felt it proper to include the entire "Reflections on Revival" as I recorded them at the time.

REFLECTIONS ON REVIVAL - 1992
~

Ephesians: 1:12—"*To the praise of his glory.*"

God created a hunger and a thirst in my heart over seven years ago for personal revival.

> *Our service for God has been barren and dry*
> *and barren it shall remain.*
> *Until we are blest with fire from on high,*
> *and the sound of abundance of rain.*

Our church was barren and dry. We needed a revival. Seeing our need led to a spirit of helplessness which moved to a spirit of desperation. I entered into Prayer 101 of God's school of discipleship.

Through a series of events, God began to burden my heart for prayer and personal revival. God put me through the Garden of Gethsemane with my sons and the incidents (not accidents) in their lives—both going down into the valley of death.

Five years ago we began to pray for one hour every Sunday morning for revival. We preached across the nation on revival through our FBF meetings. There was a remnant of men who were hungry for revival. They were crying unto the Lord, "Lord, how can I tell the next generation about revival if I have not experienced revival? Don't let me die and not experience revival."

In 1988 the personal burden for revival became so great I felt that I was going to die. I did not feel I could live another day without relief.

In January of 1989 I was burdened to pray. We took our church through the prayer life of our Lord. Luke 11:1, "Teach us to pray," became a reality. In February 1989 I became desperately ill and required two major surgeries. God was stripping me of self-reliance. He was showing me that without Him I could do nothing. I learned that pain in a Christian's life is a process with a divine purpose. This old flesh does not die easily.

In 1990 and 1991 we went through some of the darkest days in our church with the trials and testings in our schools. The physical and spiritual pressure had brought me to the point of desperation. Then God led me to preach for almost a year on "Revivals in the Old Testament," "The First Great Awakening," "The Second Great Awakening," "The 1859 Wish Revival," and so on. My burden for a divine visitation increased. Isaiah 44:3 kept burning in my soul: "I will pour water upon him that is thirsty."

The heart cry of our church has been Isaiah 64:1-2, "Oh that thou wouldest rend the heavens, that thou wouldest come down, that the mountains might flow down at thy presence, as when the melting fire burneth, the fire causeth the waters to boil, to make thy name known to thine adversaries, that the nations may tremble at thy presence!"

When planning our Congress of Fundamentalists of 1992, I felt greatly burdened to hand the mantle down to the next generation of Fundamentalists. In so doing, I invited preachers and their sons to come and preach: Dr. Bob Jones Jr. and his grandsons Bob IV and Stephen, Dr. O. Talmadge Spence and his son, Dr. Van Gelderen and his son, Dr. Paisley and his son Kyle, and my own two sons. Little did I realize what God had in mind.

During this meeting I felt a sense of responsibility building up as a dam ready to burst. On Friday night, October 30, Dr. Paisley preached on the Cross. Another preacher had been scheduled to speak following Dr. Paisley, but God seemed to say, "Stop here. You can't go any further than the cross." I told the other preacher, "God wants to do something," and I gave an invitation. There were approximately ten or twelve young people saved in that meeting and the youth meeting following the service. A spirit of revival began to break loose.

On Saturday night, October 31, Evangelist Jim Van Gelderen, one of the BJU Minutemen, spoke, and approximately thirty-five were saved.

Sunday morning, November 1, Jim Van Gelderen preached in our church and there was a great spirit of revival. Approximately two hundred Christians came forward confessing sin, making restitution, and so on. God's people were getting right with one another; God's people were getting right with the Lord; God's people were answering the call to preach, answering the call to the mission field. There was a great spirit of brokenness, and five souls were saved.

Sunday night, November 1, there was a great moving of the Spirit of God. Dr. R. L. Hymers from Los Angeles preached, and there was a divine visitation. Many people came and got right with the Lord. Fifty-seven souls were saved at this meeting—a great moving of the Spirit of God. People were getting right with one another and getting right with the Lord.

Monday morning, November 2, I asked our school administrator to give the high school young people an opportunity to give a testimony. They began to give testimonies, and without any prodding or invitation, seventy-one young people received Christ as their personal Savior. There was a great brokenness—a holy hush and deep conviction moved upon our young people.

Young people were running to find someone to lead them to Christ. We had staff members getting saved; mothers bringing their children into the pre-school, not knowing what was going on, were being saved. This went on from 8:00 A.M. until 11:00 A.M. A great holy hush came over our student body. They organized their own prayer meetings and began to pray. People were saved throughout the week. Parents were getting right with God. Parents called saying, "What has happened? We have new children!"

On Saturday, November 7, a great multitude of young people and adults went out on visitation. There were over one hundred people who went out that week. The young people did not want to quit knocking on doors. They had a hunger to win others to God.

On the following Sunday morning, November 8, I went to prayer at 8:00 A.M. with some other men. We prayed for the blessed Spirit to once again move upon His people. Needless to say, that morning we all met in the auditorium during our regular Sunday school hour. There was quite a spirit of expectation. The people, broken, began to testify. Others came to testify and to weep. A great brokenness came over the service. This service began at 9:45 A.M. and went until 12:30. The singing was unbelievable; as a giant choir the congregation sang. The hearts of the saints were unlocked and their lips were free.

When the invitation was given, twenty-seven people came forward to get saved. People answered the call to preach and go to the mission field. People were going to one another and getting things right. There was a great stirring. We had young people asking the church to forgive them. We had people making restitution, and a great stirring prevailed until 1:30. I baptized twelve people who had been saved. At 3:00 my wife and I were still dealing with people.

We returned at 4:30 and the prayer rooms were filled. People were praying for the evening service.

Sunday night, November 8, I preached a short message to one of the largest crowds we have had in many years. The downstairs was filled, and people were sitting in the balcony. The parking lots were filled and people were parked on the soccer field. I gave the invitation and fifteen more people came forward, with many rededications, and many people came answering the call to preach, to go to the mission field, and to go into the ministry. Over 250 people stood and said they would be going out on soul-winning visitation this week; perhaps one hundred said they would go out on organized visitation. I baptized another fifty people on Sunday night.

(A spirit of concern for others is being manifested. My own personal feeling is that I am awestricken. I feel worthless almost to the point of being totally helpless. I feel like a zero with the circle rubbed out. I am humbled. I am afraid in the sense that I might interfere and get in God's way. I have determined to stay out of God's way and try to be a traffic director. I want to find out which way God is going. He has it already organized. It is a sovereign, divine act. God's people are singing. God's people are rejoicing. God's people are praying. God's people are burdened. We are in the midst of a divine breath of heaven. We have never seen it in this fashion before.

Some characteristics I have noticed among our people: a call to prayer, a call to purity, a call to personal evangelism, a call to prepare for the ministry and to have a hunger for the Word. I have also noticed there is a new life in singing. Our people are singing as I have never heard before. There is an expectation, an eagerness. There are joy and excitement. There is life. God is in our midst. There is a smooth, quiet moving of the wind of God.)

One person came to me and said, "I have used God's tithe to buy things and I am going to sell them and bring the money to the church." Another said, "I have been gossiping about this church and about different people. I want to get it right." Another asked the church to forgive him for gossiping. Another asked the young people to forgive him for gossiping and having a bad attitude and bitter spirit. I worked with many men who have been called to preach the gospel and go to the mission field.

I saw one man so under conviction that he crawled down the aisle. Other men were shaking as a leaf in the wind—trembling and broken before a Holy God. I heard shouting from people who had never shouted or expressed any kind of emotion before. I saw hard cases break and melt like wax. I saw defiant people crumble into clay. I saw the stubborn resist and then break. I saw people who were never concerned over souls weeping and concerned.

The amazing thing about it all is that it is not forced; it is so easy and free. "Oh, God! May the burden increase. Plow on, O King eternal! Plow deep. Break up the fallow ground. Send revival." God has to break men and strip them of self-reliance to the place where they can do nothing but rely completely upon the Savior. The Comforter has come. He has not taken sides, but He has taken over. As Evan Roberts prayed, "Bend me, bend me, O God, bend me."

With my heart as wicked as it is, how could a holy, sovereign God breathe upon us? I feel so sinful. I feel so wicked. I feel so unclean. I must express my feeling. I feel so unworthy. I feel as though I am the chief amongst sinners. Knowing what I know about myself and then realizing that God knows so much more about me than I know, I am so unworthy of this divine breath of heaven. But then so are we all.

We are so grateful to be a beneficiary of His mercy. In the midst of judgment, God has remembered mercy. God has put His approval upon the theme of the Congress as He has passed a "burning torch to the next generation."

THE SECOND WEDNESDAY NIGHT
NOVEMBER 11, 1992

Great crowds and a sense of anticipation. The place was electrified with expectancy. I admonished the people that we were in revival. However, I was afraid that many would witness it but few would experience it. It is one thing to go through a revival, but it is another to be in a revival. God help us to be participants and not spectators.

I gave a challenge from Acts 2—"Where Do We Go from Here?" (Text: Acts 2:37-42—After revival three thousand souls saved.)

    I.   Indoctrination—Get into the Word
    II. Communication—Fellowship
    III. Commemoration—Breaking of Bread
    IV. Supplication—Prayer

After the great revival at Pentecost, the apostles continued in doctrine (got into the Word), in fellowship, in communion, and in prayer. We need to pray, be faithful, tell others our experience, and stay out of God's way.

I admonished the people that I did not organize it, I did not advertise it, and I did not supervise it. I was going to try to stay out of God's way and let Him run it. I did not give an invitation but sang the song "Pass me not, O gentle Savior, hear my humble cry. While on others thou art calling, do not pass me by." The altars were filled with a sense of soul searching and brokenness.

Sunday morning, November 15, at eight o'clock, the hour of prayer before services, four times as many men as usual were prostrate before the Lord, begging God for revival and begging God to break their hearts and help them to stay out of the way. They were weeping over their sin and begging God to save sinners.

Sunday, November 15, morning service. There were great crowds; the singing was unbelievable. There was a spirit of prayer and expectation. I preached on Luke 19:10. Many came forward, and thirteen were saved. Many came forward for assurance.

Sunday afternoon: great expectation, great prayer time. The choir sang; we sang the old songs "Sound of Abundance of Rain" and "What's the News?" Anticipation and expectation were in the air. People were burdened; tremendous crowds. We had over one hundred visitors. Rod Jr. preached on "Lost in the Church." Many came forward—twenty-seven responded for salvation. We baptized twenty-one. People rejoicing. People still coming after the service to get saved.

(There is a great spirit of revival. The Spirit of the Living God is falling afresh upon us.

God gave me a thought this morning. Singing is a matter of the heart. When the heart is unlocked, the lips are free.)

TESTIMONIES ON NOVEMBER 18 (WEDNESDAY PRAYER SERVICE)

~

One teacher stood up and said that she had to spank a little boy who had been disobedient. Another little fellow jumped up and wanted to take his place and take his spanking for him because of his love for him. I think this is evidence that our children have their minds upon the Cross.

One man gave a testimony of how he was under great conviction when he moved into a new home because every time he went into the bathroom and looked at the commode, the word *church* (the name of the manufacturer) was on the hinges of the toilet seat. The word *church* got him under so much conviction that he had to get saved.

John Monroe, our youth pastor, gave the testimony of going to obtain a permit from the City of Virginia Beach for a bonfire. The lady at the fire marshall's office asked what the purpose of the bonfire was, and John told her we were fulfilling Acts 19:19 and burning those sins which "so easily beset us." After he told her this, she asked him to write the reason down for her to keep. John did, and she got the gospel written down for her to read.

All testimonies were fresh and Christ honoring!

Wednesday night prayer meeting, November 18—Great crowds continue to come with many visitors. The altars were filled. Scores of decisions were made as hearts were convicted by the Holy Spirit. There were 535 in attendance, praying and seeking God's face.

Thursday night visitation, November 19—a great number of our people were out on follow-up visits and visiting our inactive members. One of our faithful members went out to visit with Dr. Hymers and got saved. He had been under great conviction all week.

Friday, November 20, we held an all-night prayer meeting from 7:00 P.M. to 7:00 A.M. People signed up to come in three-hour periods. Many came at 7 P.M. and stayed until 7 A.M. We had 150 people throughout the night praying for the revival fires to continue and for a host of people to be saved on Sunday. Many teens and junior high kids came with their parents. It thrilled my soul to hear them pour out their hearts to God in prayer. There is an openness and transparency in our youth that I had never seen. One young man broke into bitter tears and cried, "Oh God, please do not let my friend go to hell." God is passing the torch of true biblical Fundamentalism to this next generation.

Saturday, November 21 at 10:00 A.M., we had two hundred meet to go on house-to-house visitation. We handed out literature inviting people to come to our Sunday services. Saturday night the young people had a bonfire and invited the adults to join them as they burned "the sins that so easily beset" them—rock music, tapes, videos, literature, and so on. One lady who recently came to Christ burned over $4,000 worth of rock music. We had two teenage girls saved on Saturday night after the bonfire. Many gave testimony of their difficulty in letting go of these things, and many tears were shed as people threw those things into the fire. We praise God for the victory in so many lives. We had approximately 250 in attendance for the bonfire.

Sunday morning, November 22, our men gathered for our regular 8:00 hour of prayer. Attendance was five times the usual number. We prayed for the Holy Spirit to prepare hearts for the morning service. We were earnestly pleading for souls.

The auditorium was packed for the morning service. There were great crowds with a host of visitors. Many came to Christ that Sunday morning, and scores of other decisions were made. Sunday night we again witnessed broken hearts and conviction.

Recap for the day: twenty-seven saved, one church membership, one assurance of salvation, one rededication, and eleven surrendered to preach, teach, or go to the mission field. We baptized twenty precious souls.

Wednesday night, November 25, Thanksgiving service— great singing and spirit of prayer. I gave direction to the church on prayer and fasting.

Friday, November 27, our people were encouraged to take this day for prayer and fasting. A special prayer sheet was given for this time. Names of unsaved loved ones and friends were turned in and prayed for in earnest.

Saturday, November 28, great spirit of evangelism as young and old alike came out to go canvassing and soul winning. Our people are saying, "God is preparing the hearts of those being witnessed to as we go soul winning."

Sunday, November 29, my telephone rang at 4:30 in the morning. A lady could not sleep because she was under deep conviction all night. She had to get saved. I led her to Christ over the telephone. I invited her to come to church and make a public profession. She said she could not because she was two hundred miles away in North Carolina! She had heard about the awakening here at Tabernacle and wanted me to lead her to Christ. She promised me that she would go to her church and make a public profession of Christ.

Sunday morning, November 29, I preached on "The Lost Soul." There were great crowds, and God gave me great liberty. We had tremendous, Christ-honoring singing. Revival fires continue to burn. Eleven came forward for salvation, two for assurance, and one answered the call to the mission field.

Sunday night we observed the Lord's Table, and there were testimonies of brokenness as we had fellowship with the Lord. Sobs were heard throughout the auditorium. We baptized nine, and two came forward for salvation.

This brought us to approximately 350 people who have been saved in our school and church ministries—scores of decisions for Christ and His service.

We did not organize this meeting; we did not advertise it; we did not supervise it—we were finding out which direction the Lord was going and were going with Him.

This is the Lord's doing, and it is marvelous in our eyes. Brethren, pray for us that the wind of God will continue to blow and that Christ will receive all of the glory.

This report is being sent out to those who I know are hungry and thirsty for revival. This is not a "brag sheet" but a praise sheet. Our prayer is that this news might be an encouragement to you and that revival fires will spread. Pray for revival!

Dr. Rod Bell
Isa. 64:1-2

REVIVAL UPDATE I
~

Wednesday, December 2, 1992. There was a great spirit of prayer and a mighty moving of consecration among God's people. There was a sense of evangelism. Since the Spirit of God has done a work within, there was now a great burden to do God's work without in evangelizing. Our people were finding that when they are obedient to witness, God had already prepared the hearts. People were ready to be saved.

Our people were admonished to do three things in the stirring of this awakening:

1. Surrender to God's Will
2. Obey God's Word
3. Pray for God's Power

Saturday, December 5, 1992. The following is an example of God's preparing hearts:

There is a precious black lady in our church by the name of Wanda Lowe who loves the Lord . Wanda's grandmother went to be with the Lord last week. She had visited our church and knew we were a soul-winning church. She had requested that I preach and give an invitation at her funeral. Wanda asked me if I would come to the funeral at the Antioch Missionary Baptist Church in Norfolk and give the invitation at her grandmother's funeral.

The Antioch Missionary Baptist Church is a liberal black church. I went with a burden to be a blessing to this precious family. When I got there, I noticed it was in the ghetto in Berkeley. I saw posters of Martin Luther King Jr., Jesse Jackson, and others all over the walls. The black preachers were dressed in robes and clerical garbs with gold crosses and medallions. I felt that this was going to be most interesting.

Dr. I. J. Williams said to me, "We want you to make yourself at home."

That opened the door, and I prayed silently, "Thank you, Lord." I thought to myself, "They all know where I stand—I stand against everything they stand for. But this is a funeral, and I promised a dear old black saint of God that I would preach her funeral and give an invitation. Say what you want to say."

After much singing and eulogizing, I was asked to come and give an invitation to discipleship. It had been emphasized several times that this was an invitation for discipleship. The place was packed with the unsaved. They had never heard a gospel message. Once a year this church traditionally gives an invitation for people to join. So I felt burdened to give the salvation message. I preached for twenty minutes on "Come unto me, all ye that labor and are heavy laden, and I will give you rest." I gave an invitation for people to come to the Lord Jesus—all those who were burdened and heavy laden with sin.

As I got ready to give the invitation, a man sprang to his feet and came down the aisle. I thought, "I am in trouble, nobody knows how to lead anyone to the Lord here except me and Mr. and Mrs. Lowe" (who were sitting with the family). I stopped and gave an invitation for everybody that wanted to be saved to stand and pray publicly the sinner's prayer after me. Seventy-five or more people stood and prayed the sinner's prayer. They asked God to come into their hearts and save them and forgive them of their sin. There was weeping. There was rejoicing. There was a great sense of conviction. A holy hush fell over that place, and many precious black people accepted Christ as their personal Savior.

I wept because the field is so white unto harvest among the black ghettos. I came home burdened to try to reach them for Christ. We have heard good reports about those who have accepted Christ and want to come to our church. May God bring them and may we somehow reach into this black ghetto to get more precious souls saved. There was a great moving of the power of God upon that service.

Sunday, December 6, 1992. There was great spirit of singing and a burden of prayer and praise for the things the Lord has done. Throughout this day there was a sense of expectancy and waiting on God. Ten people were saved, eleven baptized, and others   are waiting for baptism. Two answered the call into the ministry.

Tuesday, December 8, 1992. I received calls from people wanting to be saved. Our people are witnessing on the job and taking advantage of every opportunity; their focus seems to be on winning the lost.

Wednesday, December 9, 1992. This week has been filled with a sense of burden for sinners and evangelism. A sixty-six-year-old man came to my office. He had been attending our church. One of our people had been witnessing to him. I had the joy of leading him to Jesus Christ, and he wept like a newborn baby over his sin that had nailed our Lord to the tree. He got up off his knees and said, "Oh, I have six children that need to be saved. Pray that I can win them."

Wednesday night our people met for Bible study and prayer time. There was a time of great excitement and anticipation and joy over souls they had had the privilege to lead to Christ that week. The singing was alive and free! There was a freedom and boldness in our witnessing. It was not forced. It came naturally.

Thursday, December 10, 1992. At 8:30 in the morning, I received a call from one of our navy chief petty officers, Ray Borah, who had led one of his men to Christ. He let him testify to me over the phone that he had received Christ as his Savior and would be in church on Sunday. The man said, "Oh, Preacher, I got saved, but please pray for my wife that she will be saved and come with me on Sunday."

At 10:30 that same morning I received another call from Chief Borah. He said, "I have someone here to talk with you. He wants to tell you what happened." Another fellow got on the phone and said, "I got saved. I just want you to know I was in church on Sunday and was under conviction. I should have come forward, but I didn't. I came into Chief's office today and got saved."

Our burden was to see this revival move out into soul-winning evangelism. The thing that I noticed about the soul winning and evangelism was that it was spontaneous—so easy and free, no pressure. It came from the broken, surrendered hearts of our people on the job, in the homes, with neighbors and friends. There was a quiet working and witnessing to their loved ones and co-workers. We continue to pray for the unsaved and for true New Testament evangelism.

Friday, December 11, 1992. At 7:00 P.M. we began another all-night prayer meeting. It was a cold, rainy, dreary night. God's people came to pray—women and their daughters, fathers and their sons. The prayer meeting rooms began to fill. I sensed that the hearts of my people were burdened for lost souls. Their cries were going up for individuals upon their hearts.

We had a song and praise service at 7:00 in the morning following our all-night prayer service. Our ladies came in and cooked a delicious breakfast. At 10:00 A.M. we got ready to go out on soul-winning visitation. We had cold rain pouring and wind, but the spirits were not dampened. The soul-winning fervor is high, and the burden is deepening.

Sunday, December 13, 1992. At 8:00 in the morning, I arrived for Sunday morning prayer time. The 11:00 o'clock service had good crowds. I preached a message on "He came unto his own and his own received him not" (John 1:12). Five adult men came forward for salvation; others came for rededication, and some came to pray for others to be saved. Chief Borah had two pews filled with visitors.

Sunday night we had our annual Christmas cantata, "Ten Thousand Hallelujahs." We had an excellent crowd. I gave the invitation and ten or twelve adult men came forward to be saved. Several came forward to confess sin. There was a real stirring after the cantata. Our military men were weeping over their friends to whom they had been witnessing for nine months to a year. Wives were weeping over their husbands' being saved. Children were weeping over their lost dads.

Now the soulwinning and evangelism are moving out into the communities, the neighborhoods, and the workplaces. People are being saved. People were saved after the service. One man came to me after the service and accepted Christ. I came home from the service on Sunday night, and there was a young Navy man waiting in the driveway. He was burdened about his sin, and I led him to Christ. In one and a half months approximately 375 to 400 souls have been saved.

The revival fires are still burning. Including all of Tabernacle Baptist Ministries, approximately 450 people have been saved as a result of the revival. Twenty-five have surrendered to preaching and/or missions.

REVIVAL UPDATE II

Sunday, December 20, 1992. Hour of prayer from 8:00 A.M. to 9:00 A.M. Men prayed for the Comforter to do His office work in the morning service. The weather was cold and rainy. This is normally one of the smallest crowds of the year. Norfolk-Virginia Beach is a military area, and it seems everyone goes home for Christmas.

The rain persisted, but the crowds came. The weather was cold and rainy outside but did not hamper the Spirit inside. We had one of the best crowds we have ever had on Christmas. A long, busy Christmas week came to an end. The crowds came, visitors came, our navy chief brought three families. Five men got saved, four answered the call to the mission field, and scores of other decisions were made. The altar was filled for prayer and weeping over lost souls.

The services were electrified with dads and moms being saved. The sermon preached was "The Windows of Heaven Are Open" (Malachi 3).

I. The Problem—Windows closed because of sin and judgment.
II. The Process—"Windows of Heaven" always refers to the supernatural intervention of God. Obedience opened the windows of revival, and will do so today.
III. The Product—"If you will, I will." Divine supernatural intervention; blessing will continue.

The revival fires continue to burn—250 or more came weeping, desiring surrender, obedience, and prayer for the revival fires to continue. The invitation shows a great hunger for God's blessing to continue.

In the evening service we had two men saved and one family surrender to go to the mission field. We are finding that physical thirst can be satisfied, but the more we receive of the Water of Life, the more we want. I firmly believe there is a genuine spiritual thirst for God.

Christmas Eve, December 24. One of the greatest services this year. We observed the Lord's Table. The testimonies of young converts were aflame with the love of Calvary. The singing about the "Blood and the Broken Body" has taken on a new meaning.

Sunday morning, December 27. Cold, rainy day. After I woke early and spent time in prayer, the weather still hindered my spirit. But after another hour in prayer, the sunshine in my soul broke through. Normally the crowds are the smallest this weekend because of living in a transient area. I was surprised when I entered the auditorium and heard a packed house singing "What's the News?"

The sermon preached was "Broken Cisterns" from Jeremiah 2. The altars were filled with weeping and sorrow—wanting more of the fountain of living water. Many united with the church, four visitors were saved, and two answered the call to the mission field.

Sunday evening, December 27. We had a good season of prayer with the men—expecting a moving of the Spirit of God. Excellent spirit, good crowds, many gone home for the holidays.

However, the crowd was excellent and there was great liberty in preaching.

Sermon: Luke 16:1-2—"Give an account of thy stewardship; for thou mayest be no longer steward."

About 250-300 people were deeply moved and came to the altar to pray. They did not want to lose their credibility of being a steward.

    I.   The Responsibility—The Summons (v. 2)

   II.   The Accountability—The Stewardship (v. 2)

  III. The Credibility—The Service (v. 2)

  IV. Credibility in Question—Disapproved (vv. 1-2)

Many are winning souls daily. I have never seen a congregation more desperate to be obedient to the Great Commission. As I visited one of my members in the hospital, I asked the gentleman in the next bed if he was saved. He broke and wept like a little child and said, "I was afraid you were *not* going to ask me."

I said, "Would you like to be saved?"

His response, with tears coursing down his cheeks, was "I'd give anything to get saved. I just do not know how."

I showed him how. We rejoiced! He has witnessed to all his family and his nurses of his salvation.

As we stopped in Long John Silver's Restaurant for lunch, a family of four came in to eat. I asked them, "Do you have all your Christmas shopping done? Are you ready for Christmas?"

The dad said, "I've still got to buy one more gift."

My response was, "I hope you have the Greatest Gift."

"What is that?" he asked.

"The Lord Jesus" was my reply.

The next thing I knew, they were in tears. I led all four to Christ, and they received the "Greatest Gift."

Similar situations are being experienced by our people. Oh, may God keep the flame burning. There is a freedom and boldness, a hunger and a burden—almost a holy desperation to win others. "When God intends great mercy for His people, the first thing He does is set them a-praying." —Matthew Henry

Oh, for the floods on the thirsty land!
Oh, for a mighty revival!
Oh, for a sanctified, fearless band,
Ready to hail His arrival!

New Year's Eve, December 31, 1992. Night of family prayer and fellowship, good crowds. Quality family time. I came home with a satisfied heart. I received a call from a man from the shipyard. One of our members had been witnessing to him; he had received Christ and wanted to tell me.

Sunday morning service, January 3, 1993. Seems like everybody has gone out of town. The weather is cold, and on a rainy, chilly morning our men spend one hour in prayer. One man broke and wept, "Oh, please don't let my neighbor go to hell. Save him today." God answered prayer in the morning service. The singing and crowds were excellent. We had four saved and two called to preach. Brokenness over sin in invitation. Sermon: "How to Handle Adversity," using Isaiah 43:3 as my text. Altars were filled with 100-150—a quiet moving of deep conviction. Thank God the Spirit did not go "out of town."

Sunday evening service, January 3. Preached on "Revival" from Isaiah 44:3-4. We had great crowds, many visitors. Some are coming to see what is happening. We sang "What's the News?" One man jumped up and said, "The news is I got saved." The presence of the Lord was evident—weeping and brokenness over cold hearts.

Sunday morning service, January 10, 1993. Terrible weather—many sick with flu and colds. Spent one hour in prayer from 8:00 to 9:00. We prayed for the unsaved. Good crowds; great singing. Preached on "Red Lights on Hell's Highway"—five were saved and three answered the call to preach. Many came burdened for loved ones. There seemed to be great concern to go out this week and compel people to come in. I am not organizing any kind of revival campaign. I must let Him lead, and we will follow.

Sunday evening service, January 10, 1993. There is a great burden to help our people get into the Word and pray. Cold rain, ice, or sleet. Good singing! Spent one hour in prayer. I felt the need for our people to get into the Word in 1993. We must have Bible reading and personal devotions. There seems to be a special hunger for the Word. We had four saved, 250 new "starters" on daily Bible reading, fifty new family altars started. We feel led of the Lord to have at least one all-night prayer meeting each month from 7 P.M. to 7 A.M. No church is greater than its prayer life. "Lord, teach us to pray!" I believe a sinning man will stop praying and a praying man will stop sinning.

Brethren, pray for us. I stand amazed at His work. God did more for our church in thirty seconds than we have done in thirty years.

Personal Note: Brethren, as we have witnessed the Wind of God blowing in His sovereign power, as the flame of God has melted the hardest hearts, we will never be satisfied with the stagnant waters of methodology. The leeks and the garlic are no substitute for the grapes of Eshcol.

Wednesday, January 13, 1993. As I was preparing this update, a navy chief (approximately twenty years in the navy) made an appointment with me, got off work, and came to my office. When he came in, he was shaking as if he had just come in out of a snow blizzard. He spoke as if he had just faced death. "Preacher, I can't sleep, I can't work; I must get saved!" He fell down on his knees and was saved by God's sovereign grace! Immediately, he was calm and a smile of peace and joy shone upon his face. He said, "I must go home and tell my wife and family. Thank you, thank you."

Brother Ken Dorhout, chairman of our deacons, said, "This is the Lord's doing and it is marvelous in our eyes."

God keeps the records. The actual account of souls is recorded in heaven. Within the ministries of Tabernacle Baptist Church, we have had five hundred saved and hundreds of other decisions. No man dare take any credit for this movement. To God be the glory, great things He hath done!

Sunday, January 24, 1993. We started our twenty-fifth annual missions conference: Our Responsibility for Worldwide Evangelism. Missionaries came in from eight to ten different countries. Many of the missionaries from our own church came back to give reports. A mission school was conducted throughout the day. Prayer meetings were held for our missionaries. During the evening services, slide presentations and a challenge for missions were given.

Every night souls were stirred for missions, and many teenagers came forward to surrender their lives to go to the mission field. Several were saved. The crowds were some of the best that we have ever had for a missions conference. Our Faith Promise goal was $120,000, which exceeded our goal of last year by over $40,000. God has given us the largest general offering that we have had for many years in our church.

I had the privilege of leading a sixty-four-year-old Buddhist to the Lord. His wife is a doctor who was gloriously saved. We have had approximately twenty young people surrender to go to the mission field. I gave an invitation, and there were approximately 150-200 who surrendered to go to the mission field and/or full-time Christian work. There is a burden to get the Good News to the regions beyond.

Our people are burdened for foreign missions as never before in my ministry. I stand back in amazement to see people getting involved in missions and mission projects who have never been involved before. Special prayer meetings are being held by the ladies and teens for the gospel to be sent to the regions beyond.

I told my people I was glad to see so many surrender and answer the call to go to the mission field, but please don't all go at once. I would have only my wife and family to preach to!

Sunday, January 31, 1993. An invitation was given for all those who had answered the call to full-time service for our Lord. Over two hundred people responded to the invitation. How my heart burned within me to get the Good News to the regions beyond. In the invitation, the Cambodian (Buddhist) came forward with his wife to make a profession of faith. Seven more were saved, and two came to surrender to preach; ten came for baptism, and many united with our fellowship.

We are looking forward to our Friday all-night prayer meeting. Our families will be gathering to pray for the services and for the revival fires to continue to burn in soul-winning evangelism. Pray that our hearts will be in tune with the will of God.

Sunday, February 7, 1993. I left for the mission field. We visited Cambodia, Thailand, Burma, and Singapore. Our hearts were so burdened for the millions there who have never heard because millions here have never cared. We sensed the power of God in preaching in Burma and Cambodia.

While I was gone, one of my seminary students preached on commitment. Over one hundred fathers came forward to take their place of responsibility in the home and lead their families. Four were saved, six united with the church, and four surrendered to go to the mission field.

Sunday, February 14, 1993. Evangelist Bruce Hamilton preached both services with great liberty, stressing the claims of Christ on our people. Three were saved and four united with our fellowship. The evening service was dedicated to foreign missions with the emphasis upon Russia. Our people were greatly moved.

Sunday, February 21, 1993. I returned from the Far East mission trip with fire in my soul. In the morning service the Spirit of God broke our people for missions. My sermon was entitled "Where Are the Nine?" Only one of ten was grateful for what the Lord had done, and that one was a half-breed. So many in America are like the other nine who feel God "owes" them. They take the blessing of God for granted—the ungrateful wretches! But thank God for that one healed, saved leper, who humbly bowed and became a servant.

My people were moved by the Holy Spirit in waves of conviction, and many came to confess their lack of gratitude. Fifty more family altars were started. The teens started their new Leadership Bible Studies, and new teens are coming in. They are on fire—to God be the glory!

After returning from the mission field, I am convinced that America is the greatest mission field on God's green earth. It is filled with a pagan, humanistic president (Clinton) in the White House disguised as a religious Southern Baptist, and with sodomites, perverts, baby killers, feminists, one-worlders, anti-God-believers, and Bible haters. America is under the judgment of Almighty God.

We must have revival—or we perish. So, brethren, pray for us that the revival fires will spread and burn in Virginia Beach, Virginia.

"REFLECTIONS ON REVIVAL"

November 1992 by a church member
"We never saw it on this fashion" (Mark 2:12)

The wonder of it startled even those who had so long yearned for a genuine personal experience of the spiritual consciousness of yesteryear.

Miraculous times—considered by a hostile world and an indifferent church as spurious interludes of antiquity patiently recorded in Holy Writ, piously recounted in Christian biographies, and now properly resident in the archives of church history.

Exhilarating times—when those who named themselves among the children of God rejoiced in singing pious hymns, repented in the presence of powerful preaching, reverenced the place of importunate prayer, and fervently requested the preeminence of the Paraclete in their lives.

Victorious times—when church members were moved to circumspect introspection as the burning torch of spiritual truth scorched the deepest recesses of degenerate minds, and indifferent hearts were expunged of satanic secrets.

Challenging times—when obstacles to personal sanctification were obliterated and powerful personal testimonies turned the world upside down.

Yes, "it" startled most, this long-sought-for but now fearfully, most reverently embraced movement of the Holy Spirit in our midst. Some, a pitiful few, who for almost five years had been fervently praying and faithfully witnessing, those few recognized when the Holy Spirit began working, unhindered.

To be revived is "to be restored from an inactive or unused state." Revival, in the biblical sense, is not the conversion of sinners but the restoration of weakened spiritual vibrancy, the resurgence of neglected scriptural separation, and the resurrection of dormant soul-winning power in the life of the saint. Revival starts in the church, first in the minds, then of necessity in the hearts of the people.

Lest you misconstrue what I mean, revival comes only to the child of God, a sinner saved by grace, willing to yield personal desires, abandon personal goals, and deny personal pleasures in deference to devotion to the Son of God, dedication to the Word of God, and dependence upon the Spirit of God. Once sin has been confessed, power is unleashed, for that is how God works—through the yielded believer. The church victorious has a people vehemently opposing sin. The church rejoicing has a people victorious over self. The church triumphant has a people valiantly contending for the Faith.

We do not know where the Lord will lead this people, but there is a cadre, albeit a dedicated cadre, of people in our church desperately desiring a continuance of this marvelous working of the Holy Spirit, passionately pleading for the salvation of lost loved ones and rejoicing in the victories thus far received. The people are also profoundly aware that unconfessed sin and selfish desires will assuredly quench the remarkably refreshing revival in our midst.

Would to God this tremendous power, presently directed toward inward revival, be turned outward and unleash the convincing power of the Word of God and the convicting presence of the Spirit of God upon our community, our state, and hopefully our nation.

The following are my reflections on the 1992 revival at Tabernacle Baptist Church. I will present these reflections from the vantage point of a father, a college professor, and a theologian.

Reflections of a Father

The Lord brought revival among the families of TBC. Many young people in the grade school and high school (TBS) sensed a conviction of sin and the need for repentance. There was widespread openness among the youth as many teens sought the Lord's forgiveness and one another's forgiveness. Even in my family, four of my children put their faith in the Lord and lives were changed. This openness and sensitivity among the youth is an evidence of spiritual revival, in my opinion.

Reflections of a Bible College Professor

Several students were saved or gained assurance of their salvation at Tabernacle Baptist Theological Seminary and Bible College. Several examined their baptism relative to their salvation experience and recognized their need for scriptural immersion after salvation. Prayer groups were started, and there was a deep sense of commitment to study and to the preparation for the ministry. Students became burdened for lost loved ones and for worldwide missions.

Reflections of a Theologian

No one man brought this revival to TBC. The sovereign Lord brought the revival in His own good time. Certainly the Lord burdened Pastor Bell several years prior to this for revival.

Having prayed for several years for revival, Pastor Bell was led to have protracted meetings with Dr. Ed Nelson and then Dr. Jerry Sivnksty. The Scripture memorization program of Dr. Sivnksty was incorporated into the church's memory program. A great emphasis was placed on everyone, from child to parent, to memorize a verse per week and to have family altars. Along with prayer and Scripture memorization, Pastor Bell and others utilized strong preaching to bring about an atmosphere for God to work in hearts. When church members were obedient, the Holy Spirit worked in lives.

Theologically, it seems revival came when the following requirements were met: the Preparation, the Praying, the Permeating (of the Scripture), the Place (a local New Testament church), the Preaching, the People (were obedient), and the Providence of God.

REFLECTIONS ON REVIVAL FROM OUR PRINCIPAL

~

November 2 was the most unusual chapel service ever in the history of Tabernacle Baptist Schools. Our human plan was to go to chapel and have people who were saved in the previous Sunday evening's service testify of what God had done in their lives.

We had a combined chapel of 250 students from grades K-5 through 12. The service was opened with one song, after which I led in prayer and read Psalm 107:2—"Let the redeemed of the Lord say so, whom he hath redeemed from the hand of the enemy."

After the Scripture, I asked one twelfth-grade boy to give his testimony, and I asked others to follow. This young man told how God had saved him the night before. The next person told how he was saved in the same service. The third person to testify was another senior boy. During his testimony a twelfth-grade girl got up out of her seat and went to a teacher saying, "I need to be saved; would you help me?" They left the meeting and went to the back of the church, where the young lady accepted Christ.

The next three hours continued uninterrupted, with seventy-five souls being saved and over fifty rededications. No one but the Holy Spirit of God was speaking in the service.

There was no invitation given or any encouragement from the platform. There was no break in the service for three hours. The Holy Spirit was working in elementary lives as well as the junior and senior high. About a half-hour into the service, teens began to go to their classmates. Later, young people said they accepted Christ as a result of one young man, who became an immediate soulwinner.

One young lady, a senior girl, told how she and three friends went out for pizza after the service the night before when fifty-eight people had been saved. The topic of conversation at their table was lost friends. They soon realized it was the first time they had ever been concerned about lost classmates. God was at work.

The service of children and teens was soon joined by some adults. Two school mothers came up to testify that they had received Christ that morning. Another mother came to deliver her child to the preschool. She found the hallway full of people getting saved and asked, "What is happening?" Someone told her that God had sent a revival and people were getting saved. She began to cry and said, "I need to be saved." Someone led her to Christ.

Our meeting continued from 8:00 to 11:00, with a great outpouring of the Spirit. Again, not a word was spoken to encourage anyone to come to Christ—God was doing His work through the Holy Spirit. During the testimonies, many young people surrendered their lives to Christ; some were specifically called to the mission field.

The eleven o'clock hour brought a close to the meeting. Then I encouraged each child and adult to make sure there was nothing between him and his brother. This was used of God for the next half-hour to restore fellowship among our TBS family. There was a real openness on the part of everyone in the meeting to get right with a fellow Christian.

So after three and a half hours, God ended the meeting but not the revival.

Our church family had been taught that a main factor in continuing revival is prayer. I began the next morning to have student prayer meetings before and during school. The meetings were in the hands of the students—there were no adults involved except to encourage the teens. God put a special burden on some hearts, and they continued to pray.

Teachers have remarked how attitudes and actions have changed. There is a much greater concern among teens for their classmates. Their concerns were openly expressed. One teacher related that her high school English class had written journals about how they were praying for classmates. Several of the prayer burdens have already been answered by the Lord.

The spirit in the hallways, though never "bad," has continued to just be more open and friendly. The hallways are full of young people whose countenances have changed, and the strains of the bondage of sin are gone from their faces. There have been fewer problems for staff to handle because students are allowing the Lord to work things out.

Our boys' basketball team is enjoying one of their best years ever. They play with more joy and togetherness. These things are actually observable to those of us who know these boys. Two of the three boys who seem to be leading in the school since the revival are on the team. One of them was already going to Bible college, and now the other one is seriously considering it.

One young athlete shared with his pastor, Dr. Bell, that he wanted to be remembered by the younger children in school as a spiritual leader, not as a ball player. This young man and other boys are going into the elementary classes and holding prayer times with the children. Not only will they share petitions and prayer time, but they rejoice in answered prayer.

Parents have expressed that they have seen the change in their children. Bible reading and devotions are now a part of young lives. We have tried, through the school Bible classes, to get devotional material into the hands of the students. Over one hundred children and teen devotional booklets have been distributed.

One major evidence of revival is a changed life. We have seen many changed lives at TBS. The changes have been clearly toward the things of God. The revival is still with us as teens go on soul-winning visitation. They have seen friends come to Sunday school and church.

The most recent evidence of revival was the large number of teens who surrendered for full-time service. Three students answered the call to the mission field. Several surrendered to do whatever God wants them to do. Each of the three young men who are leading in the school surrendered their lives to the Lord's will.

We are thankful at TBS to have been blessed of God in actually seeing revival. What a wonderful experience to see God move in and take over. We truly believe that as a result of this ongoing revival, future marriages will be saved from divorce, children will have better homes, and more people will be in full-time service. November 2 is truly a "mountaintop" day in the spiritual life of TBS.

Part 5:

Reflections on a Mountain Man

CHAPTER 17:
A Wife's Perspective

"LIFE IS JUST A CHAIR OF BOWLIES"

I wonder what the original cherries God created in the garden of Eden were like. Do you suppose they were all perfect, juicy, tart sweetness? They did have pits back then because all the trees and herbs bore their seed in themselves. In order to successfully grow a cherry tree in the Hampton Roads, Virginia, area, the nursery man has to spray the tree seven times each year. It must also be fertilized and pruned on a regular schedule. A plentiful harvest comes only after about five years of careful nurturing, but the fruit is worth the effort and time spent.

Can you imagine a cherry as large as an apple? What a mouth-watering thought! What an unrealistic fantasy. This was the type of thinking with which I began my life with Rod L. Bell ("Bobby Lee" to some folks). Cherries as big as apples—perfect, juicy, tart sweetness, having no thought of pits or worms. No reality at all.

Rod and I met as young teenagers, thirteen and fourteen, and attended Scott High School in Madison, West Virginia. We "dated steady" our senior year and married on August 31, 1953. My fantasy was that this tall, skinny man with big, brown eyes and an award-winning smile would be totally committed to spending his entire life listening to and heeding my every beck and call, always thinking of ways to make me happy and content. Rod's sixth-grade teacher, Mrs. Price, said his smile could win the world! This fantasy would require nothing from me but my being there.

Talk about being blissfully ignorant! To make matters worse, Rod also had the same idea—that I would do those same things for him. We had impossible expectations. "The pits" had to follow.

Our first experience with "the pits" was facing joblessness and having a baby due in July. This was a loud wake-up call for me and a frightening obligation for Rod. We had to move back to West Virginia from Baltimore, Ohio. This was a great disappointment. Our baby, Terri Lynn, died at birth. I think we ran the gamut of emotions—from shock, anger, disbelief, and sorrow to perplexity.

Although I had accepted the Lord as my Savior at ten years of age, Rod was not a Christian. In my early teen years, I was concerned only with pleasing Lenore and hoped God would agree. Words cannot express the extent of my regret for this time wasted. I can only thank God that He continued to love me in spite of myself. I had never taken into account that God had a legitimate claim on my life. Never had I seriously considered His will or direction for me.

Reality struck when our baby died. I was not in control of my life as I had thought. I was overwhelmed with guilt because, selfishly, I had not wanted a baby. (Guilt and shame are the Devil's banners; God gives forgiveness and restoration.) My sin had caused my husband grief, and I couldn't give him comfort. Rev. Bill Tate conducted the burial service for our baby. He spoke to us of God's goodness and compassion. Of course, Rod couldn't understand this at all. My life as a Christian had been so hypocritical that, as much as I desired for Rod to be saved, I couldn't reach him. Pastor Tate led him to the Lord on January

19, 1957. Soon afterward, Rod was called to preach. This was my "chair of bowlies"!

PRUNING TIME
~

I am very grateful to my parents for their faithfulness in serving the Lord. I had been in church on a regular basis since my dad accepted the Lord when I was four years old. This did not prepare me to be a pastor's wife, however. I had very little Bible knowledge. The one thing I wanted most not to do was to be the wife of a pastor. When the Lord called Rod to preach, my whole life was turned upside down.

We left for BJU in Greenville, South Carolina, in August 1958. This was the greatest decision we had ever made. Our association with the University has continued to this day; however, these years were the most difficult—*just plain hard!*—but also wonderful and exciting years of our lives. God had given us a baby daughter, Niki, on January 7, 1958. We were thrilled with her. Since Rod was so busy working and being a college student, I had many lonely evenings. Having Niki filled many of these evenings with play time, stories, and singing. Sometimes, while rocking her, I would rock myself to sleep.

The whole time Rod was in school I had a running battle with God concerning being a pastor's wife. I begged, pleaded, and tried to make deals with God—anything I could think of—to change His calling for my husband. Even as I write, I shake my head and think, "Oh, what a foolish girl!" I did not realize that God would never ask me to do anything He wouldn't enable me to do. "Faithful is He that calleth you, who also will do it" (I Thess. 5:24). I have leaned heavily on this promise.

Based on my observations of the people I had been around since childhood, I had formed a strong aversion to being a pastor's wife. I could just see myself with my hair in a ball on the back of my head; drab, shapeless, ugly clothes, and no make-up; living on the side of a mountain, up a hollow in West Virginia.

The pastors' wives I had known were scrutinized from top to bottom, including how they kept house, how they trained their children, and whether they were good cooks. If they could quote a Bible verse, they were accused of trying to act pious; if they couldn't, they were a detriment to their husbands' ministries. The Devil had sold me a bill of goods. I bought it, no questions asked. What a relief and a joy to learn that God only wanted this for my good. Ignorance of the Bible and an improper concept of God had caused this grief. Telling His story was to be our lifelong ministry. It would require commitment and diligence for the future.

Only in the ministry is the wife expected to be directly involved in her husband's occupation. Whether this is fair is immaterial. A ministry wife can choose to have a career separate from the church, but although I tried this for a while, it just was not for me. Rod and I needed to work together to promote the unity of our marriage. Did I lose myself, my identity? I hope so. I hope God took a totally self-centered, unfocused individual, whose goals were only here and now, and changed her into a profitable servant.

We attended Tabernacle Baptist Church in Greenville. Dr. Harold Sightler was the pastor at the time. It was here and through listening to Dr. Bob Jones Sr. on the radio that I learned that God had a plan of salvation. "These things have I written unto you that believe on the name of the Son of God; that ye may know that ye have eternal life, and that ye may believe on the name of the Son of God" (I John 5:13). I learned that I was secure in God's love.

Also, it was here that I learned God's plan for the home. This was quite different from anything I had learned before. Actually, I had heard about it but had decided very early on that no man would ever tell me what to do! The admonition to children was easy to understand. However, the husband and wife relationship was a different matter. I think I'll just say that God knows best, and when our understanding and relationship is right with God, His plan works perfectly. Since we aren't perfect people, it usually takes the greater part of our lives to get it right. Due to our imperfections, life can sometimes be the pits!

Understanding God's will and submitting to that will are concepts that were not easy for me to grasp. Doing things "my way" had held sway for so long, but God did give me victory. The three basic things that God uses to draw us to Himself and His plan for our lives are (1) the Word of God, (2) the Holy Spirit, and (3) circumstances. All those things worked together when my heart was willing. Why do we allow the Devil to keep us from trusting God? So often, we accept his line that God cannot be trusted. Not so!

The most liberating act of my life was when I finally surrendered to God's will, no matter what it was. Being loaded down with the garbage of anger, resentment, and self-will is too much for a body to carry. Our emotions, when running contrary to God's will, can be the death of us. My friend Pat Joyner gave me the little book *None of These Diseases* that deals with God's explanation of the sanitary instructions for the children of Israel and also what carrying anger and bitterness will do to your body. It made me realize what I was doing. I had to confess these things as sin and turn my will over to the Lord. Why did I wait so long?

OUR MINISTRIES

Mount Calvary Baptist Church in Greenville, South Carolina, was our first ministry. We met in an old garage with corrugated tin walls and a concrete floor. It took three whole days of hard labor to get the building clean enough to have services. Rod was still in school, which meant that I saw less of him than before. He worked day and night. Our two boys, Timothy Paul and Rod Jr. (Bobby Lee) were born while we were working there. After Rod Jr. was born, I became a full-time mom.

When Rod graduated from college, he went to work at Tabernacle Baptist School (Dr. Harold B. Sightler), teaching and driving a bus. Shortly after we joined the staff, Tabernacle started a Bible college. Rod taught four nights a week in addition to his responsibilities during the day and with the church. These were grueling years for both of us. Rod has always given 110 percent to any job he has. This is a wonderful character trait, but there are only twenty-four hours in a day. These jobs left no time for his family. Do you hear discontent? It was there. The Devil did his best to use these good character traits to tear down our home and ruin a godly ministry. He did not succeed, thank the Lord.

Many times it is difficult for a young man to realize that his family is his ministry as well as the church or any other legitimate occupation. This truth needs to be emphasized in our Bible colleges as men prepare for the ministry. Many pastors are put on a guilt trip if they take an evening for family time. God couldn't be pleased with this attitude.

When God called us to Virginia Beach, we were in the midst of remodeling a house in the neighborhood of Mount Calvary ("Bootleg Corner"). We had long-range plans for the ministry there. Dr. Mark Minnick, who is the pastor there now, has developed the ministry in the exact direction we had intended. It seems to be God's stamp of approval on our former work.

We realize now that our ministry was based on a lot of zeal but little knowledge. I probably committed all the errors in the book! At this time in our lives, Rod thought that if you had a planned program, God wouldn't be free to work. Consequently, our services were quite lengthy. The folks who worked with us were faithful, longsuffering, and kind. In Virginia Beach I could start with a clean slate and be a pastor's wife for the glory of God, not Lenore's. That was my greatest desire.

The work in Virginia Beach grew quickly. Rod knocked on doors several hours a day. The first year, the church office was in our home. Everyone met there for planning sessions, visitation, and so on. My precious privacy was invaded. Everyone soon discovered that I wasn't really a great housekeeper.

In 1967, the boys were ages two and three; Niki was eight. The children adjusted to the move quickly; everyone was so helpful, friendly, and loving. It was wonderful! The only negative

I recall was that I had nursery duty for two years—not exactly my favorite job! Only when I began to do this job for the Lord did I have joy in it. I still take my turn in the nursery, but now it's only one service per month.

Then I worked in each Sunday school department, starting with the beginners. I received "on-the-job training" in Bible doctrines. I was in desperate need in that area. My favorite age to teach is junior high girls. My heart is drawn to them. I want to help them make the transition from a little girl to a young lady. I've taught a women's class for several years and loved it. At this time, Rod and I are in a couples' class together. I'd really like to get back to a women's class one of these days.

In 1969 we started the day school at Tabernacle. Not long after this came the Bible institute for evening students. The institute grew into Tabernacle Baptist Bible College and Seminary. I worked in the offices as a receptionist and secretary. I loved working with Rod and really felt a part of the ministry. I did a short stint as his secretary, but I don't consider myself to be "secretary material"!

PREVENTIVE MAINTENANCE

In 1976 Rod was elected president of the FBF and had to be away from home more often, almost weekly. Wives whose husbands are away a lot know that if anything is going to break down or if the children are to become sick or get hurt, it is when Daddy is gone. A wife can choose to be angry and resentful, or she can realize that this is her calling for this time in her life. This is her ministry. I experienced some of both. However, I came to realize that if I was angry and resentful, my children would be affected. We pass our bad attitudes to our children, and they continue generation after generation.

In our church the men are employed by the military, in shipyards, in real estate, as business executives, and so on. Many men spend numerous hours and even months, if they are military, away from home. It is a necessity. The wives and children can become self-reliant and capable persons, or they can sit on their hands and bemoan the fact that Daddy isn't home. We do have a choice. The attitude of a wife may determine her husband's success in his field of endeavor. I must be honest and tell you that I have thrown my share of "pity parties." They produce only negative results. I soon learned to fix all the foods Rod didn't like while he was gone. We watched all the TV programs he didn't like, and I got involved in projects that I really enjoyed. This worked for the mutual satisfaction of both Mom and the kids!

Rod and I earnestly desired that our children know the Lord and serve Him. We never forced our calling on them, but we urged them to pray (as they got older) for God's will for their lives. This would bring true happiness. If they heard their parents bemoaning their fate and crying "poor me" on a regular basis, they surely would not want any part of the ministry, would they?

The spirit of the mother permeates and rules the home. What an awesome responsibility. We had many pleasant times together teaching the children Bible verses, choruses, and wholesome songs. The day-to-day living out of these principles would weigh heavily on my shoulders. However, Rod was always their hero, and his homecoming always brought great joy.

Contrary to the bleak picture I initially had of being a pastor's wife, my life has been far from the mountain-hollow poverty and boredom I had envisioned. God has always supplied our need, and our income has been sufficient. We had decided very early on that money and material wealth would never be our goal. If God allowed financial gain, that would be fine. If not, that, too, would be just fine.

Never did we envision the scope of our ministry being what it is today. God allowed us to take on as much as we thought we could handle, doing whatever was necessary to get the job done, and here we are. At times when I hear Rod being referred to as a great man, I totally agree; and then wonder how I fit into the scheme of things? Thankfully, God enables us. I'm so proud of

Rod, this mountain boy who so honorably wears the mantle of his great-grandfather.

BRANCHES

My first trip abroad with Rod was in 1976 to Edinburgh, Scotland, for the World Congress held at Ulster Hall. Rod's topic of address was "The Authority of the Divine Inspiration of the Word of God." This was the boy who would not have graduated from high school unless I outlined his literature book! Oh, the grace of God! Our staff, Charlie Anderson, Fred Thomson, Homer Massey, and Jo Jackson, traveled with us. Dr. Carl Bieber, the principal of our schools, also accompanied us. He doesn't enjoy flying, and he held his feet up the entire time we were over the Atlantic Ocean!

Edinburgh is a magnificent city—the city of John Knox and Bloody Mary, with buildings and streets older than the United States. Cobbled streets, beautiful gardens, and castles! Jo and I went on our own sightseeing tour. We visited a tie factory where they did screen printing, had tea in a little shop below the street, then found ourselves, of all places, in a brewery, totally lost. A very kind man gave us directions to the correct bus stop to get back to our hotel. We were never really scared, just a little bit apprehensive. What a lark! I probably wouldn't be so adventurous now.

After the meeting, we took a ferry with the Paisleys and members of Martyrs Memorial (Dr. Paisley's church) to Ireland. Ian Jr. and Kyle were about seven or eight years old and just full of themselves! Stanley and Ina Barnes took us to see the Irish Sea. All the stones and sand on the shore were black. Then we went to the Giant's Causeway and to the History of Ireland Museum. We were invited to numerous teas; the pastries were fantastic. I tried everything. (I also gained about ten pounds!)

Another time, we stayed at the Paisleys' in Belfast. Eileen Paisley took us shopping. What an experience. This was at the height of "the Troubles" (terrorist bombings). No cars were allowed near the shops. We passed through a high fence that was guarded with well-armed soldiers. The shops were all locked. We knocked to get in and were frisked and our purses searched before we could look at a thing. I think my eyes were as big as saucers! Rod preached with Dr. Paisley on a flatbed truck out in a huge field. I got quite angry at him for taking off his jacket; white shirts make excellent targets. That was all I could think about during the whole meeting. The Paisleys are godly folk who have been terribly slandered and misrepresented by the press. They are our dear friends.

On another trip, we were invited to Kings Ranch in Cody, Wyoming. It is beautiful, rugged country at the edge of Yellowstone National Park. Our hosts were the Bud Wells family. I thought for sure I was going to get their beautiful daughter, Kelly, for a daughter-in-law, but our kids had other plans. I must say that I dearly love both our daughters-in-law; Kimberly Gail and Shari Kay are just perfect for our sons. Kim and Tim have given us three grandsons: Corey, Gabriel, and Thomas. Rod and Shari have given us our only granddaughter, Brooke Taylor. Grandchildren are simply marvelous. In some cultures the parents choose mates for their children. I'm sure glad we don't have that responsibility here.

One of the national FBF meetings was in Tempe, Arizona's, Tri-City Baptist Church (Jim and Mary Singleton). The ladies' meeting was at a restaurant, where we had a section to ourselves. When I announced the title of my talk, "Victoria's Secret," I could see necks craning to hear what I was going to say. Actually, I was referring to our underlying beliefs or foundational philosophies of life. I made up the title just for fun.

Probably the most exciting trip we have taken was to Barbados, West Indies. Pastor Carl Naitrim took us sightseeing. One of the places we visited was a huge cave, large enough to travel through by tram. It was an awe-inspiring and magnificent sight, but none of us wanted to stay underground very long. Claustrophobia! Of course, our tram broke down. "Not to worry," they said, "help is on the way." It seemed like hours, but it was only about thirty minutes before we got out of there. Time really flies when you're having fun. While we were stuck underground, we sang hymns and choruses, led by a group of the island men. They have beautiful, mellow voices, and they kept the rhythm by tapping on the back of the seats. Were we glad to be rescued? You bet!

Barbados is a beautiful island in the sun. The people are English-speaking and extremely polite. The ministry is exciting. It would be an ideal place to retire. However, I would want to live on top, not under it in the caves!

SOUTH AMERICA
~

I joined Rod in Bolivia and Chile for some regional World Congress meetings. The purpose was to encourage the missionaries there and minister to the people. Rod and I were with Beneth and Bob Jones III and their son and daughter-in-law, Stephen and Erin Jones. The ladies had a morning meeting separate from the men to focus on our special interests. In the evening we all came together. These are Spanish-speaking people, so for the first time ever, I had to speak with an interpreter. Lineth, Angel Coreon's daughter, interpreted for us. She is a doll and truly a good interpreter. I fell in love with these Inca Indian people and could have stayed there.

John and Cathy Gunter have been working in Bolivia for forty years. They have established fifty native churches. Thirty-nine of the pastors—native Incas—were able to attend the meeting in Santa Cruz. We had a typical Bolivian meal in the home of Merry and Mattea Brooks. Charles and Hanna Brooks, also missionaries there, had adopted Mattea when he was a young child. He attended BJU under the Timothy Program and is now back in Bolivia as a native pastor. What a joy to see missions in action!

John and Mattea took us to some Inca ruins at the top of a mountain. The mountain is mostly stone with very little topsoil at the peak. The Incas had carved an amphitheater, where they worshiped the sun and moon; at the very top of the mountain, they had offered human sacrifices.

In Chile we were in Santiago with the Purvis and Chapman families. Theresa Maria "Chachi" interpreted for us there. She is a delightful person whose ministry is in camp work and ministering to women in prison. One day, while we were shopping, a group of men surrounded Pastor Julio Cortez. In just a matter of seconds, they robbed him, right in broad daylight, with people all over the place! I kind of lost my desire to shop at the street markets after that episode.

PRUNING

Our family is no stranger to difficulties. The decade of the eighties was our pruning time: very painful but necessary to mold and make a family for God's glory. Being a Christian does not ensure a smooth ride through this journey of life. God sends rain on the just and the unjust. The difference is that a Christian can draw comfort and wisdom from God's Word. An unbeliever has to "tough it out" all alone.

Our daughter, Niki, married a "preacher boy" who attended TBBC. Almost from the beginning, trouble reared its ugly head. Niki was almost destroyed emotionally. I could hardly bear to see her going downhill so rapidly. She lost respect for herself and became extremely careless about her appearance, even while they were still together. Four years into the marriage they separated, supposedly to receive counseling. John deserted Niki and their son "J. W." (John) not long after the separation and has not been a part of their lives for all these years. Niki's son John has been a delight. He is attending BJU to prepare for full-time Christian service. God does turn bad things into good. Niki has done a good job training him.

When J. W. was in kindergarten, I would take him home with me at 3:30 P.M. One day as he was running to the car, he tripped on the sidewalk, skinned his knee, and tore a hole in his pants. It was just a small wound, but he continued to cry and was very upset. Finally he said, "Grammy, will all my blood run out that hole?"

Poor little fellow. He thought his skin kept the blood in his body. I was able to assure him that he would be fine.

One day Tim bought John a model car. He was just dying to put it together. I knew he would need help and asked him to wait until Papa came home. He assured me that he didn't need Papa's help. He said, "I have the destructions right here!" He was such an independent little boy.

Our oldest son, Timothy, suffered a head injury while playing basketball at BJU in the spring of 1984. As a result of this injury, he had amnesia for several months. He couldn't remember us, his friends, or his past. The doctor recommended that we get a pet as a help to restore his emotional well-being. Our friends Frank and Grace Hopkins raised English bulldogs and pugs at that time. We got a pug, and Tim named him "Satch." Satch was simply adorable, and I believe he was good therapy for Tim. Satch had one problem, though—his snoring rattled the rafters! One day the boys recorded him snoring and vowed it was me. I snore too, but not that badly!

As Tim's memory returned, his emotions and mood swings were like a roller-coaster ride. We never knew what to expect. Rod was so totally devastated and emotionally involved that I couldn't let my feelings show. I learned later that because of my "stiff upper lip" in the face of this adversity, Tim thought I didn't care, which was never the case. God did bring us through this bumpy time, and we are much stronger for it.

Rod Jr. was injured in a car-truck accident in 1987 in Gainesville, Georgia. He went there every weekend to work as the youth director at McEver Road Baptist Church. My parents live nearby; my mother adored Rod and loved having him in their home. The accident occurred on McEver Road, not far from the church. When we got to the hospital the next day, the doctor told us Rod had only a 5 percent chance to live. We were stunned. We had been praying from the minute the call came telling us about the accident, but nothing could have prepared us for this. We understood he had a broken leg. Nothing had been said about his internal injuries.

God repeatedly brought to my mind the words of the song "We Have an Anchor":

> *We have an anchor that keeps the soul*
> *Steadfast and sure while the billows roll.*
> *Anchored to the rock that will not move,*
> *Grounded firm and deep in the Savior's love.*

I felt like a tiny sailboat in a cyclone, but I had an anchor! God had assured Rod through His Word (Ps. 118:17-18) that our son would live. Three weeks later we were going to take him home. Bob Jones III loaned us his car to travel from Greenville, South Carolina, to Gainesville. Bob III and Beneth came down on the University's plane. Rod drove Dr. Bob's car to Greenville and then joined us for the trip home. What wonderful friends! They had made sandwiches and drinks for us to enjoy on the way home. We turned our spare bedroom into a hospital room for Rod Jr., and I was his nurse for about three months. This episode settled once and for all my idea of a career as a nurse! Cleaning wounds and carrying bedpans was not my calling, but surely I could do it for my baby boy.

The most difficult time of our lives was Rod's illness and operations in 1989. I really thought the Lord was going to take him; Rod was at death's door many times. We were so very blessed with people praying for us, bringing food, sending cards and letters. But at a time like this, only God can give true comfort and peace.

One day, on the way to the hospital, God spoke to my heart with such tenderness. He assured me, through the words of a song written by Becky Calvert, that whether Rod lived or died, God is good.

God is good. God is good.
And He doeth all things well.
All His efforts meet success.
God is good. God is good.
Who am I to question
    the judgments that He makes?
God is good,
This I know.
God is good!

This is a very simple truth, but it really was the turning point for me. I searched Psalms for a promise, and God gave me Psalm 91:14-16. It seemed those verses were written just for me: "Because he hath set his love upon me, therefore will I deliver him: I will set him on high, because he hath known my name. He shall call upon me, and I will answer him: I will be with him in trouble; I will deliver him, and honour him. With long life will I satisfy him, and show him my salvation."

Neither one of us had prayed for God to heal him; it just didn't seem to be the thing to do. We prayed for God's will to be done. God did heal my husband, and our lives have never been the same. The doctors said he would be able to work only three half-days per week. It is amazing! His schedule has been busier than ever. My sisters Sandy and Angie were Shacklee distributors and helped me get Rod on a good nutrition program. When we brought him home, he was able to eat only a tablespoon of food every thirty minutes.

Neither of us would want to go through this episode again, but God produced much good from it. Rod is no longer the self-reliant person he was before. He has learned to depend on God for strength, wisdom, and the power of the Holy Spirit in his preaching. He is so much more kind, tender, and compassionate. Truly, he is not the same man I married! God produced good—great good—in our lives through this extremely trying time.

God's ways are wonderful. His plans are, many times, beyond our understanding.

I am so grateful that He turned a potential tragedy into a success story. Rarely does a good marriage emerge when a Christian marries an unbeliever. Most of the time such a union brings heartache and disaster because there are two totally different philosophies of life. Had Rod not accepted God's offer of salvation, this chapter and, indeed, this book would be an entirely different story. By accepting Jesus Christ as his Savior, Rod accepted God's philosophy of forsaking the world and rejecting anything that is contrary to the Word of God. Faith is a miracle. It is the ability God gives us to trust His Son, not merely partake in an emotional decision. Faith produces action, the results of which are certainly evident in Rod's life.

BOWLS OF CHERRIES

When Rod and I married, I thought he could do anything. I had total confidence that he would love and care for me all my life. He said he would, didn't he? I could put my life in his hands and never have a worry. He made me feel very secure. He still does. After forty-five years of marriage, I realize that he really can't do everything. Actually, I learned that early on. I know he didn't "hang the moon in place." He is definitely not a handyman, but we won't discuss that little shortcoming here! But he is a man who put his trust in God as a young man of twenty-two, who has used these years to learn more and more about Him. He has labored diligently and sincerely to reach souls for eternity and to be a "Barnabas" to his fellow preachers all over America and around the world. He is a preacher's preacher. Together, we have grown up, had a family, and established a fruitful ministry under the direction and through the power of the Holy Spirit. He still makes my heart sing!

If it were possible to go back in time, both of us would change some things we've done, but we would never change partners. When we gave our marriage vows, they really meant little to either of us. But they have since become precious to us as we have lived them every day for forty-five years.

The cherry tree is mature. It has survived spraying, pruning, and many winters. Now is the time of the abundant harvest. It is by God's grace. Perfect, juicy, tart, sweet cherries. None as big as apples. All of them with pits. That is how God planned it. His plan is always best.

Our walk together is not finished. The best is yet to be.

CHAPTER 18:
A Daughter's Perspective

"UNCONDITIONAL LOVE"

~

Rod and Lenore Bell would like to announce the birth of their daughter, Nikita Dawn Bell, born January 7, 1958, in Boone County, West Virginia.

The weather outside is a blizzard, and snow blankets the small town. Their hearts are warm, and the love they share for this new child shines on their faces. You see, three years ago there was another baby girl born to Rod and Lenore Bell, but God saw fit to take her to heaven, maybe because He knew they were just not ready to start raising children yet. God knew that Rod (my dad) would accept the Lord as his Savior the year before I was to be born.

I have never known life as the child of an unsaved parent. When I was eight months old, Dad packed up everything we owned and moved us to Greenville, South Carolina. There he enrolled in Bob Jones University and studied to be a preacher. It was there my life as a "P.K." (preacher's kid) began.

As far back as I can remember, Dad has always called me his "Sunshine"—Daddy's little girl. I went everywhere Dad went. I can even remember driving around with Dad in our '54 blue

Chevy. Dad was very busy, going to school full time, working, and preaching, so I didn't get to see him much.

Dad wasn't only my dad; he was my pastor, principal, and school bus driver. He tells the story about my first time going to school. "Mom cried, and Dad got something in his eye." We all know men don't cry, but that "something in his eye" was tears.

Five years went by and—you guessed it—another baby. This time Timothy Paul was born; sixteen months later, it was Rod Jr.

In the first or second grade, I remember a teacher asking, "What do you think of your dad?"

I raised my hand. "My dad reminds me of a bear."

I guess I thought of him as a bear because he scared me. He was so tall and had a loud, booming voice. Well, thankfully, I grew out of that stage.

Being a "P.K." you learn "right fast" that your dad is not there just for you. He's there for everybody, twenty-four hours a day, seven days a week. I didn't like this aspect of it at all. It seemed like he was never home. Someone could call on him and Dad would drop everything to go help that person. It didn't matter what time of the day or night. I can still hear Dad say, "They're my people; they need me." Even people who had been gone from the church for years called; I asked Dad, "Why do you go?" Dad always answered, "Because I'm still their pastor. They know where I stand and that I tell them the truth." Dad showed "unconditional love."

When the church on Bootleg Corner was in its building stage and Dad was raising money, God touched the hearts of people in unusual ways. They brought everything under the sun to the altar to be sold, and the money was given to the church. I've seen Dad give every last dime from his pockets and then take the shoes off his feet to give to the Lord's work.

As I grew up, Dad would always remind me, "Remember whose name you bear." When you told someone you went to Rod Bell's church, you either puckered or ducked—most people had a love/hate relationship with Dad! But I always knew what Dad really meant: "Don't do anything that might bring reproach upon the Lord's name."

As everyone knows, being a teenager means having periods of rebellion, and being in a preacher's home was no different. People think P.K.s should be different from other children, but we're not. Through all the rebellious stages this child passed, never did my dad turn his back on me. He has loved me unconditionally.

It wasn't until the age of seventeen that I really settled my salvation in my heart. All those years I had the "head knowledge" but not the "heart knowledge." Living in a preacher's home, it was so easy to play the role of a Christian and yet not be one. Many nights I heard Mom and Dad crying and praying for me in their bedroom. I had hardened my heart and stopped my ears to the Lord, until that night in February when Dad showed me how to be saved.

Off to college I went at the age of eighteen. I thought I would be able to make a name for myself, but even there, I was caught in the spotlight that followed Rod Bell. I didn't want to admit it, but I still harbored resentment and bitterness toward my dad. I just wanted to get out from under Dad's thumb. I attended Bob Jones University for two years. Then I met a man who was a student at Tabernacle's Bible college. In two years we were married.

The Bell family is not immune to tragedy. Four years and one wonderful son later, my marriage came to an end. Dad really tried to help us, but without success. My husband and I were separated and then divorced. I felt sure Dad would disown me and not love me anymore. All my life he had taught me differently. But Dad didn't turn his back on me, nor did he stop loving me. Through the past sixteen years of being a single parent, Dad's love has been unconditional.

John (my son) and I lived in Greenville for thirteen years. Dad has always been there for me, just like the Lord. The Lord has never turned His back on me, though I can't say I've been as faithful to Him. The tragedies that the Lord allowed in my life were permitted for a reason. Dad always said, "Let this tragedy turn into a triumph, and let the Lord get the glory in the end." That's hard to do, but with the prayers of a God-honoring Dad and Mom, I know that victory will be sweet.

Being in Rod Bell's home has been an adventure. We've had the opportunity to meet many preachers and evangelists. — Billy Kelly serenaded us with his violin; Daniel Fugi; Russ Rice, a dear friend of the family whose two oldest sons were my companions growing up; and Bobby and Francis Powell (Francis was my teacher at Tabernacle in South Carolina). Jimmy Rose's preaching style captivated me as a child—he was never still! He would jump over chairs and choir-loft banisters; I think he would swing from the chandeliers if he could.

Twice I wrecked the car and had to make that phone call to Dad. I was scared to death at what he might say, but his only concern was always, "Is everybody okay?"

"Yes, sir. But I wrecked the car."

"Niki, the car can be replaced, but you can't."

I should have seen Dad's unconditional love then, but I didn't.

It didn't matter where we moved; we always had friends. Mom says she bought me dolls all the time, but I always wanted to play with cars and trucks, climb trees, and play in the mud. Though Dad's little "Sunshine" grew up and changed in many ways, Dad has always been there with his unconditional love.

Dad's stand has always been clearly known, whatever the issue. And you never wondered, years down the road, if he had wavered or compromised. That's why other Christians and preachers come to Dad when there is a question about an issue. Dad says, "Stand true to the Word of God, and get a promise—a verse, a truth—for yourself." My verse is Isaiah 43:2—"When thou passest through the waters, I will be with thee; and through the rivers, they shall not overflow thee: when thou walkest through the fire, thou shalt not be burned; neither shall the flame kindle upon thee."

I've been in the "deep waters" of this verse many times, and sometimes felt all alone. But just as the Lord has always been there for me, so has Dad with an unconditional love.

Dad and Mom have opened their home once again for me to take shelter and regain my strength. Dad has, once again, taken the burden of my problems on his shoulders. Those shoulders aren't as broad and strong as they used to be. I have seen a change in Dad since I've returned home to Virginia Beach. No, he hasn't compromised or taken a different stand on biblical issues. He has become more like Christ. His heart is so tender, and the countless hours he spends with the Lord amaze me.

So if you were to ask me, "What have you learned from being the daughter of Rod Bell Sr.?" I would tell you, "Stand true to God's Word and love unconditionally."

Dad, I know the love of a parent. It is my prayer that I, too, will always love unconditionally.

CHAPTER 19:
An Older Son's Perspective

I was born on April 30, 1963, in the home of Rod Bell. I was four years old when I realized what my father did for a living. I can remember him preaching with a red face and sweaty brow—in the Kempsville Elementary School House, in the Kempsville Fire House, and finally in our small auditorium in the middle of a corn field. I remember sermons on heaven that were so realistic you could almost hear the sweet music of heaven— angels singing "Holy, Holy, Holy" around God's *shekinah* glory— and being almost enraptured with the excitement of going there. I can remember sermons on hell that were so hot I could feel the sizzling, snapping, liquid flames engulf my soul, as I heard the tormented cry of the damned. As a young boy, the picture of my father preaching is one of a loosened tie, coat off, sleeves rolled up, handkerchief in his right hand, and holding nothing back. One of my favorite preaching lines that I have heard him say embodies his preaching altogether—"We need to believe that God is so real that we could charge hell with a water pistol, swing over hell on a rotten corn stalk, and spit in the Devil's eye, while singing 'What can wash away my sin? Nothing but the blood of Jesus.'"

Through the thirty-six years of my life, my father's ministry has changed from being a little country church to a ministry in the city. Note that I said his *ministry* has changed—not the man. Each time it changed, so did my impression of the ministry itself. The late sixties through the late seventies marked the "birth and childhood" years of Tabernacle Baptist Ministries (TBM). During this time, Dad received his honorary doctorate from Bob Jones University; as a result, he was more in demand as a speaker. Demands on his time and attention were not just from his church but also his day school, his Bible college and seminary, and his family. He became president of the Fundamental Baptist Fellowship (FBF), which took him away even more. As I grew up seeing this and experiencing what this ministry was all about, I began to form my own thoughts and feelings about it all. I did not like it! Why? My father had less and less time to spend with me. I would ask him why he had to go again. In fact, this was a frequent topic at our dinner table the nights he was home.

He always answered by saying, "If I don't go, who will? You see, Son, I am in debt. I owe a debt I can never repay."

"But, Dad, you are burning the candle at both ends!"

The answer was always the same. "I would rather be burned out for Jesus than to never be a light at all."

There is one distinct characteristic, if you have not yet noticed, about my father—his strong will and "bulldog tenacity" for the truth. And if protecting truth meant burning himself out, so be it. If it meant losing friends (this hurt him, I know), so be it. God's business was his business, and he was doing God's business, or so he sincerely thought. He determined to go until he dropped in his tracks.

From the late seventies through the mid-eighties, he traveled around the world to mission fields and conferences, ever "busy with the Lord's work." He received another honorary doctorate. This one did not mean very much to me either because I felt I did not know who my father was. Many times I would not see him for days, sometimes weeks. I would ask my mom, "Where is Dad?"

"He's still at the office," or "He comes home after you are in bed."

This part of his ministry almost cost him his life (through health problems) three times. I was always very proud of my father and all his accomplishments, but I had to look to other men (like my coach) as "father-figures" during my teen years. I always knew when my dad was at my ball game—not that I saw him. I knew he had nearly broken his neck to get there, just getting off a plane or back from a trip. I could hear him yell from the crowd, "Go get 'em, T. Paul! That's my boy!"

I will never forget when I was sixteen years old and Dad took me hunting for the first time. It was bitter cold that weekend, and we slept outside in a truck that had a camper on the back. I lay freezing in the front seat, while he and another friend were in the camper, nice and warm! I was shivering so badly that Dad finally took me back and put me between them. I was as snug as a bug in a rug. I killed my first deer on that hunting trip. Dad tells people that he heard several shots while he sat in his stand, and then he heard me yelling, "I got one! I got one!" Those memories are few, but they're priceless.

Let me recount the day my dad became great in my eyes. One night, he called a family meeting in our home. He started out by telling us how he had been raised in the mountains of West Virginia by his father—a hard disciplinarian, a rough, rugged drunkard. Dad had a love-hate relationship with his father; Dad loved his father with all his heart, but he was "eaten up" with anger for years. His father and grandfather demanded instant, unquestioning obedience, but they didn't know how to show love or proper discipline. All they knew was to slap, knock, beat, yell, scream, and curse. Dad admitted he had acquired these traits and thought that was the way it was done.

With tears coursing down his cheeks, Dad said to each one of us, "I'm sorry. I have not disciplined you correctly. I will never raise my voice or yell again. Please forgive me. I want to be the right kind of Dad. I'll not pass on to my children this wrong kind of discipline. I want to chasten and treat you as our heavenly Father treats His children."

From that day on, Dad corrected, chastened, and loved us as our heavenly Father does, and we revere him for it. That day, Dad became more like the Lord. He taught us the biblical way to nurture our children; and by God's grace, we'll hand these principles down to them.

Thank God, he was man enough to admit he was wrong and to apologize and to correct himself. He became a giant in my eyes that day.

I'm so thankful Dad has grown "from glory to glory" in his Christian character and conviction. I've watched him grow into one of the most balanced men I know. Sure, he makes mistakes, but he's always ready and eager to correct them, regardless of the cost. He's taught us that our family is our primary "ministry." He's imparted to us his life's theme, "Not I, but Christ."

When my father asked me to help him with his book, I could not believe it. He asked me to write about what it was like to live in a preacher's home. "Be honest and transparent; maybe we can help other parents avoid some pitfalls and enjoy some mountaintop experiences."

"Is this going to be a two-volume book?" I asked.

How could I explain what it was like growing up in *the* Dr. Rod Bell's home? One might think of Rod Bell as a defender of the truth, a contender for the faith, or "Mr. Fundamentalism," but I think of him as "just my dad." Though he is all those things, and sometimes I expect to see a comic book "super hero" come through the door, he is and will always be my dad. In my biased opinion, he is the greatest preacher that ever walked in shoe leather. No one can preach with such compassion and conviction, no one can tell stories like he can, no one can take up an offering like him, and absolutely no one can sing like him (for which we are eternally grateful)!

Some might think that living in a prominent preacher's home has many advantages. Well, it does have its perks. I would like to share a few of them:

1. You get to meet some of the greatest preachers God created, such as Dr. Monroe Parker, Dr. Oliver B. Greene, Dr. Harold B. Sightler, Dr. Bob Jones Jr., Dr. Bob Jones III, Dr. Ian Paisley, Dr. Gilbert Stenholm, Dr. Jimmy Rose, Dr. Tom Ferrell, Dr. Myron B. Cedarholm, Dr. G. Archer Weniger, Dr. John McCormick, Dr. Ken Connolly, and the list goes on and on.

2. When these speakers would come into town, I knew we were going out to eat!

3. Anywhere you go with your dad, you are treated like royalty.

4. You always like the reaction you get when you tell people who your dad is!

That last perk brings to mind the disadvantages:

1. You'd better be ready to pucker or duck—Dad is either greatly loved or hated!

2. Your dad is always gone . . . somewhere.

3. Your life is lived under a magnifying glass, not because you were such a bad kid but because of who your dad is.

4. Your emotions get the best of you when someone you don't even know attacks your dad because of his stand for the truth (which in this house was quite often). Death and bomb threats, fistfights to defend his honor, biased TV and newspaper reporters calling him names—it all comes with the territory.

5. The expectations of your life are set so high by others that it is impossible to even begin to live up to them.

6. To whom do you go when you have a real spiritual problem and you don't want your dad to know? Most people go to their pastor, but when he's your dad . . . ?

7. If you are a son in a preacher's home, you are automatically put in the "future preachers' club." There is nothing wrong with being put in that position just as long as *God* put you there and not someone else.

8. Many think that in such a prominent leader's home there is no lying, no stealing, no bitterness, no yelling, no hateful or hurtful words, no rebellion, and certainly no disrespect. Well, maybe in your home, but not in mine. Now I'm not saying this was the norm at the Bells' home, but with three children in various "growing up" stages, those times did occur.

What was the discipline like? Let me share one story with you. I was about sixteen years old, and I was not saved. I was rebellious and bitter and resented the rules and standards in our home. On this particular day, I was cutting the grass with an old, broken-down lawn mower, and the motor kept cutting out on me. My brother watched me, and every time it cut out, he would just laugh. Well, I lost my temper and cursed him out real good! What I didn't know was that my mother was listening the whole time. She called me in and tried to spank me, but it didn't hurt, and I let her know it. She told me that my father would take care of me when he came home.

I knew he would probably whip me good, so I tried to get psyched up for him. He came home, and she told him the story. Then I heard those familiar words, "Son, go into my bedroom." I knew this could be very hazardous to my health.

My dad was a very big man at that time—let's say 270-280 pounds. He began taking off his coat, then his tie, then his shirt; but when he took off his tee shirt, I began to see my life pass before my eyes. I knew I was "dead meat"!

He reminded me that he had already spanked me, had put me on restriction, and had taken away as many privileges as he possibly could. Now it was time to see how discipline really feels. He took his big leather belt off and laid it on the bed. Then he lay facedown on the bed with his arms stretched out. He told me to pick up the belt and give him five lashes across his back.

"No! No! I can't do that!" I could never hit or hurt him.

He looked at me and said, "Someone has to be punished, and since it doesn't bother you, then I will take your whipping."

I got mad at him and hit him one time. Then I looked on his back and saw the stripe. I dropped the belt and started crying.

He picked me up and held me tightly. "Now you see how I feel when I spank you. I love you, Son, with every fiber of my being, and I just want to see you do right."

Not every whipping was that dramatic, but for me it was the best thing that could have happened. I don't remember ever needing another "whipping" after that.

Many events in my life have involved my dad in one way or another. I was sixteen years old and did not know the Lord as my personal Savior. I had made several professions, but none of them were real. I either wanted attention or I needed to get out of trouble. The year before I had won the district, state, and national preaching contests, and I saw many get saved through this preaching, but I was as lost as could be. I had met with my principal the week before basketball season, and he basically told me that I was on a one-way path to hell. My coach knew it, and my dad did too. I was too stubborn, though, to surrender to the Lord.

The best part about Dad knowing was that he never pressured me into making any kind of decision, especially concerning the ministry. (For any parent, especially preachers: Don't pressure your children into a decision, whether a spiritual or a practical one. Pray that God will use the Holy Spirit and the right circumstances to draw them to Himself.) I was under such conviction that every time I went to bed at night, I just knew I would wake up in hell. One Sunday Dad preached a message on the Cross, and for the first time in my life, I realized the love of Jesus Christ and how many times I had rejected the Lord. On November 19, 1979, I bowed my head in the principal's office and accepted Christ as Lord of my life. When I did that, it seemed as if the weight of the world was lifted from me. Dad was preaching in Phoenix, Arizona, at the time, so I couldn't tell him what had just happened. The principal, Dr. Bieber, asked if I wanted to call him and tell him the good news.

"Of course," I said.

When Dad got on the phone, he said, "Wasn't that Dr. Bieber? Are you in trouble again?"

"No, not this time. I just got saved!"

"Son, I have been praying for you for the last two hours. And I knew today would be the day."

The power of prayer in my family's life, as well as mine, has been so evident that no one could doubt God is in control.

My sister, my brother, and I have all had traumatic experiences. With each one, Dad has always been there and helped us through. Again, let me say that you don't need to work your children's problems out for them. Let them depend upon the promises of God and rely solely on Him to guide them through their trial. They don't need anyone to tell them that they are a victim of circumstance. Instead, they need to hear how wonderful the riches of God's amazing grace are. Share with them how God worked in your life.

In 1984 I was a sophomore at Bob Jones University, and the pressure I was under was really working my body over. I was struggling with my studies and with playing ball. I had responsibilities in my society. Dad had been chosen "Alumnus of the Year" my freshman year, and he was a favorite chapel speaker. Many people knew me or knew of me. I was not alone because my brother (a freshman) was with me that year.

I was struggling in my spiritual life, and I really did not want to be a preacher or have anything to do with ministry. My reputation on campus was not a very good one. God was about to put me through His "School of Discipleship."

It all started when I was hit on the head during a basketball game. I dived for a ball at the same time my teammate went for it. Our heads collided, with mine getting the worse end of the deal. My very close friend Vernon got up and walked away, but not me. I was out on the floor, wondering what truck just hit me. The next thing I knew, Dr. Taylor, the referee, was standing over me saying, "Can you hear me? Do you know where you are?"

All I heard was the voice of Charlie Brown's teacher (you cartoon watchers know what I'm saying). They carted me away to Barge Hospital, took some x-rays, and let me go the next day. I had a small cut over my right eye and a bump on my head; other than that, I was feeling okay.

I went to church that Sunday night, feeling just fine. It was when I got up the next morning that my head felt like it was going to explode. I was taking Tylenol like candy, and nothing seemed to take the pain away. That Monday night I went to work, cleaning up the Administration Building. We were having a party before work with a Hawaiian theme, and everybody was having a great time. Dad had just been to Haiti and brought me back a straw hat that was just a size too small. I squeezed it on, and it made my head feel a little better.

Around 11:45 P.M. I was dusting some desks, and the whole room started to move. The next thing I remember was a co-worker asking me what was wrong. I was curled up in the corner, crying. That's when it hit me: I didn't know where I was, how I got there, or who I was. Panic set in, accompanied by a ton of fear.

Within minutes, campus security and my other co-workers surrounded me. They stared at me like I was some kind of freak. They all kept asking the same questions over and over: "Who are you? Where are you? What's your name? Do you know who I am?"

My only answer was "No!" I was so frightened; my heart was about to beat out of my chest. I kept asking myself those same questions: "Who am I? Where am I? How did I get here? Who are all these people yelling at me?" I was so scared I thought I would pass out.

Again, I found myself in Barge Hospital. This time I was surrounded by doctors and nurses and a few security men. A few days passed, and many tests were run by top neurologists. Then a doctor named Bo Clark came in and told me what had happened. He said that I was well on my way to a nervous break-down. When I received the blow to the head, it sped everything up and my brain just shut down. He told me the brain is like a computer, and when there is too much information in it, it shuts down. They called this problem Conversion Reaction Amnesia. My memory would come back in seven to ten days.

A week passed, and I was still the same. Then two weeks, and still nothing. That's when they told me it could actually be months before my memory came back. There was 25 percent brain wave activity on the right side and 85 percent on the left of my brain. I couldn't read very well, and I couldn't remember anything about how the problem started. I couldn't write (except in stick figures), I couldn't play any sports (I couldn't remember how), I couldn't ride in a car without getting motion sickness.

Everyday around noon I would become extremely lethargic and "thick-tongued." The nurses did things to make me stay awake. I kept hearing that I had the greatest dad in the world and that many people respected him. Oh, your father preaches all over the world, he's wonderful! My thoughts were, "Where in the world is this great man everybody is talking about? It's been days and I haven't heard a word from him." I didn't know he was calling everyday from Newfoundland, getting an update on my condition. They told him not to worry—I just had a blow to the head, and I would be okay.

I finally received a phone call, after a week or so of no change in my condition. I heard this voice (Dad) telling me over the phone that he loved me, that he was praying for me daily, that I was in the Lord's hands and all things work together for His good. The only problem was, I had no idea what he was talking about. Who was this Lord? And why was it so good to see me suffer? I didn't know Dad had been calling every day. He was told my amnesia was only temporary and that I would regain my memory in a few days. But I wasn't getting better. The amnesia lasted six months, and I had to leave school and come home.

I can honestly say that although my father said he loved me, I did not feel it because I could not remember what it felt like to be loved by someone. I truly felt all alone. No family memories, no memories of friends, of bad times, of good times— nothing.

Through this physical experience, I saw my dad pour his life into me. Not a day went by that he didn't tell me he loved me or that he had prayed for me or that he found a verse of Scripture for me to "hold on to." Sometimes he really "smothered me" with love, but I knew he was only trying to help. Many were the seeds he planted.

One night he read half of the book of Psalms to me. Some nights I could hear him in the hallway outside my room, weeping over me. He must have claimed over a hundred verses of Scripture, not just for me, but for himself as well. In one of Dad's Bibles he claimed a certain verse for the days from March 17 through July 9. Psalm 34:19—"Many are the afflictions of the righteous: but the Lord delivereth him out of them all." In verse 20 he has the first part underlined—"He keepeth all his bones: not one of them is broken." In the margin by those verses he wrote, "Tim will remember again. He [God] is faithful; He keeps His Word."

Allow me to share with you some of the personal things Dad has written in the margin of his Bible: sayings such as "A day at a time," "Take your hands off!" "Tim's and my verse." Psalm 119:67-71—"Before I was afflicted I went astray: but now have I kept thy word. Thou art good, and doest good; teach me thy statutes. The proud have forged a lie against me: but I will keep thy precepts with my whole heart. Their heart is as fat as grease; but I delight in thy law. It is good for me that I have been afflicted; that I might learn thy statutes."

Other little notes went like this: "God will deliver," "Lord, You promised!" "Pray not, *When* am I going to get out of this trial? but *What* am I going to get out of this trial?" "Real character is forged under pressure; there is no such thing as instant spirituality."

Along with all those things, he recorded every date that he claimed those promises from the day of my concussion until the day I regained my memory. On that date, he circled it and drew an arrow back to Psalm 34:19 and wrote, "God is faithful."

I never knew he had done all this until many years later, when he gave me that Bible. I was sitting in church when I saw what he had written. I began to cry and thank the Lord for allowing me to be used in such a way to bring my father closer to Him.

As I look back on that time, I can see how God was preparing me for the ministry I have today. I have learned, firsthand, that a good Gethsemane experience makes a good Calvary preacher. He has brought me out of the city and put me in the beautiful mountains of Tennessee. I am under the care of Dr. Wayne White. He has been a Godsend to my family and me. He is my "Paul" in the ministry.

The love I have for my father now is far greater than any love that I have for any man on this earth. Dad is my close friend, my trusted advisor, my encourager in times of trouble, and my strength when I am weak; he is my hero of the faith, the prince of all preachers, but most important of all—he is my dad.

So what's it been like to live in the home of *the* Rod Bell? What's it been like watching God turn a fledgling church of five families into one of the largest independent, fundamental, Bible-believing Baptist churches on the East Coast? It's been both exciting and frustrating, but most of all, it has allowed me to be introduced to the King of kings and Lord of lords—my wonderful Savior, Jesus Christ. I would not trade places with the king of any empire.

At the end of every letter and most phone calls, Dad quotes this verse to us: " 'I have no greater joy than to hear that my children walk in truth' (III John 4). Remember, I love you."

Dad, your children are walking in truth and, by the grace of God, will remain in the truth that you have passed on to us. This mantle, God willing, will be passed on to my children and my children's children. Thank you, Dad, for such a great heritage.

CHAPTER 20:
A Younger Son's Perspective

Where in the world does one begin when asked to describe what it's like to be raised in a preacher's home? One could easily begin spouting off about "victimization." Sure, growing up in a preacher's home has its challenges, but isn't life itself a challenge? I could have been born into the home of a drunkard or a prostitute or within reach of any other variety of "pagan vice," but no! By God's marvelous grace I was born into the home of a struggling young preacher. My mother was doing her very best with my older brother and much older sister. My sister really should have been named "Rod Jr." because she is the real "chip off the ol' block." My brother? Well, we told him he was adopted because he didn't look like any of us. Finally, the best of the three (me?!) came along, and the *real* testing of Dad's faith began.

The "victimization theory" almost begs my acceptance because then I wouldn't have to accept the personal responsibility for my own selfishness, jealousy, and other sins. The problems that come with being a preacher's kid are basically the same as every other kid's problems. We are all sinners, but some are saved and some are unsaved. Why should a preacher's kid not expect to have the same problems as the unsaved? The difference between a preacher's home and an unsaved kid's home is that Satan knows just how to magnify conflict in the preacher's home. He will shine the spotlight on all the inconsistencies of the pastor/parent, causing serious doubt and confusion in the lives of the children. The doubts arise from the spiritual need in the heart of the child. We've all seen the bumper sticker "Christians aren't perfect, just forgiven." Well, we all believe that adage, except when it comes to our own families. We seem to forget that God is performing a work in and through us to cause us to become more like His dear Son.

I was such a child—doubtful and confused. I must have been pretty hard to understand. I capitalized on the weaknesses of my siblings and parents and was very quick to point out the inconsistencies I saw in their lives. I was a modern-day Pharisee. I had a great "cover" on the outside, but inside I was full of dead men's bones.

So what's it like living in a preacher's home? Pretty much the same as living in most homes where the parents are sinners who have been born again.

I was jealous of anyone who had more of my dad than I did. It was hard for this unregenerate son to forgive Dad's shortcomings and unkept promises. Now I can appreciate that Dad was having quite a struggle—trying to balance home, church, the Fundamental Baptist Fellowship (FBF), board meetings, Bible Conferences, evangelistic meetings, our school and college. I only wish I had made it easier for him instead of resenting him. I'll never forget coming into his office one day and telling him I was angry with both him and God. "God," I emphatically declared, "has you more than I do, and I'm tired of it!" This incident was one of the bricks that would help build a monumental wall between Dad and me.

Another incident that made an impression on me occurred on a Sunday when I was younger. Church was over, and we were about to head home for a dinner of macaroni and cheese and "beany-weenie." (It was a lean week.) Just then, a member in the church gave Dad twenty dollars to take us out. We were thrilled!

"KFC, here we come!" We got all the fixin's, got home, and sat down to pray when the doorbell rang. Dad met a young mother whose family had not eaten all day. Dad had no money to give her, so he quickly came in and filled the KFC bags with our food. We kids were not too happy about macaroni and cheese and beany-weenie, but God had given to us so that we could give to others. If there is one thing Dad taught us, he taught us about giving. He has always been one to give "everything" away, but God has always provided and met our needs. We learned that day to hold loosely those things that are not eternal—even if it means your fried chicken!

I probably was the most opinionated of the three Bell kids. I was very careful not to be too direct or disrespectful—ever the diplomat. As I look back now, I'm afraid one of Dad's greatest challenges in life was growing up with me.

One of the heart's desires in any Christian home is that the children accept Christ as Lord and Savior of their lives. What child wouldn't want to spend eternity with his parents in heaven? Or, to look at it another way, what child would want to go to hell? I made a profession of faith and was baptized when I was five. This decision, however, was a masterpiece of Satanic deception. I had continual struggles in my life. Through my teen years, I maintained the "front," but inside I grew more and more miserable. To whom could I speak about such things? In whom could I confide? I really didn't even consider telling my parents because I didn't want to hurt them or to receive the consequences on my backside. I was a good kid—I passed out tracts to my whole neighborhood and brought people to Christ. And yet the battle still raged within.

I'll never forget how close we came to losing my dad in 1989, when he had bleeding ulcers. Many times I wondered what would happen to us if Dad didn't make it. I blamed Dad and all the various ministries with which he was involved. I had seen dear family friends "lose" their dads in the ministry, and this really scared me. Each bout with physical problems seemed to slow him down for a moment, but just enough to regroup and get going again. Dad never has been one to allow any grass to grow under his feet.

Another great memory was when Dad enrolled me at Bob Jones University. I was not a happy camper. As a matter of fact, I resisted the whole way, even as I carried my belongings up to my dorm room. Upon returning to the car for the "last supper," Dad informed me, with tears in his eyes, that I could go home if I wished. Perhaps he knew my stubbornness, or maybe he was just using some kind of "reverse psychology," but I chose to stay. Our family was growing up, and the baby was leaving the nest. All I was worried about was who would get my bedroom at home.

Over the next several years, God would count the Bell family worthy of many tests and trials. God also permitted Satan to "stir the pot" as well. My sister, Niki, went through a traumatic separation from her husband. Tim, my brother, was hurt playing basketball and had amnesia for six months. Then in February of 1987, I was involved in an auto accident in Georgia. Dad was on his way to Burma to help establish a Bible college there. All the doctors knew at the time was that my leg was broken in several places. Dad had planned to come to Greenville and see if I was all right, but God was getting ready to change Dad's plans. When Mom and Dad saw me, I was in critical condition. The doctors gave me only a 5 percent chance to live. My parents got alone with God and prayed for God's perfect will. That night, Dad asked God for a promise from His Word. By morning, Dad had his promise: Psalm 118:17—"I [he] shall not die, but live, and declare the works of the Lord." For twenty-two days and twenty-two nights, Dad stayed by my bed. For the first time I could remember, I finally had Dad to myself.

God was preparing us for yet another incident in His plan for our lives. Two years later, in February 1989, Dad was at the point of death. He had internal hemorrhaging and required major surgery, taking fifty-four units of blood in one night. We realized that Dad was probably going home to glory. Our family was drawn closer than ever; our church family went through it with us. But God wasn't finished with Dad yet, and He raised him up. We have never experienced so much love; prayers, cards, and flowers came from all over the world. When we went through other such incidents before, Dad had taught us to get with God and claim a promise from His Word. We called Dr. Ian Paisley, and God gave us a promise through him: Psalm 91:14-16—"Because he hath set his love upon me, therefore will I deliver him: I will set him on high, because he hath known my name. He shall call upon me, and I will answer him: I will be with him in trouble; I will deliver him, and honour him. With long life will I satisfy him, and show him my salvation."

I cannot begin to tell you what our family went through during that experience, except to say that the old quip "The Christian life is not just a bowl of cherries—it comes with the pits" became a reality to me. God was molding and making a man, a family, and a ministry.

At the time, I was still deceived by Satan. All these events were sending mixed signals—I appeared strong on the outside, but inside I was a wreck. I began to see that God's master plan would be performed in our lives.

Dad's preaching seemed to be with more fervor—as a dying man preaching to dying sinners. The Spirit that saturated his preaching shot like an arrow, piercing through my best façade straight to my heart. I will never forget sitting in a restaurant in South Carolina with my sister, Niki. My dad walked in and told us he couldn't preach that Sunday if there were anything between us. He first looked at Niki and described a discipline situation they had gone through twenty years before. He pleaded for her forgiveness in the middle of the restaurant, as though we were the only ones there. He brought up incident after incident that God had revealed to him, showing him how he had handled them wrongly. We forgave Dad that day. Boy, did this blow our minds! God was showing Dad what Satan had been using to push us all in another direction over the years. But my "growing pains" were still not over.

Finally, in 1992, two things happened in my life as a direct result of my pastor's prayers. God brought my wonderful wife to me in 1990, but even she soon recognized just how miserable I was because of the inner turmoil in my life. It was my parents' and my wife's consistent prayers for me that brought about my own salvation. For the first time in my life, despite being a preacher's kid and even an assistant pastor, I submitted to the Almighty and was gloriously saved. Not only did He save me, but He called me to preach. My dad was shocked, and so was the church, but finally I had the peace for which long I had sought. Now I could regard my dad as my pastor. I can look back now and see how God, through a series of "incidents," was "growing my dad" and drawing me unto Himself.

I really began to grow up with my dad after I was saved. The "wall" came down because we were finally on the same team. My only regret is that, because I had remained so distant from Dad, I don't have many cherished memories from my childhood with him. That was my fault, not his. Since 1992, things have certainly been different in our lives. I know I cannot make up for my selfish childhood, but I thank God for bringing Dad and me together in the autumn of his life. I'm finally getting to grow up with my pastor, even as we both grow in the Lord.

Thanks, Dad, for being my pastor. Thanks, too, for your willingness to correct those faults that were once part of the wall between us.

One thing I can say about my dad: He's not the man he used to be, praise the Lord! But throughout the past thirty-four years he has never compromised. He has never changed his message. But he has been willing to be used up for God. He has become more and more tender in "doing God's work God's way" but with the same old bulldog tenacity with which he started his ministry. It is becoming increasingly clear that the image of the "mountain man" is continually being changed to reflect the image of our precious Lord.

I have had many heroes in my life: Dr. Oliver B. Greene, Dr. Gilbert Stenholm, Dr. Bob Jones Jr., Dr. Harold Sightler, Dr. Roy Harrell, Dr. Ken Connolly, Dr. Ian Paisley, Dr. Bob Jones III, Dr. Bob Wood, to name a few.

All these great men have become so endeared in my heart, but none of these men could ever be the parent, the pastor, or the partner you are to me, Dad. Thank you for pouring your life into me. Thank you for giving your life for the cause of Christ. It is my prayer that God would allow me to be at least half of the parent and pastor you are. You are my hero!

Chapter 21:
A Grandson's Perspective

When I was asked to contribute something to this work, I thought about the role my grandfather has played in my life. He has been like a father to me, and I will probably never know the extent of his influence on who I am now. He came from a different world than I did—a world where right and wrong were more easily defined, a world where life was harder than it is now. In that world "boys were boys," and there were certain things every boy needed to know.

I have many fond memories of the summers I spent with him and my grandmother. My grandfather was the one who taught me how to swim and how to ride a bike. He took me out on the church grounds and showed me how to shoot targets with my pellet gun. Later on, he took me on my first hunting trip (by the way, I was the only one to get a deer). He played catch with me, took me fishing; and when it came time, he taught me how to drive. Of course, these are all things that fathers do with their sons, and I am grateful he was there to fill that role.

Aside from all the temporal things, probably his greatest influence upon my life has been his Christian testimony. He imparted to me a pattern of godliness that has taught me much. Leaving the wealth and wonder of the world behind, he set his eyes on that Heavenly City and sought "first the kingdom of God." He encouraged me to do the same and to follow God's leading in my life. He would often take me aside to teach me spiritual principles. He instilled in me a love for God's Word. He gave me an example of what a godly Christian man should be, and I know that God has greatly blessed him for doing this.

Another reason God has blessed him is his steadfast stand against compromise regarding the Word of God. It did not matter if the issue at hand was popular at the time or if it drew crowds and filled the pews in his church. If something was important to God, it was important to Rod Bell. He is a man of conviction. Like Noah, he preaches the truth without hesitation, even when he is scorned and ridiculed. He faithfully shows sinners and saints alike the way to salvation from the coming destruction. No room is left for compromise. He is constantly warning his flock to beware of the wolves that have donned sheepskin.

In all of this, my grandfather is humble. No matter how many years he has been preaching or how many positions he has filled, he has never become comfortable accepting honor from men. He would often say, "I'm just a crooked stick that God is trying to draw a straight line with." He never forgets his humble beginnings nor his debt to the Savior. "If I had ten thousand more lives, I'd give them all to God," he would tell me. If I know him well, I know that those lives would be spent serving others and spreading the gospel, even when those whose feet he washed would spit in his face.

Thanks, Pop, for being a godly influence in my life.

CHAPTER 22:
A Secretary's Perspective

What is it like to be Dr. Bell's secretary? That is a loaded question. Dr. Bell is one of a kind. I teasingly remind him that there are two kinds of people in the world—Rod Bell and everyone else! He is first and foremost a pastor, not only to his own people, but also to many other pastors all across this nation. He also is a man of vision with a keen discernment for issues and trends. He "takes off" in many different directions at one time and leaves the rest of us panting and "picking up the pieces" after him. That is where I and others come in.

It is a great privilege to serve this dear man of God, to keep him pointed in the right direction at the right time, having all the necessary "pieces" in hand. Oftentimes after he has left for the day and I am in his office, whether it be straightening his desk or crawling *underneath* his desk, picking up all those little candy wrappers from his "Sweet Counsel" drawer or paper clips that just didn't quite make it to the wastebasket, I think of the great honor of this office—that of a great preacher, one of God's anointed—more honorable than the office of the president of the United States.

That God's hand is upon Pastor Bell is evident. He is a man of great strength and tenderness of heart at the same time. When it comes to matters of truth and right and wrong, there is no bending or moving one inch on these issues. As Pastor Bell so aptly says, "Some things are just not for sale." Then there have been times I have seen him weep with joy over a great victory in the life of one his people or, on the other hand, be dead tired from lack of a night's sleep because of being so burdened for one of his "sheep."

One of the great blessings in my responsibilities is to type Pastor's sermons. The process begins with Pastor handwriting his sermon outlines and then reviewing them with me to ensure that I understand what he has written. (Occasionally, even *he* will have a difficult time figuring out one of the words he himself has written. At such times, if I should be able to recognize the word first, I will boast of my greater knowledge of Greek or Hebrew!) The blessing comes in this reviewing process, for Pastor will get so excited as he goes over his sermon that he will begin "preaching," right then and there. It is at those times that I realize, once again, the privilege it is to serve at the right hand of God's anointed and be in the place to receive the "first drippings," as I call them.

You cannot know Pastor Bell without having an admiration and love for him. He is just himself. When I think of some of the great men of God in our day, each very different from the other, I wonder what it is that knits their hearts together in friendship. One may be a mountain man from West Virginia while another a member of British and European Parliaments, yet they share something much greater than themselves. It is that they all love the Lord and stand unashamedly for His Truth. If you love the Lord and His Word, you cannot help loving Rod Bell, for his love for the Lord is genuine, and his loyalty to the Word of God is proven.

CHAPTER 23:
A Deacon's Perspective

November 1969 brought us to the Tidewater area, thanks to the United States Navy. I came with a wife and a one-year-old daughter. Both my wife and I were new Christians. Looking for a church was quite an ordeal. By February 1970, Tabernacle Baptist was the tenth church we had visited.

At first, I was very uncomfortable coming to this "type" of church. I had grown up in the Midwest—ultra-conservative, no show of emotion in church, and never was an "Amen!" heard. My wife, on the other hand, was familiar with Dr. Bell's style of preaching and felt right at home. In fact, she had grown up in Kentucky, only about three hours away from where Dr. Bell grew up.

Something kept drawing us back to Tabernacle; we just kept going. Dr. Bell was always generous with his pulpit. Dr. Oliver B. Green was one of the first "special speakers" we heard at Tabernacle. And away from church, we had many visits from folks in the congregation. Pretty soon, my wife was baking two days per week—Tuesdays and Thursdays—because we knew someone from church would be coming over on those evenings. Consistency!

Soon we were getting a little involved in church activities. Encouragement came from the pastor and his staff. When you are in a new place away from home, your church community becomes your "family." Each month found us doing a little more at Tabernacle.

Time flies! On January 1, 1971, God blessed us with a son. We were more involved than ever in the church's various ministry activities. I was becoming accustomed to Dr. Bell and his style of preaching, and finally beginning to feel at home. We got to help with the church's "homecoming" events; we got to help with the tent meetings when Billy Kelly came. They even allowed us to help with vacation Bible school, in the nursery, and in so many other areas. The church was growing. We got to help the newcomers. Involvement! Responsibility!—two more valuable qualities.

In 1974 Pastor approached me and told me he had observed me for two years and was pleased with the growth and maturity he had seen. He asked if I would become a deacon at Tabernacle. I told him I would discuss it with my wife, and we would pray about it. Helen and I discussed it and prayed about it for a few days. During this time, our daughter became very distressed, proclaiming that she did not want Daddy to become a deacon at church. When we asked her, "Why?" she replied, "Pastor said from the pulpit that 'the reason the preacher's kids are so mean is because they have been playing with the deacons' kids!' " We all had a good laugh, but the pastor learned that even young kindergarten children listened to what he said. I took the position and now am chairman of our deacon board.

To describe my pastor is really quite simple: He is a biblicist. From the top of his head to the soles of his feet, his desire has always been to do God's will, regardless of the cost. I have seen him in some very serious situations, and his prayer was always, "God, please give me wisdom to make the right decision." Then he would search the Scriptures for the answer and march forward without reservation or apology. He has taught me that the Bible has the answer for any problem in my life.

His leadership is second to none. I believe if he had been in the army, he would have been the greatest general of our time. I know that is saying a lot, but I honestly believe it. His loyalty to his "Commander in Chief" is unquestioning. He is also loyal to his deacons. I could never believe him capable of saying a bad thing about any of us (though I have given him many reasons to justifiably do so). I thank God that He saw fit to give me a ministry under Pastor Bell.

Pastor is never quick to believe anything bad about anyone without absolute proof to back up the allegation. I remember one time someone had removed a picture from his office of an individual who had been unkind and who had spread false rumors about him. When he returned to his office, Pastor immediately missed the picture and wanted it returned to him. He said he loved that person and prayed for him every day. Pastor is long-suffering with people and always looks for a way to help, rather than bruise them. It never seems to bother him when people spread false rumors about him, though. I have heard him say so many times, "God keeps the books, and He makes no mistakes."

I have watched my pastor go until he could go no more. Sometimes I think he pushes himself too much. It's as if he feels he is the only one to do what needs to be done. "Only one life, 'twill soon be past; only what's done for Christ shall last" has certainly been a fitting motto for him.

He has been most generous with his pulpit. Some of the greatest preachers in the world have preached at Tabernacle Baptist Church. Many preachers, fearful of being "upstaged," are not so inclined to allow others to share their pulpit, but not Pastor Bell. When he hears a good preacher, he wants us to share the blessing. There is absolutely no jealousy in him.

He is a man of great principle. Our church has never had to guess on what side of an issue we would stand. Most of the time, it hasn't been the popular thing to do, but he has always determined to "Do right 'til the stars fall." I recall the first time Billy Graham came to town. Almost every church in Tidewater supported him—but not Tabernacle. Our pastor raised money to run a full-page newspaper advertisement, citing the reasons we could not support Billy Graham. When the sodomites "came out of the closet" in Norfolk and protested Anita Bryant's appearance at Norfolk's Scope Auditorium, Pastor Bell took our congregation right downtown and preached against the sin of homosexuality. Doing the "popular thing" has never been a consideration with Pastor, but doing the "right thing" is always in fashion at Tabernacle.

Over the years, Pastor has changed some of his methods and approaches to issues, but his core values have never changed. "Doing God's work God's way" is truly his desire. I believe he is the greatest warrior for God in this century.

Part 6:

Conclusion

CHAPTER 24:
Challenges of the 21st Century

Some of the issues that biblical Christianity faced in the twentieth century must cause us to look ahead and assess where we are going now. Every Fundamentalist needs to think most carefully at what Paul meant when he wrote, "Perilous times will come." I'd like to list some of the challenges that the twenty-first century Fundamentalist will face:

1. **Preach Christ**—I see the need for a clear understanding of the gospel and what it means to preach Christ. This has a particular reference to the doctrines of justification, sanctification, and the righteousness of Christ imparted to the believer, especially as these doctrines affect the believer's motivation to holiness and service. There is a need for a proper emphasis on these doctrines, from the pulpit down to the pew, in contrast to the current-day pervasiveness of "guilt motivation"—living out so-called principles, which are usually just man-made regulations, bolstered by verses taken out of context. Such guilt motivation produces a legalism, trying to make man fit into a misguided "standard" of true holiness.

2. **Prayer**—E. M. Bounds said, "Apostasy always starts at the closed door of secret prayer." We must be men and women of prayer. I see a real need for prayer in the life of the individual and in the church. We need to re-establish the family altar and a personal prayer life. We need to pray for a mighty revival and for the fullness of the Holy Spirit. Many Fundamentalists have allowed the much-hyped Charismatic "experiences" to scare them away from the fullness of true Holy Spirit living that early Fundamentalists cherished and experienced. We need to ask God for a burden for great revival. Such revival is to be distinguished from the evangelistic efforts of the local church. There are none living in America who have seen a nationwide or area-wide moving of the irresistible power of the Holy Spirit of God. There must be a return to old-fashioned Bible preaching on the sovereign moving of the Spirit of God in revival. Unless God directly intervenes in the affairs of America, Christianity as we know it will never survive. Our children will be enslaved; our preachers who stand for God's truth will be imprisoned. "Wilt thou not revive us again; that thy people may rejoice in thee?" (Ps. 85:6).

3. **Preachers**—Another challenge we will face in the next century is the need to develop a generation of preachers whose sermons are saturated with the Lord Jesus Christ, rather than an exercise in "Christian psychology" designed to meet the congregation's "felt needs," human problems, and earthly concerns.

The pulpit must be the focal point of the local church ministry. We must maintain the centrality of the pulpit, preaching Christ and Him crucified. We are becoming desensitized to sin and are accepting watered-down messages that give the crowd what they want, not what they need. The church has become a place for entertainment. God help us to have the right emphasis and not to lose the fire of evangelism nor allow intellectualism to become our idol. We must have preachers who will fill their horns with oil and go anoint the King. Oh! How this old world needs Christ!

4. Proper Balance—I was taught by Dr. Bob Jones Sr. that there is unity in the essentials of salvation; there is fellowship in the non-essentials of salvation; there is charity to all believers. We are to go as far as we can with a brother on the right road, without compromising biblical orthodoxy.

I see unnecessary fragmentation in Fundamentalism today which, if left unchecked, will destroy us from within. There must be a proper balance on the "text" issue. At Tabernacle, we maintain a strong position regarding the Authorized Version as being God's preserved Word for the English-speaking nations today. We believe that we have, in the Authorized Version, God's authoritative Word and that the A.V. is the best translation available to the English-speaking world today. However, we do not make a theory or method of "preservation of God's Word" a test of fellowship or a test of orthodoxy.

A proper balance in evangelism: We must stir the fires of evangelism that are diminishing in our churches, and we must carry out the Great Commission. Cults are putting Fundamentalist Christians to shame. There must be a rekindling of the old-time religion, a renewed preaching about the judgment of God, about sin, and about hell. Messages like Jonathan Edwards's "Sinners in the Hands of an Angry God" are conspicuously absent from our pulpits. People have no concept of the holiness of God, nor are they well acquainted with the God of the Bible. "It is a fearful thing to fall into the hands of an angry God." He is infinitely Holy.

A proper balance regarding the church: The rapid advance of technology and communication threatens the very life of our local church and biblical Christianity today. We are able to worship God at home, and we are "forsaking the assembling of ourselves together." I can see in the not-too-distant future (indeed, it is already here) that people will use their homes, their televisions, and advanced technology to worship. Such technology is taking the place of the local church and the assembling of the εκκλησια, God's "called-out assembly," called-out to propagate the gospel through the local church. The local church has been de-emphasized because of our technology and because of the improper balance and emphasis on evangelism.

A proper balance regarding music: Another battle Fundamentalism faces is the lack of God-honoring music—music that is Christ-centered and Christ-honoring. God is music. To say that music is amoral is heresy.

A proper balance regarding the Lord's Day: One of our greatest needs is a hunger and thirst for God. He that hungers and thirsts shall be filled. We need a hunger and thirst for revival. Society is influencing the church, and the church is yielding to society's pressure to dishonor the Lord's Day. We cannot give up against this frontal attack being waged against the Lord's Day; it is an attack upon both the Lord and His church.

5. **Personal Piety**—I see a significant decline in the personal piety of our leadership—a loss of dedication, devotion, and depth of life as seen in the biographies of such saints as David Brainerd, Matthew Henry, John Owen, Adoniram Judson, Hudson Taylor, C. T. Studd, William Carey, A. W. Tozer, Robert Murray M'Cheyne, and other great men of God.

6. **Power of Rome**—I see an alarming increase in government regulations, crafted by the unseen hand of Rome, designed to undermine our religious freedom. Such an enemy silently works behind the scenes to cause those who believe and practice the Bible to be perceived as extremists, as the enemy of society. We are being castigated and identified as "religious-right extremists." We must keep the right balance and fight the good fight of faith. The Roman Catholic system (a theological-political-economic entity), as it builds the "one-world church," is one of the greatest enemies we face. Rome is like a lamb when she is seeking power, but like a lion when she is in power. In America now she is as both a lamb and a fox, but in the twenty-first century—watch out for the lion.

7. **Pragmatism**—"The end justifies the means." It is the idea that worth is determined by practical consequences. If methods or a course of action has a desired effect, it is good. The corollary is also true: If it doesn't work, it is not good.

The pragmatic mindset will inevitably clash with the Word of God. The "majority vote at the polls" is not a test of truth (John 17:17).

The pastor of the twenty-first century will be pressured to change. The church-growth "experts" and the church-marketing "racketeers" are already telling us that the old-time religion does not work in the twenty-first century. The pressure will mount to stop preaching against sin, hell, and judgment. "Make the sinner feel more comfortable." God help us to preach with compassion—but preach so that Christ is exalted and sinners are convicted. They will tell you to be, not authoritative, but "user-friendly." You must promote an atmosphere that attracts the "non-Christian seeker."

God never intended the church to be a place for entertainment or frivolity. Friendly, yes. Frivolous, no. God is a God of wrath, who hates sin but loves the sinner enough to give His Son as a sacrifice for our sin.

The pragmatist asks, "What will work?" The Fundamentalist asks, "What saith the Lord?" Preaching with the Holy Spirit unction, not pragmatism with entertainment, will get the job done to the glory of God.

CHAPTER 25:
The Future of Fundamentalism

The abundance of materialism in the last half of the twentieth century has produced an apathetic spirit among Christians. This apathy has created a vacuum that Satan has carefully filled with apostasy. The apostasy will eventually lead to anarchy, and anarchy, in attempting to achieve justice, will surrender liberty and ultimately be led into slavery under the Antichrist. The only alternatives are revival or judgment. However, for the believer, the future is as bright as God's promises. "Let God's Word be true and every man a liar." The truth will stand. We have God's eternal, infallible, inspired, authoritative Word that gives us over six thousand promises! His Word is pure. We have a sovereign God who is in control.

Dr. Monroe Parker, one of the greatest evangelists of my lifetime, used to tell a story about Truth and Error going "skinnydippin'." One real hot Alabama day, Truth and Error were walking down the road. They came to a swimmin' hole.

Truth said to Error, "Let's go swimming."

Error replied, "I don't have a bathing suit."

"That's okay; we'll just go skinnydippin'."

They jumped into the cool water and swam for a while. Soon, Error got out and put on Truth's clothes. When Truth got out, he saw Error's clothes lying there, but being an honest sort, he wouldn't put them on.

So, today, when you see error, it's always clothed in truth. That's why "naked truth" can walk down the street of any city in America and never blush.

The best way for us to face the challenges of the twenty-first century is to face them with pure, unadulterated, naked truth: the Word of God. We face the same Devil, and he uses the same tactics—the lust of the flesh, the lust of the eyes, and the pride of life—to tempt us.

I see within Fundamentalism today four different mindsets:

1. The Unlearned: Those who believe the leopard can change his spots, that the Modernist and Liberal controversy can be resolved. They don't realize the great Fundamentalist/Modernist battle of the early 1900s has been fought by our fore-fathers. We lost our institutions, our seminaries, our pulpits. We lost a battle, but we did not lose the war. Men like Dr. A. J. Gordon, Dr. Bob Ketchman, Dr. Bob Jones Sr., Dr. T. T. Shields, Dr. J. Frank Norris, Dr. G. Archer Wenigar, Dr. Myron B. Cedarholm, and others paid the price. They took the separatist position. Ecclesiastical separation is the doctrine that keeps all other doctrines pure.

In the Modernist/Fundamentalist controversy, black was black and white was white. There are those today who seem not to have learned the lesson. For example, we have seen since 1979 that the "great Southern Baptist Convention takeover" is only a "make over." The SBC is more apostate in 1999 than it was twenty years ago.

You cannot compromise on the matter of ecclesiastical separation; you can only surrender it. When you try to mix the seeds of wheat and tares, or when you plow using an ox and an ass, you are in clear violation of the Word of God. The boundary lines of the distinction are being rubbed out today by Billy Graham's ecumenical evangelism. Men today, claming to be Independent Fundamentalist Baptists, are moving the ancient landmarks of ecclesiastical separation and taking their churches back into the conventions and associations of the Baptist World Alliance, an arm of the World Council of Churches and a key element of the one-world church. When we see self-proclaimed Fundamentalists returning to apostasy, we realize that they have not learned that "a leopard cannot change his spots." The enemy is using them to rub out the lines of ecclesiastical separation.

Let's not be unlearned Fundamentalists, but let us learn from the past. Our birthright is not for sale. God help our future generations to be like Naboth: "And Naboth said to Ahab, The Lord forbid it me, that I should give the inheritance of my fathers unto thee" (I Kings 21:3).

The only remedy for apostasy is judgment!

2. The Arrogant: I am afraid that there are some Fundamentalists who feel they must keep Fundamentalism pure. They fight for piety, but their problem is their philosophy. They are going to stay separated from Modernism and Neo-evangelicalism, but they see every brother as afflicted with the symptoms of Neo-evangelicalism. Therefore, they are arrogant. They are fighting battles with outdated implements. The Adversary hasn't changed his tactics, but he has changed his weaponry. These arrogant ones continue to fight all the same battles of a previous generation of Fundamentalists. They fight the same battles their Fundamentalist "idols" fought, battles of yesteryear. The "idols" of yesteryear were right, and they fought their battles correctly. But if we're not careful, we'll find ourselves fighting each other and "shooting ourselves in the foot." Eventually, this group will become so separated, so independent, that they'll fancy themselves to be the only island in the stream of Fundamentalism. This island is called the Island of Isolationism. It's not enough, brethren, to fight the symptoms; we must fight the cause.

What has caused the church to be in the world and the world to be in the church today? This question is where the battle lies. Those living on the Island of Isolationism want to be the savior of our great heritage, but they want to play only one note on the harp—the note of "Separation! Separation! Separation!"

Now, don't get me wrong. I believe in separation, but I see a danger in becoming isolationists over *preferences* and not over *biblical principles*. An isolationist will find himself separating from every brother who has an approach or technique different from his. God made us all different as individuals. But if we are united as Fundamentalists, we're all members of the same body. We just have different functions and appearances. We all need each other in order to function in a coordinated manner and accomplish the mission God gave us to do.

Let's allow for each other to be just a little different, not in doctrine or truth, but in manners, methods, and techniques. Let's not be so ignorant and pious that we separate from everybody and start a First Isolationist Baptist Church in our town.

This is a serious danger in Fundamentalism as we face the twenty-first century. Just as the great Civil War general Stonewall Jackson died from wounds mistakenly inflicted by Confederate troops, too many of our men are being wounded and falling because of "friendly fire."

3. Intellectualism: This group is always trying to define Fundamentalism by debating philosophies, and theologies, and emphasizing the intelligentsia. Every sentence must be a masterpiece of great, expository preaching taken from the depths of the Hebrew and the Greek. I don't believe that for a minute!

It's one thing to be intellectual, but it's quite another to bow at the shrine of intellectualism. The Lord knows we need all the scholarship we can muster, and I am all for good schools and seminaries. We need good, Fundamentalist scholars who know their theology and know how to use it and make it practical. How I thank God for the great scholars of Fundamentalism. God didn't call all of us preachers to be "brains." It's good to have a brain and not be "brain-dead"! The danger in our seminaries is the lack of balance. We can have all the facts in our head but have no fire in our heart. Seminaries should remove any Fundamentalist scholar who is full of facts but no fire, who can't wrap his arm around an old sinner and weep after him, who has no burden for lost souls. Keep the fire of evangelism in the heart and the facts of theology in the head. "Evangelistic unction is what makes orthodoxy function!"

These enemies of Fundamentalism bow at the shrine of intellectualism and say that everyone else who doesn't is ignorant. They can conjugate the Hebrew and chase the Greek verbs; they "go down deep but come up dry." I remind you of the Scripture, "Ye shall know the truth, and the truth shall set you free." It's not merely the intellectual knowledge of the truth that liberates us; it is the experiential knowledge. This is knowledge gained by personal experience through the Holy Spirit's power, while that person is surrendered in obedience to the Holy Spirit. By obeying and practicing the truth, we experience the freedom of the truth and power of the Holy Spirit. The letter of the law kills, but the Spirit makes alive. "For it is God which worketh in you both to will and to do of his good pleasure" (Phil. 2:13). God gives both the "will" and the power "to do" His good pleasure. Theology and doctrine are neither dry nor dusty; it is the professor who is dry and dusty.

We Fundamentalist Baptists in America have a great heritage that predates the Revolutionary War. Men like John Bunyan and Benjamin Ketch, and learned scholars like John Gill and Andrew Fuller wrote with both passion and purpose. They wrote with the fire of heaven in their souls.

The religious historians have labeled our forefathers as "miscreants begat in rebellion, born in sedition, and nursed in faction." Our forefathers were excluded and cast out; by law, they were separated from the English Universities. Independent Baptists took their place "outside the camp" and developed their own pastoral and preaching institutions. They wrote their own hymns, preached their own sermons, published their own confessions (e.g., Baptist Confession of 1688). They battled and fought apostasy in all religious schools of thought. They attacked Rome with "broadsides of God's eternal truth." They defended their beliefs against skeptics, heretics, and rival religious groups of all kinds. Wandering from prison cells to dens and caves, these great scholars wrote their beliefs, recorded their exploits, and shook both kings and kingdoms alike.

My cry is to scholars, editors, writers—*"Pick up your pen in the twenty-first century and write! Isn't it time we left this great heritage to our next generation? Pick up your pen, young men, and write. Pick up your sword and fight! Pass it on! Pass it on!"* "If ye know these things, happy are ye if ye do them" (John 13:17). The joy of the Lord is our strength.

God made us all to be individuals; none of us are the same. God took this sapling from the mountains of West Virginia, and I'm like no one else. God has need of the giant redwoods in the Fundamentalist movement, but He also has need of the small sapling when He needs to "tan somebody's hide" or make a basket to carry some bread or use a reed to pass some oil down to the candlestick. Don't ever let the redwoods become so tall and dense that they shut out the small sapling who wants to see the "Son."

4. The Informed Fundamentalist: He is in pursuit of purity. He's facing a new century but the same old enemy—the Devil, the Deceiver. He also has the same book- the Word of God. He's not going to get tangled up in the textual criticism battle; he's going to use the truth that he knows and demonstrate practical Christian living, realizing that Satan uses the same methods but dresses them up in a new disguise. The informed must be willing to learn from both the past and the present. The informed must be willing to change tactics of warfare and not be a "loose cannon" on the ship, fighting everything or everyone who doesn't agree with him.

Should he stop fighting? No! No! Ten thousand times, No! Paul said, "I've fought a good fight." We're soldiers; we're militant; we're in a war for the truth.

We must be able to discern the wiles of the Devil. The word *wiles*, from which we get our word *methods*, is an interesting word. It means "battle strategy, military tactics." Those tactics are to use the lust of the eyes, the lust of the flesh, and the pride of life. [We see the god of materialism that, like the Laodocean church, has infected Fundamentalism today.] We have need of nothing, but we're blind; we've lost our spiritual vision. That's how we live today; like Gehazi, who wanted what the world had to offer, Fundamentalists are seeking the tokens of materialism.

The church at Ephesus grew in knowledge and abounded in faith and wisdom, but the Ephesians left their first love. Even Adam gained wisdom, but he lost his fellowship with God. If we're not careful in the twenty-first century, we'll bow at the shrine of intellectualism. This is not a personal attack on our seminaries. We have one at Tabernacle, but the day our seminary ever loses the fire in its heart and thinks it has a corner on the market of truth, I'll kick it into the Chesapeake Bay!

As we approach the twenty-first century, may we be Fundamentalists who are able to "fight the good fight" of the faith. God has allowed this mountain man to rub shoulders with some of the greatest giants of the twentieth century. I owe so much to so many. I feel like Laban who said to Jacob, "God has blessed me because of thee." These great men have shown Christ to me in the walk of life.

The Company I Keep
by Beth Moore

Let me be known by the company I keep
By the One Who determines each day that I greet
From the moment I wake 'til He rocks me to sleep
Let me be known by the company I keep!

Let me be known by the company I keep
When the valleys are low and the mountains are steep
By the One who holds fast when swift waters are deep
Let me be known by the company I keep!

Let me be known by the company I keep
By the One Who implores me to sit at His feet
And quickens my soul to discern what is deep
Let me be known by the company I keep!

Let me be known by the company I keep
Eclipsed by Your presence that I may decrease
'Til all You have chosen this traveler to meet
No longer see me but the Company I keep.

What we can expect in the next century will be false christs, political distress of the nations, famines, pestilence, earthquakes, false preachers, Christians growing cold, crime, self-indulgence, divorce, an increase in knowledge, false doctrines, riches, apostasy, and men who are lovers of themselves, blasphemers, unthankful, disobedient to parents, without natural affection. Homosexuality and lesbianism will be rampant. Truce breakers will cry, "Peace! Peace!" The truth will become a lie, and a lie will become the truth. Those who stand for truth will be thrown into jail, while those who propagate lies will be the popular leaders, unrestrained. Luke 21:28 says, "And when these things begin to come to pass, then look up, and lift up your heads; for your redemption draweth nigh."

One of the greatest needs of Fundamentalism as we stand at the brink of the twenty-first century is that we might have an understanding of the times and that we may have a knowledge of Jesus Christ, not merely a knowledge of His saving power. Oh, that we might know Him and the power of His resurrection! We need the same thing the first-century Christians needed—a baptism of the Holy Ghost and instruction by Christ Himself. Christ pleads with us, "Come, and learn of Me."

We must stay in the Book, stay on our knees, and preach the Word without fear or favor, without compromise, with power, whether popular or unpopular. I believe Fundamentalists of the twenty-first century will be faced with three opportunities: martyrdom, compromise, or great revival.

God help us to faithfully hand this mantle down to our children and our children's children. Psalm 78:2-8 says

I will open my mouth in a parable: I will utter dark sayings of old: Which we have heard and known, and our fathers have told us. We will not hide them from their children, showing to the generation to come the praises of the Lord, and his strength, and his wonderful works that he hath done. For he established a testimony in Jacob, and appointed a law in Israel, which he commanded our fathers, that they should make them known to their children: That the generation to come might know them, even the children which should be born; who should arise and declare them to their children: That they might set their hope in God, and not forget the works of God, but keep his commandments: And might not be as their fathers, a stubborn and rebellious generation; a generation that set not their heart aright, and whose spirit was not stedfast with God.

I have tried to help hand down from our generation this great, godly heritage. I feel many times I have failed the next generation so miserably. It's so easy to lose the race when I put my confidence in men. My prayer is that I will finish strong in the Lord. "But I am poor and needy; yet the Lord thinketh upon me: thou art my help and my deliverer; make no tarrying, O my God" (Ps. 40:17).

However, as we try to pass on the mantle that has been given us by our fathers, God help us not to fail the next generation. They must see in us a holy fervor in prayer. They must see fire in the pulpit. They must watch us finish the race with a faith that is anchored within the holy of holies. David ministered unto his generation and rests with his fathers. One day, I will cross the river and rest beneath the shade of heaven's trees. One day I shall see Him; it is my earnest prayer that I may hear Him say, "Well done, thou good and faithful servant."

Eventually, as more information becomes available and many more "disasters" occur in our lives (maturing and making us in His likeness), I will try to ask myself, "What miracle is our loving, heavenly Father fashioning from this 'incident'?"

Instead of wondering, "Why, Lord?" I have learned to say, "Thank you, Lord." I've learned to wait until all the evidence of God's divine, purposeful hand comes in, realizing that I will be satisfied only when I awake in His likeness. Therefore, I anticipate Glory.

Let's close with the theme of the 1999 World Congress of Fundamentalists—"Entering the next millenium in the arms of Him who has been there."

> *I am leaving, I am leaving*
> *For the country of my King.*
> *Let not word of grief be spoken.*
> *Let not heavy hearts be broken.*
> *Let joy bells ring.*
> *For earth's wintry life is changing*
> *into Everlasting Spring.*

And Christ is that bright glory. It is the Lamb who receives all the glory in Emmanuel's land.

> *Christ and I in that bright glory,*
> *One deep joy we soon shall share—*
> *Mine, to be with Him forever,*
> *His, that I am there.*

Appendices

Appendix A:

Who Is Lord of the Church—Caesar or Christ?

WHY TABERNACLE BAPTIST CHURCH CANNOT RECEIVE A LICENSE

This sermon was preached at Tabernacle Baptist Church, Virginia Beach, Virginia, on December 7, 1986, during the church's battle in the courts over the issue of licensure of the church's preschool and daycare center for children. The legal battle lasted eleven years, and the church's position not to accept licensure by the Commonwealth of Virginia was affirmed by the Supreme Court of the United States when it let stand the ruling of the U.S. Court of Appeals.

TEXT—Matthew 22:21, Mark 12:7, Luke 20:25

Matthew 22:21 says, "Then saith he unto them, Render therefore unto Caesar the things which are Caesar's, and unto God the things that are God's." The Russians quote the first part but leave off the second part.

This passage is found in Matthew, Mark, and Luke, but it is not found in the Gospel of John. I believe the reason is that in Matthew, Jesus Christ is presented as the *King of the Jews*; in

Mark, He is presented as the *Servant;* and in Luke, He is presented as the *Son of Man;* but in John, He is presented as the *Son of God.* He is the *Supreme Authority.* He is the Head, and we see that He is the one who is the *Creator of all things.*

"Render therefore unto Caesar, the things which are Caesar's." When you read of Caesar, it always refers to the Roman emperor, the governmental authority of the day. "And unto God, the things that are God's." The first thing this verse teaches is that there must be a complete separation between Caesar and Christ. The government is not to be over the church, and the church is not to be over the government.

In our country's constitution the first article of the Bill of Rights reads, "Congress shall make no law respecting an establishment of religion, or prohibiting the free exercise thereof." The principle of separation of church and state has been a fact of life for every believer in America. Books have been written on the subject. Societies have been formed to propagate its truth and to protect its heritage. The courts and lawyers have argued about it. The politicians and statesmen have debated whether it should be preserved or destroyed. The Baptists have believed it. They have preached it. They have practiced it. They have defended it and been the great champions of separation of church and state. We do not believe in the separation of God and state. In other words, our interest should be in the government and we should have a proper relationship with the government—not regulation. There is a difference between regulations and relationships. We believe that you ought to have the proper relationship.

Approximately two-thirds of the world's population does not enjoy the freedom to participate in their government. They do not have freedom of speech, freedom of religion, or freedom of the press. Americans have been given a great heritage that we need to understand. Our forefathers gave us a political system whereby men would have a voice in their government. Freedom's purest meaning is freedom under and through God for every individual.

Freedom is a person's having the liberty to do the best or the least that he is able, to pursue any calling, any trade, any profession, or do nothing at all, as long as he does not trespass on the equal freedom of other people. In other words, I have complete freedom—all I want—to swing my fist until my fist comes to the end of another's nose. Then my freedom ceases! I am infringing upon another's freedom. Everyone else has the same freedom. He can come down the street swinging his fist. He is free to do that until his fist comes to the end of another's nose, and that is the place where freedom stops! He is infringing upon another's freedom. We need to understand that. Freedom is liberty with a fence around it.

At the Constitutional Convention, a lady asked Benjamin Franklin the following question, "Well, Dr. Franklin, what have you given us?"

Dr. Franklin turned to her and replied, "We have given you a Republic, Madam, if you can keep it."

You, the people, are the key to good government. We have freedom to render to Caesar the things that are Caesar's, and it is just as important to render to Caesar the things that are Caesar's as it is to render to God the things that are God's. We must keep the proper balance.

We do not have a democracy. We have a democratic system. A pure democracy is "majority ruled." The word *democracy* comes from two words which mean "people" and "rule." People ruled. Really, pure democracy is nothing more than mob rule. In America, our forefathers did not give us a democratic government. They gave us a democratic form of government. What they gave us was a republic, and a republic is a democratic system in which the people rule the people by a constitution. We have a constitution, and we operate in compliance with that constitution. So a republic is people ruled by a democratic form of government that is controlled or governed by the constitution. That is the reason that we love, respect, and appreciate the Constitution of the United States of America. That is the reason there are so many attacks upon the Constitution. Our forefathers were tightfisted when it came to giving the government power. Therefore, they gave restricted power to the government by a well-designed constitution. They gave it just enough power to be a protector of their God-given liberties or rights. The government's power is ever chained to the restrictions of the Constitution and the will of the people. We are not the servants of the government; the government is the servant of the people.

We don't "shine the bureaucrats' shoes or the government's shoes"; they shine *our* shoes! They are to protect us, and we give them the power that we want them to have according to the Constitution. The First Amendment, as well as the entire Constitution, tells the government what it can and cannot do. When government policy goes against or violates the principles of the Constitution, which is in accordance with the Word of God, it steps over the fence and needs to be put back in its place. We, the people, must do this through the political process that is provided in the Constitution of the United States of America.

God has blessed America more than any other nation on this earth, and we are "the land of the free and the home of the brave." However, freedom is not "free." The freedom we enjoy in America cost a great price. Today is December 7, 1986. You men who, forty-five years ago, were at Pearl Harbor or were in the service are the men who paid the price or saw the price that was paid. In the wars preceding World War II, our blood ran freely. We have all had to pay the price. Freedom that we enjoy in America cost a great price. Our forefathers, for example, fought, shed their blood, and gave us the freedom that we enjoy in this land. It will cost us an even greater price to enjoy freedom in the years to come. Oh, God, help us to see that we are about to lose it all!

Believers must accept responsibility and get involved. We, the people, have become complacent, unconcerned, fat, and lazy; we have not let our voices be heard through the ballot box. The kind of government that is in power is a product of the people.

An irresponsible, unconcerned people will produce that kind of government. A corrupt, greedy, godless people will produce after its kind. If we are to be under subjection to every ordinance of man, as I Peter 2:13 says, then we are to make sure that the ordinances passed will not hinder our freedom to propagate the gospel. In Romans 13, we are admonished to "be subject unto the higher powers." We should make sure that the "higher powers" we elect to represent us are rulers who are not "a terror to good works." We dare not be negligent in this awesome responsibility to build a nation in keeping with the basic Bible principles upon which it was founded.

When a government makes laws and policies that stop us from carrying out the Great Commission, we must obey God rather than man. Should we, as a local New Testament assembly of born-again, baptized Baptist believers, receive a license from the government to exist and carry out and propagate the Great Commission, or do we already have a license? Do we already have an authority or power over our church that has given us the right to exist and has given us our command and our mandate, or should we be subservient to government? Let's look at three areas:

1. The Lordship—What does the Bible teach about the Head of the church? Who is the Lord? What does history teach?

2. The Law—What is our relationship to the law of the land?

3. The License—What the government wants and what we can or cannot give. God knows I want to be a good citizen of both countries; I want to be loyal to both authorities. Therefore, it is so important that their laws do not conflict. I want to be a good citizen of both countries—don't you?

THE LORDSHIP

What does the Bible teach about the lordship of our church? Well, let's find out what it teaches about our Lord Jesus Christ. First, He is the God of Creation. John 1:1 says, "And the Word was God." Hebrews 1:8 says, "But unto the Son he saith, Thy throne, O God, is forever and ever." First John 5:20 says, "His Son Jesus Christ. This is the true God, and eternal life." John 8:58 says, "Before Abraham was, I AM." John 1:3, "All things were created by him; and without him was not anything made that was made." In Colossians 1:16-18 we find, "For by him were all things created, that are in heaven, and that are in earth, visible and invisible, whether they be thrones, or dominions, or principalities, or powers: all things were created by him, and for him; And he is before all things; and by him all things consist. And he is the head of the body, the church: who is the beginning, the firstborn from the dead, that in all things he might have the preeminence."

Second, He is the God of Salvation. He forgives sin—Luke 7:48, "And he said unto her, Thy sins are forgiven." Only God can forgive sins. First Timothy 1:14, "Christ Jesus came into the world to save sinners." Matthew 26:18 says, "All power is given unto me in heaven and in earth." All power in heaven and in earth is given to Jesus, and that was given just before the Great Commission.

Third, He is the God of Administration. Matthew 16:18, "And upon this rock I will build my church." He is the Head of the church. He is the Commander in Chief. He is the Supreme Authority. He is the Lord.

In Ephesians 1:21-23, He is "far above all principality, and power, and might, and dominion, and every name that is named, not only in this world, but also in that which is to come: And hath put all things under his feet, and gave him to be the head over all things to the church, Which is his body, the fulness of him that filleth all in all."

He is the head of the church; He is the head administrator; He is the Commander in Chief of our army in verse 23. He is

Lord. He has given us our mandate in Acts 1:8. Mark 16:15 says, "And he said unto them, Go ye into all the world, and preach the gospel to every creature." We belong to Him because of creation; we belong to Him because of salvation; and we belong to Him and owe Him allegiance because He is the Administrator. He is over this church. He is the head of the church, and we owe our allegiance to Him! He is Lord! He is Lord!

He said, "Suffer the little children to come unto me, and forbid them not: for of such is the kingdom of God." He said, "It were better for him that a millstone were hanged about his neck, and that he were drowned in the depth of the sea [if you offend one of these little ones]." This is serious business when we start letting someone tell us where we may preach, what to preach, to whom we can preach, and when we can preach. He is Lord. He bought them with His precious blood. He died upon the cross for them. He was buried and He arose again. He is the Lord!

THE LAW

Romans 13:1-4 reads, "Let every soul be subject unto the higher powers. For there is no power but of God: the powers that be are ordained of God. Whosoever therefore resisteth the power, resisteth the ordinance of God: and they that resist shall receive to themselves damnation. For rulers are not a terror to good works, but to the evil. Wilt thou then not be afraid of the power? Do that which is good, and thou shalt have praise of the same: For he is the minister of God to thee for good. But if thou do that which is evil, be afraid, for he beareth not the sword in vain: for he is the minister of God, a revenger to execute wrath upon him that doeth evil."

It is not the power that you are resisting; it is God that gave the power to the government. Every policeman, every public official, every judge is a minister of God to good and is to be a terror to evil. We should have the right kind of men in those places. We are to be subject to the law. But what happens when the state demands that we obey the state instead of the Scriptures?

We Baptists are God-fearing, God-honoring people. We are to obey every ordinance that is of God. A good Baptist will do that. There will come a time when you will not be allowed to obey God by an ordinance of man. What do you do when you come to that time? This is the "gut" issue.

I want to read to you the first article of the Constitution of the U.S.S.R. (adopted January 23, 1918):

> The church is separate from the state.

> It is prohibited to enact on the territory of the Republic local laws or regulations which would put any restraint upon or limit freedom of conscience or establish any advantages or privileges on the grounds of the religion of citizens.

> Each citizen may confess any religion or no religion at all. Loss of any rights as the result of confession of a religion or the absence of a religion shall be revoked. The mention in official papers of the religion of a citizen is not allowed.

> The actions of the government or other organizations of public law may not be accompanied by any religious rites or ceremonies.

> The free performance of religious rites shall be granted so long as it does not disturb the public order and infringe upon the rights of the citizens of the Soviet Republic. In such cases, the local agencies are entitled to take the necessary measures to secure public order and safety.

> No person may evade his citizen's duties on the grounds of his religion. Exceptions to this provision and only under the condition that a certain duty of a citizen shall be substituted by another, may be permitted by the decision of the people's courts.

> Religious oaths shall be abolished. In cases where it is necessary, only a solemn vow may be given.

> The school shall be separate from the church.

> The teaching of religion is prohibited in all state, municipal, or private educational institutions where a general education is given.

All ecclesiastical and religious associations are subject to regulations pertaining to private societies and unions, and shall not enjoy any advantages or receive any subsidies either from the state or from local self-governing institutions.

No ecclesiastical or religious associations shall have the right to own property. Such associations shall not enjoy the rights of a legal entity.

On April 8, 1929, sixty-four new laws were passed that were amended on January 1, 1932. Some of these new laws are as follows:

Religious associations of believers of all denominations shall be registered or licensed as religious societies or groups of believers.

A religious society is a local association of not less than twenty believers who are eighteen years of age or over and belong to the same cult, faith, or sect, unified on the common satisfaction of their religious needs. Believers who are not numerous enough to organize a religious society may form a group of believers. Religious societies and groups do not enjoy the rights of a legal entity.

A religious society or group of believers may start its activities only after the registration or license of the society or group by the committee for religious matters at the proper city or district Soviet.

The churches in Russia must be registered or licensed by the government, and here is a point that we need to understand. The greater always licenses the lesser. The state is over the church in Russia.

Second, they defined what is a church. This is happening today in America. What constitutes a church?

The licensure or registration with the government puts the church under the state. When the state says you must be licensed, you can be sure that with that license there will be regulations. It will tell you whom you may hire, whom you cannot hire, the kind of curriculum you can use, and the philosophy that you need to teach.

I have in my files a publication called *Twenty Reasons Why You Should Not Spank A Child*, which deals with the state's regulation on our preschools. You will really warp them! This is antibiblical. We must not yield to such philosophy.

But what happens when we run into this conflict? What happens when the law of the state and the law of God—God's Word—come into conflict? What should we do as Christians?

In Exodus 1:15-20, the king or the pharaoh made a decree that the midwives would kill all of the male babies. The Word of God says that the midwives feared God and obeyed God rather than the king. In the verses following, it says that God blessed them and gave them homes of their own because they were going to obey God rather than the king. The Bible says, "Thou shalt not kill." The government says you should kill. They said, "We will not do it."

In Daniel 6:7-10, the king said that there would be no prayer. He made a decree. The Bible says in verse 10, "Now when Daniel knew that the writing was signed, he went into his house; and his windows being open in his chamber toward Jerusalem, he kneeled upon his knees three times a day, and prayed, and gave thanks before his God, as he did aforetime." He disobeyed the king and obeyed God.

Peter and John, in Acts 4, were told not to teach or preach in the name of Jesus. What did they do? Acts 4:19-20 says, "But Peter and John answered and said unto them, Whether it be right in the sight of God to hearken unto you more than unto God, judge ye. For we cannot but speak the things which we have seen and heard." They had to obey God rather than man.

Hebrews 11 records the heroes of the faith. Hebrews 11:36-37 says, "And others had trial of cruel mockings and scourgings, yea, moreover of bonds and imprisonment: They were stoned, they were sawn asunder, were tempted, were slain with the sword: they wandered about in sheepskins and goatskins; being destitute, afflicted, tormented; (of whom the world was not worthy:) they wandered in deserts, and in mountains, and in dens and caves of the earth." They obeyed God rather than man. Whenever the government said, "You can't do it," they said, "We must."

What about our Baptist forefathers? Please read the history of the Baptists. You will see the price they had to pay. The Baptists have carried the torch, and their historical past is truly a trail of blood.

How many of you have ever heard of John Bunyan? John Bunyan is the man who wrote *Pilgrim's Progress* and many other beautiful allegories and wonderful stories. *Pilgrim's Progress* has probably influenced more people than any other book in the world outside of the Bible.

John Bunyan was a Baptist preacher in Bedford, England. The state said, "You cannot preach unless you are licensed by the state." John Bunyan went to jail. He served twelve years in jail. He had four children, one of whom was blind, and a precious wife. That family was sick and at the point of starvation.

A piece of paper was placed in his cell. He was told that all he had to do was sign it and he could go home to his sick family and help them to be relieved from their poverty. The ink and quill were also placed there and left in his cell. John Bunyan told the jailer, "If I get overcome by emotion, or if I lose my sanity, and you see me reach for the ink and the quill, you have permission to cut my hand off."

It is said that John Bunyan's wife went to make a plea to get her husband out of jail. The men were kind, but turned her down. They said, "Just tell him to quit preaching or accept a license." She said, "I could never do that; I would never do that." She turned and began to weep. One of the men who was more kind than the others said, "What's wrong? Don't weep for John. He'll be all right." She said, "I am not weeping for John. I am weeping for you wretched souls who will have to stand at judgment and answer for what you are doing to 'poor' John's Savior."

They would bring the little blind girl to visit her daddy. She loved him very much, and he loved her. When he kissed her goodbye, she would take her little hands and feel his cheeks to see if he was crying. If there were tears, she would say, "Daddy, please don't cry. We'll be all right."

Little Mary died before John got out of prison. John said that the two things he wanted to see most were the Lord Jesus and little Mary because she was in heaven watching for him to come home.

Our Baptist forefathers have paid the price. In America, during the seventeenth century, right here in Virginia, there are forgotten facts of history. From 1607 to 1786, the church-state situation was firmly entrenched. You had to have a license to preach. The Baptists refused to accept a license, and they went on preaching without licenses. They saw converts won, they baptized, they taught individual liberty of conscience in the matter of doctrine and faith. They were thrown in jail, they were beaten, and they were abused in colonial Virginia.

They did not believe that it was wrong to resist the state. The Bible passage they often used was Acts 4:19-20: "Whether it be right in the sight of God to hearken unto you more than unto God, judge ye. For we cannot but speak the things which we have seen and heard." So they were put in jail.

The county court records of some of these men are represented in the following accounts:

> In Fredericksburg, Virginia, on June 4, 1768, Lewis Craig, John Waller, James Chiles, James Read, and William Marsh were arrested for preaching and allegedly "disturbing the peace." Read and Marsh were from another area and complied with the magistrate's offer of release if they promised not to preach in Spotsylvania County for a year and a day. Craig, Waller, and Chiles, however, refused to make such a promise, and were kept in jail for forty-three days for preaching without a license.

> In Culpeper, Virginia, November 15, 1769, James Ireland, having been warned that he would be arrested if he kept another preach-

ing engagement, recalled, "I sat down and counted the cost, freedom or confinement, liberty or prison? Having ventured all upon Christ, I determined to suffer all for Him." (That is from Ireland's biography. He preached as scheduled and was arrested while praying. He was subjected to considerable harassment, including attempted poisoning, burning sulfur fumes, threats of explosions, and so on, in what has been described as the worst case of persecution during that period of history in Virginia. In spite of all, Ireland preached through the bars of his cell and wrote letters headed "From My Palace in Culpeper." Ireland was in jail almost six months and, because his health was permanently injured, was never able to have the active ministry he could have had. Today, a Baptist church rests on the exact spot where Ireland's jail cell was located!)

Ruther Glen, Virginia, June, 1771: John Young admitted his preaching without a license and was jailed until November in the Caroline County Jail.

Spotsylvania County, July, 1771: Lewis Craig was put in jail for preaching without a license.

Fairfax, Culpeper, Orange County, Chesterfield County, Essex County, Accomac County, and many other counties saw about 150 preachers jailed for preaching without a license. Thank God their suffering was not in vain!

There was a Baptist preacher by the name of John Leland who got involved. The Commonwealth of Virginia was not going to ratify the Constitution of the United States. John Leland told James Madison that the reason they refused to ratify it was that there was no guarantee of freedom of religion. The Bill of Rights was drafted and presented to Madison, and they told him that religious liberty must be guaranteed. John Leland and James Madison met outside Orange, Virginia, and today there is a park and a monument where they made their agreement. Leland said, "We Baptists will support you if you will get the Bill of Rights and we will ratify the Constitution." This Madison did, and now we have the Constitution of the United States of America and a Bill of Rights.

There is a marker that stands on Highway 20, where Leland and Madison held their historic meeting. Historian Joseph M. Dawson has this to say, and I quote, "If the researchers of the world were to be asked who was most responsible for the American guarantee for religious liberty, their prompt reply would be 'James Madison'; but if James Madison were asked, he would as quickly reply, 'John Leland and the Baptists.' "

So what happens when the law of the state comes in conflict with the law of the church or the Word of God? We obey God rather than man.

THE LICENSE

The Constitution guarantees religious freedom in America. But when we have a conflict, what do we do? Let me give you a little history of our case.

1. We Negotiate

We try to settle it. We are not "rabble-rousers." We do not advocate going against our government. We love our government. We are not "red necks." We sit down and negotiate. We did that from 1976 to 1979. During that time, Virginia's governor, John Daulton, told me point blank, "Bell, I'll put you in jail." He then said, "We will have to arrest you and put you in jail. If you break the law, I must arrest you." I said, "That is not so. Why don't you arrest the prostitutes that are within a block of this capitol?" Anyway, we butted heads. However, most of the time, you can work things out by sitting down and negotiating!

2. We Legislate

We have a process that we work through. During 1978 and 1979, we legislated. We spent thousands of dollars, thousands of man hours. We traveled thousands of miles. I left my pulpit, my people, my family, and almost stayed in Richmond, Virginia.

3. We Litigate

Now we are back into litigation. They have taken us back to court, and we have been in court for almost seven years (1979-1986). I'll tell you, it wears on the old body. You run up and down the roads and across the country. It wears on you.

4. We Incarcerate

I have in my notes: "negotiate, 1976-79; legislate, 1978-79; litigate, 1979-86;" and by "incarcerate," a big question mark!

House Bill No. 276 was a law passed in 1979 that exempts us from licensure. It does not exempt us from fire, health, and safety regulations. We want to make our place safe. But we don't want the state to tell us that we can or cannot exist. We don't want the government to tell us what we have to teach. We cannot and will not live with that.

In conclusion, what is a license saying? The license is saying that the state is over the church. The state will tell you what you can do and what you cannot do. We cannot preach without the state giving us permission. We cannot teach the little children without the state's permission. We must be licensed by the state or we cannot exist. The state is saying "you cannot exist." The Savior is saying, "You must exist. You can preach. You can teach. As a matter of fact, it is a commandment, you must preach." Caesar says, "You can't"; Christ says, "You must." So what are we going to do?

Let me read to you what the late Honorable D. Dortch Warner, U.S. District Judge, said at one of the hearings. We have been in court since July. I do not come to the pulpit like this often, and you visitors, please bear with me. This is the first time I have ever taken a message to do anything like this. I don't come to the pulpit and waste precious time preaching on politics and so on. I carry that burden because it is not for the church to carry. It is my burden. I am the pastor. But now, I am laying the burden on you because it is time.

The ramifications of what the judge said are devastating. He said, "If you lose this case, then the day of the parochial school is finished; the day of the Sunday school is in danger; the day of tax exemption is gone; the day of freedom of religion is gone."

We, as a church, and I, as a Baptist pastor, cannot receive a license from the state.

1. I'd be selling out my birthright.

I would be worse than Esau. I would have to face John Bunyan. I would have to face little Mary. I couldn't face Mrs. Bunyan. I have been given a birthright. I have been given a great Baptist heritage. I owe my allegiance to my Lord. He is my King and Lord, not Caesar. He is God, not Caesar. The state says you can't; the Savior says you must. I would be selling out the birthright of New Testament believers—my Baptist forefathers. I cannot and I will not, by the grace of God, bow to the government. I was born free and I will die free!

2. I'd be selling out my calling—John 15:16.

The Lord said to preach the gospel to every creature. "Suffer the little children to come unto me, and forbid them not." The government and the state say, "You can't unless we give you permission and unless you do it the way we say to do it." I am not trying to dramatize it. I am trying to lay it on the line.

3. I'd be ignoring the Great Commission—Matthew 28:19-20.

My Savior is Lord, and He has spoken! He has given the order. I must obey! I dare not retreat. I cannot back up. He has already told me what to do. "Go ye and preach . . . to every creature."

4. I'd be a traitor to my Commander.

My commander is the Lord. A good soldier always obeys his commander.

5. I'd be a coward to my countrymen.

Men who have left their homeland and spilled their blood on the sands of Iwo Jima or in the jungles of Vietnam or on the hills of Korea or at sea have died to give me this freedom to preach without fear or intimidation. I cannot and will not be a coward to my countrymen. Their blood would cry out against me. That was their day to stand up and be counted. Today is my day. Today is the day that God has "brought us to the kingdom for such a time as this." We will not, and we cannot back up or change our convictions. Just as they stood in their day and did their job, we must stand in our day and do our job.

I talked to Brother Lester Roloff, and with tears running down his cheeks, he said, "Do you know the biggest heartbreak that I have had to face? It came from some of my own people, who wouldn't stand with me." I can understand some of that. I have called, I have visited, I have begged, and I have done everything that I know to do to find preachers to stand with us in this thing. They say, "Well, it is not affecting us. We don't want to get involved and get into any trouble."

Get your head out of the sand and see where this is going to lead! This battle is not going to be fought with bullets and bombs. It is going to be fought upon our knees.

6. I'd be guilty of child abuse and spiritual neglect.

I think that spiritual neglect is far more serious than physical neglect. I said to the attorneys, "You speak of child abuse. Aren't you concerned about spiritual neglect and spiritual abuse?"

7. I'd be making Caesar lord over this church.

I've got news for you. Caesar didn't die for this church. Caesar didn't have one thing to do with saving me or you. Caesar didn't die for the church. Caesar didn't bleed for the church. Caesar is a usurper of authority that is not his. He wants to tell us what to do.

The humanists who are in our government, along with the atheists, fear only that which they cannot control. You cannot control a society or nation until you control the educational system. They cannot control it thus far. They have already taken the absolutes out of the state schools. There is no more Bible. They can't say this is wrong or that is right because they have no absolute that says this is wrong or that is right. They have taken God's Word out. They have taken prayer out. Now they want me to get our schools in the same shape that their schools are in, and we will never do it. Never! Never! No surrender!

I am convinced that this is the greatest test that I have ever faced in my thirty years in the ministry. This is our "hour." We have come to the kingdom for such a time as this.

One day in years to come, our children and grandchildren will look us in the eye and say, "Mommy, Daddy, where were you the day that freedom died in America? Where were you when this issue came up? What did you do, Mommy? What did you do, Daddy?"

It may be that we will have to suffer. If so, we have counted the cost. The die is cast, and we will not bow. If the state says we do not have the right to exist, we will follow His command, without question, without hesitation, without equivocation. He has spoken and we obey. He is Lord. We have willingly counted it a privilege to suffer for the cause, and we will gladly pay the price. To be born free is a privilege. To die free is an awesome responsibility.

May it be said of the body of believers of Tabernacle Baptist Church that they stood and that they loved not their lives unto death. May they say in unison that He is Lord; He is Lord; He is Lord.

Dr. Bell called the Tabernacle Baptist Church to order and presented the official "Notice to Potential Class Members." The church voted unanimously to stand with the pastor.

IN THE EASTERN DISTRICT COURT
FOR THE EASTERN DISTRICT OF VIRGINIA
Richmond Division

NOTICE TO POTENTIAL CLASS MEMBERS

This action, presently pending before this Court, involves a challenge by three licensed child care centers to the constitutionality of Va. Code, section 63.1-196.3, which exempts any child care center "operated or conducted under the auspices of a religious institution" from the licensing requirements contained in Va. Code 63.1-195 through 63.1-202. Plaintiffs claim that the exemption statute violated the First Amendment to the United States Constitution as an "establishment of religion" by the State. The Commonwealth contends, in defense of the exemption statute, that the licensing statute would, if applied to child care centers operated or conducted by a religious institution, violate the First Amendment as an infringement of the free exercise of religion of such institutions.

By a decision of the United States Court of Appeals for the Fourth Circuit dated February 7, 1984, based on the record that was then presented, the exempting statute as it currently exists was found to be constitutionally overbroad in violation of the Establishment Clause of the First Amendment.

Pursuant to that decision, religious institutions that operate or conduct child care centers were allowed to intervene in this action as a class representative in order to assist the defendant in defending the constitutionality of the exemption. On November 21, 1986, the United States District Court for the Eastern District of Virginia conditionally certified a class of defendant-interveners as parties to this action. The class members are (1) all child care centers that are exempted by Va. Code Section 63.1-196.3 from State licensure and from certain regulations that govern licensed child care centers in Virginia, and (2) all child care centers that have filed notices to obtain that exemption. You have been identified conditionally as a member of the class.

The licensing statutes and regulations, if applied to exempt child care centers, may infringe First Amendment rights to the free exercise of religion. The purpose of a class action is to deal with the issues in the case and the rights of the exempted child care centers in an efficient and conclusive fashion. The class representatives will present to the Court the views of class members as to how licensure and/or regulations, if applied to the sectarian child care centers, would have infringed the members' free exercise rights, to show that such rights should be protected and to show that the General Assembly had a valid basis for protecting and/or accommodating those concerns.

Licensure would make applicable to exempt child care centers the statutes and regulations applicable to all licensed child care centers, currently found in Va. Code 63.1-195 through 63.1-202 and in the Virginia Department of Social Services' Minimum Standards for Licensed Child Care Centers. A copy of the statutes as of July 1, 1986, is attached. Sections 63.1-196(a) and (c), 63.198, and 63.198.1 of the Virginia Code, and Sections 1.6, 2.3, 2.4, 2.7, 3.1, 3.11(3), 6.2, 6.20, 6.28, and 6.34(2) of the Minimum Standards, are among those that have been identified as areas which, through licensure, would raise free exercise concerns. You may identify any additional statutory provisions or regulations not identified above that might interfere with your free exercise of religious beliefs and notify counsel for the class. You also have a right, by notifying the clerk of the Court as directed below, to be excluded from the class and not participate.

The judgment of the United States District Court, whether favorable to the class or not, will include all potential class members who do not request exclusion by January 2, 1987. Any member who does not request exclusion may, if it desires, enter an appearance through counsel, no later than January 22, 1987.

The interveners who have been appointed as class representatives are Grace Baptist Church of Petersburg, Tabernacle Baptist Church of Virginia Beach, Berean Baptist Church of

Salem, and The Rock Church of Virginia Beach. They are represented by the law firm of Mays & Valentine in Richmond. Anthony F. Troy, Esquire, serves as lead counsel.

If diverse religious groups respond to this notice, the Court will consider creating and certifying subclasses in order to establish for the record the varying free exercise problems caused by licensure and/or regulations if applied to sectarian child care centers.

If you choose to be excluded from this class, you **must** respond in writing to the Clerk of this Court, no later than January 2, 1987. The attached form should be returned by first-class mail, postage prepaid, to the Clerk, United States District Court, Eastern District of Virginia, Tenth and Main Streets, Richmond, Virginia 23219. You are **not** required to respond in any way if you choose to be a member of the class and thus be represented by the intervener churches and their counsel, named above. If you remain as a member, you will, as indicated, be bound by the judgment of the Court if favorable or unfavorable.

A final hearing on class certification will be held before this Court at the above address on January 7, 1987, at 9:00 a.m.

Dated: November 26, 1986
Signed: Richard L. Williams
United States District Judge

RESPONSE TO NOTICE TO POTENTIAL CLASS MEMBERS

TO: Clerk
United States District Court
Eastern District of Virginia
United States Courthouse
Tenth and Main Street
Richmond, Virginia 23219

FROM: Dr. Rod Bell, Pastor
Tabernacle Baptist Ministries
717 N. Whitehurst Lndg. Rd.
Virginia Beach, VA 23464

YES I wish to be included in the class and to be represented by the class representatives and their counsel.

Signed: Tabernacle Baptist Ministries
By: Rod L. Bell Sr., Pastor

This Notice to Potential Class Members was read to the members of Tabernacle Baptist Church on Sunday, December 7, 1986. The vote was unanimous to be included in the class and to be represented by the class representatives and their counsel.

APPENDIX B:
Divine Authority: Inspiration, Infallibility, and Inerrancy

Sermon preached by Dr. Rod Bell
at the World Congress of
Fundamentalists
Edinburgh, Scotland
June 15-22, 1976

My text is II Timothy 3:16 and 17—"All scripture is given by inspiration of God, and is profitable for doctrine, for reproof, for correction, for instruction in righteousness: That the man of God may be perfect, throughly furnished unto all good works."

As I approach my subject, I feel like Moses on the back side of the desert of Midian. Moses saw a burning bush and drew near. But God spoke to Moses out of the bush and said, "Draw not nigh hither: put off thy shoes from off thy feet, for the place whereon thou standest is holy ground" (Exod. 3:5).

The burning bush in the desert is a type of the miraculous presence of God speaking to men. The Bible is as truly miraculous as was that burning bush. The bush had natural branches, but they burned with the supernatural fire of God. The Bible has human language, natural branches, but it nonetheless speaks with the Voice of Deity. The Bible had human writers, but those human writers wrote God's words of fire. So let us pray as we approach this holy ground that God will once again speak to us out of His burning Word in this desert world of sin.

Just as the Living Word—the Lord Jesus Christ—was both human and divine, so is the Written Word both human and divine. The Living Word was perfect in every aspect, and so is the Written Word.

In order to explain the infallibility of the Bible, I feel that it is necessary to define some terms.

The first term is *inspiration*. This may be defined as the inward work of the Holy Spirit in the hearts and minds of chosen men who then wrote what God wanted to be written. We also mean that the Word is divinely trustworthy and authoritative. The two Greek words that are translated "God-breathed" suggest the in-breathing of God into men, thus qualifying these men to receive and to communicate divine truth. In other words, it is God speaking through the Holy Spirit, through men, to men. It is the Word of God through the Spirit, in men, enabling them to receive and to give forth divine truth. It makes the writer infallible in the communication of this truth, whether this truth is previously known or not. It causes the message to transcend human power and become divinely authoritative. So the Holy Scriptures are God-inspired, God-breathed—the product of the all-powerful and creative breath of God. It is the same power that spoke the heavens into existence. As someone has said, "No breath, no syllable; no syllable, no word; no word, no book; no book, no salvation."

When we speak of inspiration, we do not mean that it merely contains the Word of God, but that it *is* the Word of God. Because the Bible is the Word of God, even the smallest Hebrew letter is inspired. Matthew 5:18 refers to the smallest Hebrew letter—the jot: "For verily I say unto you, Till heaven and earth pass, one jot or one tittle shall in no wise pass from the law, till all be fulfilled."

I agree with the statement that "the Bible is none other than the Voice of Him that sitteth on the throne. Every book of it, every chapter of it, every verse of it, every syllable of it, every letter of it, is the direct utterance of the most high."

The second term is *plenary*. What is meant by plenary inspiration? Plenary means "full, complete, entire, extending to every part." So plenary inspiration means that every part of the Bible is inspired and equally inspired.

The third term is *verbal*. Verbal pertains to words. Therefore, verbal inspiration of the Word of God means that the Holy Spirit so directed men in their choice of subject matter and in their choice of words that their writings contain exactly what God desired and all that He desired. This is the Doctrine of Superintendence, or guidance; that is, God so guided in the writings of the books of the Bible that the words are *His* words in the style of the writers. In other words, the Bible is God speaking. Second Peter 1:21: "For the prophecy came not in old time by the will of man: but holy men of God spake as they were moved by the Holy Ghost."

The fourth term—*inerrancy*—connotes the characteristic of Scripture that renders it *without mistake* and therefore infallible—not only in religious matters, but also in matters of historical and scientific fact.

The fifth term is *absolutely sufficient*. I believe that all we are required to know about heaven, hell, salvation, faith, and practice is within this blessed Book.

What am I saying? I am saying that as Fundamentalists we believe that we have an infallible Book that is perfect in every respect. We believe, my friends, that every one of the 31,173 verses of the Bible is a direct message from Almighty God and that we need to believe it, obey it, practice it, defend it, and preach it as never before.

The sixth term—*infallibility*—bespeaks the fact that the Bible is free from error in the whole and in the part; that it is completely trustworthy and authoritative; that it is inerrant in that it is not false, mistaken, or defective; and that it can be completely relied upon as being true and completely free of error. If the Bible is not infallible, it is not authoritative, inerrant, or inspired. And if a man does not believe that the Bible is the inerrant, infallible, inspired Word of God, he is not a Fundamentalist.

The seventh term is *divine authority.* I believe that the Bible, not the pope or the church, is the ultimate authority. The writings of Paul were received and accepted as being the Word of God. First Thessalonians 2:13 explains: "For this cause also thank we God without ceasing, because, when ye received the word of God which ye heard of us, ye received it not as the word of men, but as it is in truth, the word of God, which effectually worketh also in you that believe." God has spoken, and we do not submit to a "Holy Father" of an earthly church, but to a holy, infallible Book—the Bible. This is the battleground, and the battle is raging. All the forces of Satan and all the armies of hell have joined together in one master attack to discredit, distort, and destroy the Word of God. All the winds of hell are blowing against it, and all the wicked minds and depraved hearts are trying to ravish and rape this sacred Book—this divine inerrant Word of God.

The point of controversy is this: Is the Bible the infallible Word of God? Upon the answer to that question everything you and I hold dear stands or falls. As Fundamentalists, we believe that the Bible is the divinely authoritative, verbally inspired, inerrant, infallible Word of God. Inspiration cannot lie, cannot be in error. It involves infallibility from start to finish, and we accept the authority of the Scriptures as being final. We need not be troubled by any *theory* of inspiration. Inspiration is not a theory; it is a fact. I am not wasting my time theorizing how we got what we have; I am enjoying what we have, and that is the infallible Word of God.

Let me cite five reasons that I believe the Bible is the infallible Word of God. First, the Word is infallible because of its *dogmatic declarations.* The Bible does not speak in generalities or uncertainties or loosely, nor does it use ambiguous terms. There are several things about which the Bible makes dogmatic declarations. The first is the *sovereign act of creation*. Genesis 1:1 declares that "in the beginning God created the heaven and the earth." That is God's breath; it is the product of the creative breath of God. Genesis 1:3 says, "And God said, Let there be light." According to Psalm 33:6, "By the word of the Lord were the heavens made; and all the host of them by the breath of his mouth." God's breath is the irresistible outflow of His power. The same God Who spoke this world into existence spoke this *Word* into existence. Turn to Hebrews 11:3: "Through faith we understand that the worlds were framed by the word of God, so that things which are seen were not made of things which do appear." God said, "Let there be light; and there was light." The Word of God, the Bible, the Scriptures, did not confer behind closed doors with the evolutionist, the skeptic, or the Modernist professor to see if it would be offensive to them or to consider the best way to start the Word of God. Scripture dogmatically and authoritatively declares that "in the beginning God created."

In Genesis, chapter 1, the phrase *"and God said"* is used ten times; *"and God called"* is used three times; and *"God blessed them, saying"* is used one time. Isaiah 1:2 says, "Hear, O heavens, and give ear, O earth: for the Lord hath spoken." What do we understand by all of this? We understand that God has created by the power of His Word. John 1:1-3 says that "in the beginning was the Word, and the Word was with God, and the Word was God. The same was in the beginning with God. All things were made by him; and without him was not any thing made that was made." Colossians 1:16 states that "by him were all things created, that are in heaven, and that are in earth, visible and invisible, whether they be thrones, or dominions, or principalities, or powers—all things were created by him, and for him."

My friends, God stepped out on nothing and, by the power of His Word, created worlds. It was the creating power of His Word that flung the stars into space, set the earth and her planets in their orbits and made them to rotate on their axes, and caused the sun to shine. It was the creating power of His Word that mashed out the valleys and scooped up the mountains. It was by His Word that the earth was covered with plush green carpet and tacked down with little white daisies. It was the creating power of the Word of God that wove a rainbow into a scarf and wrapped it around the shoulder of a dying storm and put it to sleep in a cradle of peace. It was the Word of God that sprinkled the world with brilliant-studded diamonds to kiss away the darkness of night and to declare the glory of God. When He had finished, God said, "Stay there!" And, my friends, creation has obeyed Him for all these centuries.

Also, God is dogmatic about the *sovereign act of salvation.* In Romans 3:23 God declares that "all have sinned and come short of the glory of God." The guillotine of judgment falls on all. God is not a respecter of persons. With one sovereign decree He condemns the souls of all mankind: "As it is written, There is none righteous, no, not one" (Rom. 3:10). Hebrews 9:22 authoritatively states that "without shedding of blood is no remission [of sins]." In John 6:37 our Lord dogmatically declares that "all that the Father giveth me shall come to me; and him that cometh to me I will in no wise cast out." And John 3:16 dogmatically declares that "God so loved the world, that he gave his only begotten Son, that whosoever believeth in him should not perish, but have everlasting life." This is dogmatism.

In the second place, I believe that the Word is infallible because of its *definite development.* The Word of God is not an afterthought but a divine blueprint written by the Supreme Architect of the universe. Note its clear unfolding. The development of the Bible, in its order, in its detail, and in its unity, is one of the greatest evidences of its supernatural origin. Its definite unity or unfolding staggers the mind. The Bible contains sixty-six books, was written by some forty different authors, and involved more than fifteen hundred years of writing. The first writer, Moses, died about 1450 years before the last writer, John, was born. At no time did the writers ever have a conference on what they were writing about. The Bible was written in three different tongues, yet they all agree. The writers used the same basic theme, but there are no contradictions and no disagreements—which proves that behind this one Book is one Divine Mind.

When we see the definite development of the Book, we cry with the psalmist (138:2): "Thou hast magnified thy word above all thy name." Where is the man who would try to teach the book of Hebrews without a knowledge of Leviticus? Where is the man who would try to teach the book of the Revelation without a knowledge of the books of Daniel and of John? Where is the man who would dare to teach the book of Ephesians without a knowledge of the book of Joshua? Where is the man who would try to teach the book of Romans without a knowledge of the book of Numbers?

My friends, it took longer to write this Bible than any other book. Webster spent thirty-six years in the writing of his dictionary. Gibbon took twenty years to write *The Decline and Fall of the Roman Empire*. But God spent a period of more than fifteen hundred years in writing His Word. God's Book is more important than the universe, for we read, "In six days the Lord made the heavens and the earth and all that is in them."

Notice also the Word's *complete* unity. It is a unity that overwhelms the soul. Some of the sacred writers were lawyers, some were captives, some were subjects, some were farmers, some were fishermen, some were scholars, and some were shepherds. The seed is planted in Genesis, it is cultivated in the Gospels and the Epistles, and it is harvested in the Revelation. "In the Old Testament, Christ is concealed; in the New Testament, He is revealed." Redemption's scarlet cord is seen in every book. The central theme of the Book is that "without shedding of blood is no remission." In Genesis we have the book of commencement, and in the Revelation we have the book of consummation. The Lamb is promised in Genesis, the Lamb is produced in the Gospels, and the Lamb is proclaimed King in the Revelation. In the Old Testament we have revelations of outward forms developing inward principles. In the New Testament we have revelations of inward principles developing outward forms.

In the third place, I believe that the Bible is the infallible Word of God because of its *divine demonstration.* Consider the Word's transforming power. Romans 10:17 says, "So then faith cometh by hearing, and hearing by the word of God." One of the greatest evidences that the Bible is the Word of God is that it can make of a man a new creation and cause him to change his habits. The saving power of the Word is a divine demonstration of its origin and claim. Second Corinthians 5:17 explains that "if any man be in Christ, he is a new creature: old things are passed away; behold, all things are become new." The Bible can make the harlot pure, the drunkard sober, the crooked straight! It can turn a sinner into a saint, a hell into a heaven, a sorrow into joy, a beer into bread, a house into a home, and rags into riches. It is by the preaching of this old Book that people get saved. No other book has this power, and no other dares to make this claim. Call out your authors; march out your philosophers; get their wisdom. There is not another book that makes prophecies and promises and produces them as the Bible does.

God is not looking for more methods on file; He is looking for more men on fire to thunder forth His blessed Word to a lost humanity. Peter declared that men must be "born again, not of corruptible seed, but . . . by the word of God" (I Peter 1:23). The Word will transform a person from the Kingdom of Darkness into the Kingdom of Light. It will pick up the gutter rat from the garbage pile of human ruin and clothe him in the righteousness of the Son of God and make him a child of the King. Some books inform and some books reform. *This Book transforms!* Every person who is saved by divine grace testifies to the infallibility of this blessed old Book. Christian friend, you are one of God's trophies. Your life demonstrates to the world that the Bible does what it says it will do.

In the fourth place, I believe that the Bible is the infallible Word of God because of its *determined durability.* Isaiah 40:8 declares that "the word of our God shall stand forever." Repeatedly, we are told that His Word shall never pass away. Ponder all the scorching attacks. The one outstanding fact of all time is the durability of the Word of God. No other book is as universally attacked as is the Bible, yet it not only survives the attacks, but it also comes out in the highest place of permanence. Ezekiel 12:25 says, "The word that I shall speak shall be done." All the powers of hell have tried to destroy this Book. All the winds of unbelief have blown against it. Princes, philosophers, politicians, and poets have all conspired against it. It has been insulted by the scorn of fools and has become the jest of infidels and the joke of skeptics. Consistently and persistently it has been assailed by professed scholars and has been made the butt of the critic. Like the three Hebrew children, it has been in the fire; and like them, it has been wonderfully preserved—there is not a smell of burning upon it. The fire has yet to be lit that can destroy the Word of God. The steel has yet to be forged that can scar it, the kingdom has yet to be built that can overthrow it, the scholarship has yet to be developed that can discredit it, the weapon has yet to be created that can demolish it, and the plan has yet to be devised that can annihilate it. All the cunning of hell and the craft of earth have combined against the Bible, yet it stands unmoved. As W. E. Gladstone, one of England's greatest premiers, said, "It is the Impregnable Rock of Holy Scripture." God's Word is indestructible. No criticism will dilute it or discredit its effectiveness. Listen to the psalmist: "The words of the Lord are pure words: as silver tried in a furnace of earth, purified seven times. Thou shalt keep them, O Lord, thou shalt preserve them from this generation for ever" (Ps. 12:6-7).

When God's man stands in the pulpit and uses this old-fashioned, King James authorized edition, he makes a clarion call from the preserved Word of God. The Modernist blushes, the "Liberal" squirms, the Devil flees, and all hell shudders and shakes. The Bible has withstood the hottest broadsides of hell, and it will not be affected by the slingshots of modernistic theologians. Voltaire boasted that Christianity would be a museum piece. Voltaire thought that he had destroyed the Word of God. But as Voltaire passed screaming out into eternity, the Bible marched on. Voltaire's press was used to print the Bible and became a depot for the Geneva Bible Society! My friend, the sun will go out like a candle in the wind, the moon will turn to dripping blood, the sea will burn like fire, the sky will roll back like a scroll, and the stars will fall like cinders. Yes, heaven and earth shall pass away—*but God's Word shall never pass away.* The Word of God shall stand, though assailed on every hand. Its foundations are eternally secure.

It will bear the critic's test and the idle scoffer's jest. Its saving truth forever shall endure. The psalmist says, "For ever, O Lord, thy word is settled in heaven" (Ps. 119:89). Peter says in I Peter 1:25, "The word of the Lord endureth for ever." Because of its determined durability, I believe that the Bible is the Word of God.

Some time ago I read in the paper an illustration that touched my heart. It seems that there was a great blast in a Midwestern town. The blast destroyed the city and caused massive damage for at least three blocks. The sky was lit up like an inferno. The next morning as the smoke died down and the ashes smoldered, there was an investigation to find the cause of the explosion. Walls were crumpled and ruined, steel was twisted, and ashes were everywhere. The only thing left standing was a shelf, and standing upon the shelf was a dusty Bible. The next morning the paper gave this headline: "Library Destroyed, City Rocked, the Bible Left Standing." You think of the ink of infidels, the scissors of criticism, the darts of hell. I want you to know that the Book still stands. *And thank God she will continue to stand!*

> Century follows century—There it stands.
> Empires rise and fall and are forgotten—There it stands.
> Dynasty succeeds dynasty—There it stands.
> Kings are crowned and uncrowned—There it stands.
> Emperors decree its extermination—There it stands.
> Storms of hate swirl about it—There it stands.
> Atheists rail against it—There it stands.
> Unbelief abandons it—There it stands.
> Thunderbolts of wrath smite it—There it stands.

An anvil that has broken a million hammers—There it
stands.
The flames of hell are kindled about it—There it stands.
The tooth of time gnaws but dents it not—There it stands.
Infidels predict its abandonment—There it stands.
Devoted minds of lust despise it—There it stands.
Some read it and believe it; some read it and don't believe
it—*There it still stands!*

No wonder saints of God can sing,

"How firm a foundation, ye saints of the Lord,
Is laid for your faith in His excellent Word!
What more can He say than to you He hath said,
To you, who for refuge to Jesus have fled."

Rejoice, ye saints of the Lord! We have a durable, infallible
Book.

Finally, I believe that the Bible is the infallible Word of
God because of its *devastating destruction*. The Word is devastating to those who oppose it. It grinds its enemies to pieces and to
powder. In Jeremiah 23:29 God asks, "Is not my word like as a
fire? saith the Lord; and like a hammer that breaketh the rock in
pieces?" In view of all the attacks, all the unbelief, all the apostasy, all the new translations, what will happen? My friends, the
Bible is like a lion in a cage. Open the door and let it loose, and
it will take care of itself. The psalmist says that "He sendeth out
his word, and melteth them" (Ps. 147:18). The Word of God
melts the hardest heart and breaks the stoniest will. According
to Proverbs 13:13, "Whoso despiseth the word shall be destroyed:
but he that feareth the commandment shall be rewarded."

We do not treat lightly the Word of God and get by. We do
not toss it aside like a toy. The Word is God's dynamite, God's
hydrogen bomb, God's TNT, and God's power. Let us
Fundamentalist preachers from all over the world unleash this
mighty source of power from our pulpits in every hamlet, village,
city, and countryside. Oh, how sin-hardened hearts need this
Book! It is food for the hungry—bread that will never get stale.

It is water that will never get stagnant. It is a hammer for the laborer, light for the pilgrim, a weapon for the soldier, fire for the cold, detergent for the unclean, water for the thirsty, seed for the sower, good news for the sin-sick soul, and the Rock that will never be shattered.

May it be said of us at this Congress, "Thou hast kept my word, and hast not denied my name." When the battle is over, the enemies of the Word shall be slain in the dust of defeat. When the sun is setting and the war is won, the Word of God, this infallible Book, shall be marching victoriously over the heap of human ruin. In light of all this, may I humbly offer this admonition from Paul: "Preach the word; be instant in season, out of season; reprove, rebuke, exhort with all longsuffering and doctrine" (II Tim. 4:2).

I did not feel that I would be able to come to this Congress because of my mother's illness. However, she came to me the day before we were to leave and said, "Son, your dad and I have an agreement that if anything happens to me while you are gone, we will not contact you. It is far more important for you to preach the Word than for you to come back to preach my funeral. Son, go and preach the Word. You have a great responsibility; you be faithful to your calling and preach."

My friends, I believe that we have an infallible Book and that we have a divine calling. I feel that we should expound this Book fervently, factually, and faithfully. I believe that God would have us to expose sin and wickedness in every place where it exists. This Book is to be loved because of its purity, its power, and its promises. Let us preach the Word when it is popular, when it is unpopular; in our cities, in our jungles; in weakness, in strength; in prison, in palace; in life or in death. Even if our heads roll from the chopping block, our flesh feeds the flames, our bodies become racked with pain or rot in a forgotten jail, our congregations turn against us or fail to stand with us—*let us preach the Word*. God help us not to yield to pressures to be silent but to thunder forth as the ram horn of God! May we be uncompromising in approvals and in criticism. May we be obedient unto death! We dare not, we cannot, we must not, alter our position, policy, or preaching of this infallible Book.

God bless you!

Appendix C:
Word of Appreciation

I wish to express my deepest appreciation to the people of Tabernacle Baptist Church, who, in their faithful and sacrificial service, have allowed their pastor to be "on the road" for the last twenty-two years as a twentieth-century circuit-riding preacher. They have done so without complaining and have given me the opportunity to have a national and international ministry in starting over sixty churches throughout America, and hundreds in other countries through our Missionary Agency. They are the ones who deserve the credit, not I.

The people of Tabernacle Baptist Church have been most cooperative: I have not had one negative vote in my thirty-two years here. I am truly a pastor who is greatly blessed and most beloved by his people. As Laban said to Jacob, "God has blessed me because of thee."

To two of our starting members who still serve with us today:

Mrs. Joyce Stern
Mrs. Myrtle Chappell

To my loyal deacons and their wives (and their faithful yokefellows):

Bob and Bev Bechtel
Jonathan and Stacey Carpenter
Lowell Chappell (deceased)
Ken and Helen Dorhout (Chairman)
Lee and Reo Dyson

Pete Forhand (deceased)
Henry and Gwen Jackson
John Lovelace
Bob and Sheila McGee
Eric and Lisa May Melvin
LeeRoy and Nora Pace
Bruce and Becky Rhew
Dean and Marie Slape
Milton Snell (deceased)
Charlie and Shelby Stallings
John and Linda Turner
John and Alice Wells
Don and Barbara White

And to my faithful and loyal staff, to whom I would render great injustice should I forget one name in any attempt to name them all. They are all servants and love their Lord and their undershepherd. Thank you for your labor of love.